A JOHN CATT PUBLICATION

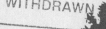

THE LEARNING RAINFOREST

·················

GREAT TEACHING IN REAL CLASSROOMS

TOM SHERRINGTON

ILLUSTRATIONS BY OLIVER CAVIGLIOLI

First Published 2017

by John Catt Educational Ltd,
15 Riduna Park, Station Road,
Melton, Woodbridge IP12 1QT

Tel: +44 (0) 1394 389850
Email: enquiries@johncatt.com
Website: www.johncatt.com

© 2017 Tom Sherrington
Illustrations © 2017 Oliver Caviglioli

ISBN: 978 1 911382 35 5

Set and designed by John Catt Educational Limited

Praise for The Learning Rainforest

"What is truly astonishing about this book is the amount of distilled wisdom packed into it. It combines a huge amount of significant research with decades of Tom's own invaluable experience of working at the chalk-face to form a coherent, practical and thought provoking book that will be an indispensable guide for years to come. Simply put, this is the book I wish I had read when I started teaching."

Carl Hendrick, head of research, Wellington College

"Packed full of practical wisdom about classroom teaching. The content includes presentation of research-informed pedagogy gained from the world of cognitive science successfully combined with down-to-earth examples of how research theory can achieve powerful impact within the busy classroom. Written in an entertaining style using the extended metaphor of a 'managed rainforest' this book provides a useful and compelling read for anyone interested in education."

Dame Alison Peacock, Chief Executive, Chartered College of Teaching

"'The Learning Rainforest' is a piece of work underpinned by humility – nothing ever goes quite to plan. Well, that's a relief, because I thought it was just me. Tom uses the personal to explain the bigger picture and makes the case for humour, compassion and heart being at the centre of our work. Tom has managed to balance the big picture with detail, the theoretical with the practical, and has produced a work which everyone, at whatever stage in their career, will find invaluable."

Mary Myatt, education adviser, author of
High Challenge, Low Threat and *Hopeful Schools*

"I found Tom's book wise, balanced, practical, and grounded in research. I'm confident it will help teachers not only to choose the best guidance but to implement it and what's more to coordinate it with other sounds ideas. It's a compelling road map to building a successful school."

Doug Lemov, author, *Teach Like A Champion* and *Reading Reconsidered.*

"In the time I have known Tom Sherrington – in person and online – I have learnt so much about pedagogy and classroom practice from his blogs and tweets. Now it's a treat to have a compendium of his experience, wisdom and insights, all rooted in such an optimistic view about why great teaching matters. This is likely to be an indispensable book for classroom practitioners at all stages of their career."

Geoff Barton, General Secretary, Association of School and College Leaders

"I recently re-read Ron Heifetz' argument that leaders must 'get on the balcony above the dance floor ... to see what is really happening' - one of my favourite leadership metaphors. In this great book, Tom takes us all both up to the canopy and down onto the rainforest floor."

Roo Stenning, Head of High School,
St Andrews International School, Bangkok

"Tom Sherrington is a rare thing – a headteacher who can write, not just elegantly, but intelligently. One would be valuable enough. Being capable of both make him and his work essential reading for school leaders everywhere. He also has the gift of not only a career full of experience, but the capacity to unpack his experience in such a way as to make it not just intelligible, but relevant. One of the reasons for this is that he embraces the complexity of the school leader's role without losing sight of the overarching moral purposes to leadership. Rather than writing a book – as so many books on leadership are – of 'here's what I did and you should do it too,' he assists the reader in developing their own journey through what may or may not work- and in what contexts. Accessible without being reductivist, intelligent without being opaque, this should be on the bookshelves of any school leader interested in reflecting on what they do."

Tom Bennett, Director of ResearchEd

"Just as the rainforest is beautiful, Tom's book is uniquely visual. Just as the rainforest has its dangers, Tom does not shirk from the difficult educational debates of our day. As much as we need to preserve our amazing rainforests, we should treasure this book and share Tom's insights about teaching and learning far and wide."

Alex Quigley, Deputy Head, Director of Research, Huntington School, York

"A beautiful articulation and drawing together of the concepts, ideas, philosophies and issues that head teachers like myself grapple with in order to achieve the best possible education for their students. It's like a Bill Bryson 'short' of everything teaching related! Part 2 is a 'godsend'; the explanations and ideas within each strand (C, K, P) and the emphasis on mode A teaching is brilliant."

Sam Gorse, Headteacher Turton High School, Bolton

"This book is a big leap forward in transcending the sterile debates between traditionalists and progressives. Hacking through the undergrowth of academic research and passing fads, Tom takes his readers on a journey (through the rainforest) to the sunny uplands of classrooms in which powerful learning and rich experiences can flourish. Whether you agree with every word here is not the point – this is a book that will get you thinking, reflecting, changing the way you teach, and questioning the very essence of effective teaching."

Peter Hyman, Executive Headteacher, School 21

"Teachers have been thrashed by changing tides of policy and ideology for decades. They have been bamboozled and confused by consultants and theories trying to shape them into this fad and that. They are tired and what they need is a light. A sensible, balanced, well informed light. Tom's book is that light for many teachers - especially for those in the secondary sector. It offers a way through the arguments and debates that sometimes polarise education, and in a clear, intelligent and open way, offers practical and thoughtful solutions."

Debra Kidd, teacher and author

CONTENTS

TOM SHERRINGTON

" I WORKED AS A TEACHER AND LEADER IN SIX VERY DIFFERENT SCHOOLS OVER 30 YEARS AND I LEARNED SOMETHING NEW IN EACH CONTEXT.

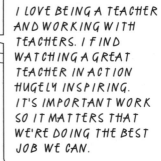

I LOVE BEING A TEACHER AND WORKING WITH TEACHERS. I FIND WATCHING A GREAT TEACHER IN ACTION HUGELY INSPIRING. IT'S IMPORTANT WORK SO IT MATTERS THAT WE'RE DOING THE BEST JOB WE CAN.

THE WORLD OF EDUCATION RESEARCH HAS BEEN ANOTHER MAJOR SOURCE OF INSPIRATION IN RECENT YEARS, HELPING ME TO SHAPE THE IDEAS BEHIND THE LEARNING RAINFOREST.

WRITING MY BLOG TEACHERHEAD.COM AND ENGAGING WITH TEACHERS ACROSS THE WORLD VIA TWITTER AND THROUGH MY CONSULTANCY WORK HAS BEEN EXTREMELY REWARDING. I LOVE BEING PART OF A GLOBAL COMMUNITY OF TEACHERS SHARING IDEAS AND WRESTLING WITH THE SAME PROBLEMS.

FOREWORD

Tom Sherrington is first and foremost a teacher, his enthusiasm for education shines through every page in this book. He is also a leader and blogger and it is his breadth of experience that captures the interest as a reader of this book. Whether you agree or disagree with some of the points within, you can't say that his opinion hasn't been honed with thought, care and reflection and anyone with this breadth of experience deserves to be taken seriously because he has lived and breathed education in a number of different environments.

It is environment that leads Sherrington into his chosen metaphor – 'The Learning Rainforest' – and one is struck by the organic vision this conjures up, his ideal school seems far away from the 'exam factory' of common conception. Is the rainforest school a place in which children roam free to explore? Are you about to read a book full of sixties hippy idealism in which anarchy and chaos are just one step away? Fortunately not. However, there is a belief in people, in colleagues and pupils. Sherrington believes in trust but also in challenge and in allowing a variety of approaches rather than centralised top-down dogma. A belief in professionalism borne of an environment in which all are valued for their contributions is central to his ethos.

Importantly, he is also acutely aware that this approach might be challenging, what to do if everyone is free to be as mediocre as they want to be? This is where another metaphor that of 'plantation thinking' is introduced. Here the constraints of the contemporary school are brought into play – inspection, data, performance measures – are not treated as unfair intrusions, Sherrington is aware of the importance of accountability and rather than seeing these things as a threat to his vision he sees them as an opportunity. Context is all and leadership is about traversing different contexts, in different places but also, importantly, at different times.

Sherrington sees the importance of a knowledge rich curriculum, he is invigorated by ideas extolled by such as Peter Hyman and his appeal to an education for 'Head, Hand and Heart' and also, for which I am most grateful, to my work on the Trivium. Here the book looks at the great debates at the heart of teaching and learning and he puts an emphasis on the importance of curriculum, its content and sequencing.

As a science teacher Sherrington is a knowledgeable person to have at your side when it comes to interpreting data and research, here he is unapologetic about his support for teacher led instruction and those who might have been thinking that this book was going to be all group work and 'creativity' might be disappointed. But, they needn't be, the author is thoughtful, and judges his critique carefully so as not to deliberately trample on people's beliefs. He doesn't hold back either, if he thinks something is wrong, he tells us.

His chapter on assessment is particularly strong in this regard, here he draws on the work of such luminaries as Christodoulou and Wiliam, to emphasise the importance of 'authentic assessment' where it is used to assist pupils' learning and giving rich data through which children can be assisted to move forward in their learning.

This is all part of Sherrington's principles – a good school is rooted in the establishing conditions – where behaviour and curriculum are key, on to which is unapologetically added the techniques that build the knowledge of their pupils so that they can begin to explore the possibilities of what it is like to be an educated person.

The second half of the book then goes on to explore how these three areas are carried out in practice. It is this part of the book that I can see people might return to again and again. Here is a useful handbook, a 'Haynes Manual' of teaching and learning. With Oliver Caviglioli's excellent diagrammatic thinking to guide us, one can happen upon something that will help us in our school, in our classroom, straightaway, whether we are a leader or a classroom teacher.

I am sure this book will be treasured by many who read it and will help all of us in education find our way through the forest where clarity of thought and vision is so often lacking. Reading this one is struck by the compassion and insights of one who has a lifetime of experience in schools and is willing to share his thinking, not in a dogmatic way, but in a way that allows us and challenges us to reflect on our own practice too.

Martin Robinson
Author of Trivium 21c

REAL CLASSROOMS, REAL STUDENTS REAL TEACHERS

" THE LEARNING RAINFOREST METAPHOR IS AN ATTEMPT TO CAPTURE MY UNDERSTANDING AND EXPERIENCE OF TEACHING. INDIVIDUAL SPECIMENS IN THEIR DIVERSE GLORY CREATE BEAUTY AND INSPIRE AWE; COMPLEXITY, DIVERSITY AND UNPREDICTABILITY ARE UNDERPINNED BY SCIENCE.

EXPLORING POSSIBILITIES

BUILDING KNOWLEDGE

ESTABLISHING CONDITIONS

" THE ELEMENTS OF EACH TREE IN THE RAINFOREST REPRESENT A DIFFERENT ASPECT OF THE LEARNING PROCESS:

- THE ROOTS: ESTABLISHING THE CONDITIONS FOR GREAT LEARNING;

- THE TRUNK AND BRANCHES: BUILDING THE KNOWLEDGE STRUCTURE;

- THE CANOPY: EXPLORING THE POSSIBILITIES.

EACH ONE SUPPORTS THE OTHERS; NONE EXISTS WITHOUT THE OTHERS.

" PART 1 OF THE BOOK EXPLORES THE KEY DEBATES AND INFLUENCES THAT SUPPORT THE MODEL: TRADITIONAL Vs PROGRESSIVE PHILOSOPHIES; THE CURRICULUM DEBATE AND THE LEARNING FROM EDUCATIONAL RESEARCH.

" PART 2 HAS THREE CHAPTERS WITH 20 SUB-SECTIONS; STRATEGIES AND IDEAS THAT SUPPORT THE DEVELOPMENT OF THE THREE PARTS OF THE TREE MODEL. YOU CAN DIP INTO EACH SECTION SEPARATELY OR READ THE BOOK FROM START TO FINISH.

'Trees are poems that earth writes upon the sky.'
Khalil Gibran[1]

'I love teaching; I love being a teacher; I love working in schools.'

The opening line from my previous book, *The Joy of Teaching Science*[2], is still true. That is how I've felt throughout my career. Teaching is a joyful job. The better you get at it, the more joyful it becomes. One of the reasons I wanted to write this book was to inspire teachers to continue to love their jobs and to inspire others to join our wonderful profession. A big part of this is sharing ideas about how to become a better teacher and ultimately a great teacher – a goal that remains throughout your career. It's the relationship between a love of teaching and the quest for great teaching that informs a lot of what I hope to convey through the idea of the Learning Rainforest.

Since I started writing my blog about the realities of teaching in real classrooms, I've found that organic, ecological metaphors are extremely useful for getting ideas across. All analogies and metaphors have their limits so it's important not to get too carried away with the details. It's the spirit that counts.

The Learning Rainforest metaphor is an attempt to capture various different elements of our understanding and experience of teaching that I will set out in detail as we progress through the book.

Here is a quick introduction:

If we picture a rainforest, it is a beautiful, almost magical place, dripping with possibilities, teeming with life. It's an exotic organic display of light and shadow, sound and movement, shape and structure revolving around its central protagonists – the impressive, awe-inspiring trees standing tall and dazzling with their diversity and strength, their character. How is this like a classroom?

- The rainforest is a collection of individual specimens sharing the same space; there is a degree of interdependence between individuals and there are sub-species with common characteristics within the overall community of plants. Each individual can be extraordinary and dazzling on their own terms.

- There is lush, glorious diversity in the forms plants take. New possibilities evolve in different contexts, each with the potential to thrive and flourish

---

1. Gibran, K. (1926) *Sand and Foam*
2. Sherrington, T. (2014)

in a unique way, each specimen making a valuable contribution to the ecosystem as a whole. At the same time, the science of growth and reproduction is universal and has relevance to every plant, regardless of its exact form. We can learn to understand what makes them all thrive.

- Each tree in a forest has three interconnected components that are necessary for its existence:

  - a root system tapping into a nutrient-rich soil providing the conditions for healthy growth; the nurturing environment in which each individual feels they belong and has their basic needs met.

  - a solid trunk providing the structure that allows the tree to reach great heights before branching off; this represents knowledge in all its forms.

  - a canopy of leaves spreading out in different directions, responding to the (motivational?) stimulus of sunlight; the range of ambitions and learning possibilities.

Each element supports the other; strength in one allows strength in the others; weakness in one undermines the others. There is no canopy without the trunk but, as the canopy develops, so too does the trunk. They grow together. Just as with real plants, the substance of the trees comes as much through the leaves as through the roots. Crucially, there is no shortcut to the creative, diverse educational outputs without building a strong core of knowledge to support them; that's a central feature of every plant, every tree in the rainforest.

- There is a high level of complexity in the relationships between the nutritional inputs, a plant's genetic make-up, the proximity of other plants and the level of success a plant enjoys in reaching its climax form as a specimen. The science helps to explain some patterns and trends but, with so many variables, the outcomes for any individual remain unpredictable in the detail. A rainforest represents the symbiosis of art and science in understanding and delivering great teaching and deep learning.

- The vibrant rainforest experience generates plants and trees that create beauty and inspire awe in a way that is joyous and surprising. However, there is a flipside where some plants fail to thrive: where they are crowded out or find themselves in soil that is insufficiently fertile; there are dangers and diseases, competitive pressures and pitfalls. There are risks.

The rainforest metaphor is one I come back to repeatedly, but it isn't without its flaws. Teaching in a regular classroom is possibly more directed, systematic and ordered than a rainforest might suggest. It could be that a plantation would be more accurate as a metaphor. Here the diversity is virtually eliminated. Trees with certain desirable features are reproduced on a grand scale, row after row in straight lines. In a plantation there is much more emphasis on securing order, controlling the inputs, ensuring individuals conform to certain expectations and reach certain minimum success goals. I will return to this in Chapter 1.

Plantation vs Rainforest has served me well as a reference for considering the nature of learning and the wider aspects of school systems and culture. Over time, my thinking has been influenced by research evidence, by engaging in various debates about curriculum, pedagogy and assessment and by my own experience as a teacher and school leader in different contexts. All of those influences have resulted in a shift from a position of rejecting the plantation model outright to embracing aspects of it more warmly. What I am really proposing is that a 'managed rainforest' might be the optimum metaphor, taking the best of both.

Central to any rainforest are the trees. A Learning Tree works as a metaphor for an individual's learning experience in any context – plantation or rainforest. I have found this a very useful concept over the years as I've sought to deepen my understanding of teaching and learning and tried to be a better teacher myself. In particular, I have found it helpful to resolve various debates that seem to present teachers with an either-or choice between traditional or progressive ideas; between direct knowledge-led instruction and student-centred, hands-on activities; between firm no-excuses discipline and a nurturing ethos full of love.

Through the Learning Tree metaphor, I think it is possible to find sympathetic, symbiotic relationships between each of these apparent poles. This isn't simply a mushy compromise that seeks to deny the debate; however, neither is it a set of simplistic binary choices. My argument is that navigating the contradictions and tensions in these debates is not about choosing sides; it is about finding the most effective sequence and relative emphasis in a student's learning at any given point on their educational journey. In particular, I find that the trunk of knowledge is especially powerful as a focus. This places traditional knowledge instruction at the core of great teaching. However, it is not enough in itself; it doesn't work effectively without maintaining a nurturing environment or without exploring the possibilities in the leaf canopy where learning is applied and explored in pursuit of ambitious goals, where diverse, unpredictable outcomes are possible and celebrated.

The subtitle for the book is Great Teaching in Real Classrooms. My ideas about what constitutes great teaching are drawn from my experiences as a teacher and a school leader over the last 30 years, alongside everything I've read and all the debates I've engaged with during that time. Those ideas have changed a lot in response to different contexts, new learning, fresh research and all the successes and challenges with different students and classes. Even looking back to blogs I wrote five years ago, I find myself not quite agreeing with what I was saying then. I've shifted in various different directions. All of that is healthy. It's part of the process – that search for truth on the road to becoming a great teacher, avoiding getting stuck in a silo of dogma.

An opening line of many of my workshop presentations and keynotes about teaching is that none of my lessons ever goes according to plan. To some extent, that unpredictability lies at the heart of my love of teaching. That's the magic of the rainforest. It's partly your students' capacity to surprise and delight you but, for me, it's also the continual intellectual challenge of making sense of such a complex process that is so rewarding. Without doubt, with every new teaching situation I've encountered, I've developed new insights as my intellectual, rational understanding of what should work has come face-to-face with the real-world complexity of each classroom. The result is an ever-improving understanding of what great teaching is alongside my capacity to deliver it.

My journey as a teacher has run in parallel with numerous evolving debates about curriculum and pedagogy across the teaching profession. Some of these debates will have been unique to England but most are universal. My time as a Headteacher coincided with the rapid development of a community of people using Twitter and blogging to share educational ideas. I quickly became hooked into this world when I realised that I could learn so much and engage directly with officials and teachers across the system. I also discovered that people would read what I wrote, share resources, offer critique and promote ideas I hadn't encountered before. The concept of teachmeets and the excellent ResearchEd movement sprung from this dynamic online dialogue between professionals, researchers, academics, commentators and policy makers. Without question, Twitter and blogging have massively influenced my thinking about great teaching and this continues week by week.

I started writing my blog – now called teacherhead.com – in May 2012 as a way of helping me to organise my thoughts about teaching and school leadership. After introducing blogging to my students, I felt that it would be useful to try it myself. To my great delight, I've found that there are people interested in my perspective on teaching and school leadership and now, after five years, my blog has had 3 million views with some from nearly every country – a fact that continually astonishes me. Blogging is largely a tool for self-reflection; it's me thinking aloud. It has also been a superb medium for sharing ideas with others, offering some insights, commentary and critique across a range of educational issues. Through blogging and the power of social media, I have found that many of the challenges we face in our own classrooms are shared across the world. We're all part of a global community of people trying hard to solve the complex puzzles that teaching and learning present us with every day. I love that.

To some extent, this book represents the best of what I've tried to capture on teacherhead.com, organised in a way that might be helpful. In places, I've reproduced whole blog posts as they were originally written – simply because I can't do a better job of getting the ideas across than I did the first time. However, most of what I've written is new so hopefully the book offers much more than just teacherhead.com's greatest hits.

In Part 1 of the book I will walk through each of the areas of influence that have led me to the Learning Rainforest:

- My personal experience of teaching and learning at school
- The traditional-progressive debate and the Trivium
- Core knowledge and the curriculum debate
- Evidence from research
- Assessment Thinking

We will pause here to take stock, revisiting the Learning Rainforest to see how all these ideas come together.

Part 2 is the Learning Rainforest in Practice. Here I will set out the practical ideas and strategies for great teaching in a real classroom based on everything I've learned so far including my rough shorthand for two distinct teaching modes: Mode A, based on traditional knowledge instruction; and Mode B, which captures everything else.

I am very conscious of the time pressure teachers are under and that, if a book like this is to be useful as well as one that provokes some thinking, it needs to be easy to engage with. I'm also aware that, unless ideas are presented simply and clearly, they are unlikely to penetrate teachers' armour of ingrained practice. It's actually incredibly difficult to change our practice as teachers. It requires making a deliberate decision to make a change and then to persist with it until our default ideas and habits shift.

With this in mind, Part 2 consists of three chapters, each of which contains 20 ideas or strategies that teachers might consider in taking their teaching forward:

Chapter 7 – Establish the conditions: C1-C20

Attitudes and habits for excellence, relationships and behaviour, planning the curriculum

Chapter 8 – Mode A teaching: Building the knowledge structure: K1-K20

Knowledge instruction: explaining, modelling, questioning, feedback and assessment.

Chapter 9 – Mode B teaching: Exploring the possibilities: P1-P20

Hands-on experience, projects and group work, student-led learning, oracy; going off-piste

The intention behind the structure of the book is that it should work as one you can read through from cover to cover as well as one you can dip into. Each chapter and each of the Part 2 strategies should stand alone, offering insights into specific aspects of the teaching and learning process. The chapter summaries illustrated by the magnificent Oliver Caviglioli capture some of the key points.

I hope you enjoy your walk through the Learning Rainforest as much as I have enjoyed writing it. It's been a labour of love. There will be a page on teacherhead. com devoted to this book where you can leave comments and ask questions. This is by no means a definitive text but I hope that it makes a positive contribution to the ongoing debates around curriculum, evidence-informed instruction, assessment and teaching and learning.

Thank you for reading.

Tom Sherrington

September 2017

PART 1: THE LEARNING RAINFOREST METAPHOR

MY RAINFOREST EXPERIENCE

" MY OWN SCHOOL DAYS HAVE INFLUENCED ME. WHERE IT WORKED BEST, A CHALLENGING TEACHER-LED KNOWLEDGE-RICH CURRICULUM WAS BLENDED WITH THE OPPORTUNITY TO DO THINGS FOR MYSELF.

" 30 YEARS AT THE CHALKFACE HAVE TOLD ME DIFFERENT CONTEXTS REQUIRE DIFFERENT PRIORITIES. MOST OF THE BEST LESSONS I'VE EVER SEEN WERE AT KEGS BUT I'VE MET GREAT TEACHERS IN EVERY SCHOOL.

" GREAT TEACHERS ARE DRIVERS, NURTURE RELATIONSHIPS, TAKE JOY IN GOING OFF-PISTE, CELEBRATE INTRINSIC REWARDS, ARE PRINCIPLED ABOUT PEOPLE AND ARE EFFECTIVE CURRICULUM DESIGNERS.

" REAL STUDENTS ARE DIVERSE AND COMPLEX WHILST STILL HAVING A LOT IN COMMON. ALL THE COMPLEXITY IS THE SOURCE OF THE CHALLENGE OF TEACHING BUT ALSO THE JOY OF IT.

" RAINFOREST Vs PLANTATION? OUR MANAGED RAINFOREST SHOULD ENSURE EVERY STUDENT IS ALLOWED TO GROW, LEARN AND FLOURISH; IT SHOULD ALSO FEEL LIBERATING, INVIGORATING AND INSPIRING.

*'Among the scenes which are deeply impressed on my mind,
none exceed in sublimity the primeval forests.'*

Charles Darwin[3]

'...there ain't no journey what don't change you some.'

Zachry Bailey, Cloud Atlas[4]

School days

It's inevitable that our own school experiences inform our thinking as teachers
– even if we're conscious of the pitfalls that surround nostalgic reflections. That
'it didn't do me any harm' bravado you sometimes hear about the disciplinarian
practices of the past is an important example. I remember seeing Mark Johnson
being given the slipper by the Headmaster on the stage in front of the whole
school as his punishment for shoplifting. He was 11. We all knew who was
more in the wrong – and these things stick in your mind. In educational terms,
I don't think there were any 'good old days'. The same applies to rose-tinted
extrapolations by successful people who didn't do well at school; the maddening
survivor delusion whereby people extol the virtue of a bad education making
them the person they are today. As if this helps as a motivational message for
young people.

My bias is that I always loved school but, just like everyone else, my perspective
stems from my own atypical experience. I went to the local primary and local
comprehensive school in leafy Farnham, Surrey. Hardly the mean streets but
it was more socially comprehensive that many people assume. I was a bit of a
problem; not freakishly clever but I found regular school a bit too easy. I was
given IQ tests; packed off on nightmarish socially awkward weekends for 'gifted
children' to play Hexagonal Chess and generally worried over. In the end I was
moved up a year and went to secondary school and university early. Eventually,
it all came good and I'm not really complaining. But it took about three years to
stop feeling emotionally out of my depth at school – and I was still routinely at
the top of the class and often rather bored along with my counterpart Michael
who was on the same journey with me. Being moved up a year certainly made
a difference but ideally what I needed was to be intellectually and mentally
challenged in lessons and to grow up socially and emotionally at the same rate
as my peers.

3. Darwin, C. (1839) *Journal of Researches: into the Natural History and Geology of the Countries
Visited During the Voyage of H.M.S. Beagle Round the World*, ch. XXIII, 604-5.
4. Mitchell, D. (2004) *Cloud Atlas*, Sceptre

The truth about my school days is that, within the comprehensive framework, it was still very much sheep and goats with full-blown banding in place. I never had lessons with Terry, Eddie and Jane in my tutor-group. They did CSEs in pottery, rural science and metalwork and would not have studied French, history or physics.

I had lots of strong teachers and plenty who were just ordinary but, generally, my education was not a string of *Dead Poet's Society*-style inspirational lessons; it was solid, traditional teaching peppered with a few stand-out experiences. What do I remember:

Physics, taught by Mr King, was excellent. A strongly knowledge-driven curriculum was underpinned by an excellent textbook. You could rely on Abbott[5] if you needed to check your understanding. We had to learn the equations of motion and electromagnetism by heart and we had lots of tests to make sure we did. There were some demonstrations and routine experiments. In all their hyper-traditional ordinariness, I loved these lessons. Mr King, smartly dressed and very formal, was an inspiration in a marvellously understated way; his seriousness about the subject gave it credibility. We were in the pursuit of some serious learning about the fundamentals of the universe. It felt good.

The stand-out experiences here were two projects we did. In one, I made an 8-note electronic 'organ' which was basically a line of tuned circuits with variable capacitors you could turn to tune to a note. I have a soldering iron burn-scar on my wrist to remind me. We got as far as 'Three Blind Mice'; it sounded terrible but it was fun to do and we learned a lot about electronics. We also had an extended block of lessons in the Fifth Year (Year 11, 10th Grade) to explore an area of interest; a project which was not assessed as part of the exam. I spent the time trying to link a motor kit to a generator kit and back again in a bid to find out why perpetual motion was not viable. We knew it wouldn't work but we wanted to try anyway. Mr King encouraged it. Other kids were launching projectiles and making magnetic levitation vehicles; it was joyous. I had my heart set on a degree in physics from then on.

From my perspective, as a successful learner, this was the Learning Tree in action. Mr King nurtured us as learners: he was caring and inspiring. The knowledge was the driving force: absolutely at the core of everything, clearly laid out, challenging, deep, traditional. But we were allowed to go off-piste: the diet of activities was varied with some special moments of real exploration, built around the knowledge foundation. All of this fed back into the more formal learning process.

---

5. Abbott, A. F. (1977) *Ordinary Level Physics.*

Similarly, I remember biology with Mr Taylor. Not only did he have his Ford Capri painted red with a full-works Starsky and Hutch white stripe (plus a massive tie, flares and facial hair to match), making him genuinely cool in 1979, he loved dissection. I pinned out a rat's intestines on a board as a live demonstration during a parents' evening, having enjoyed doing it in class; unforgettable. A constant companion was Mackean[6], a glorious large-format textbook with a distinctive blood-red cover with a picture of a skeleton ribcage and associated blood vessels. All the knowledge you needed was in there. In an age before PowerPoint, textbook images were vital – but that wasn't all. They were ours to take home; they were our companions.

In English, we learned the technical skill of how to write a precis but mainly I remember the reading. Here's an excerpt from one of my blogs:

> For me – and I won't be alone – reading at school was really very important. It meant that I did actually have to read. I remember reading **'The Rime of the Ancient Mariner'** in the 2nd Year (Year 8) and we studied *Twelfth Night* in the 3rd Year. We also read from *The Odyssey*. The teacher played an important role in making them seem both exciting and important in some way. The selection at O Level seems pretty bizarre to me – it did then and it does now: *My Family and Other Animals and The Woman in White* (gosh that was long) were a real drag. We'd have killed for a bit of Steinbeck! Thankfully we did *Henry IV Part 1* which we all loved. My friends and I would learn all the in-between lines as quotes for fun. *'Good Sire, we shall sup tonight at Eastcheap'*. All of that bawdy bardiness was very appealing.
>
> Best of all, by far, was the *Penguin Science Fiction Omnibus* edited by Brian Aldiss. About half-way through the year the teacher confessed to us that she'd misread the syllabus. We were only meant to read 10 of the stories but by this point we'd nearly done them all. For me, this was perfect. Short stories. Science Fiction. Punchy and potent. This was me. I can still remember the stories now – each with a surprising twist, human dilemma or moral message of some kind: **'Lot', 'Skirmish', 'Half a Pair', 'Grandpa', 'Track 12'**. We even named our Sixth Form band after that story (adding a Germanic twang: *Tract Nein* – oh how clever!)

I also remember the trouble I had with creative writing. The feedback was always so unhelpful. 'B minus. The ending is rather corny.' More like a stinging review than constructive guidance for improvement. What was I meant to

---

6. Mackean, D. G. (1973) *An Introduction to Biology.*

have done differently? There was no chance to improve it and we'd move on. Retrospective feedback was the default. I don't think I ever got an A. For me, there was too much 'hit and hope' in English literature and creative writing. You never knew exactly what to do. In fact, my whole experience of learning poetry was of feeling that everyone else was in on a secret that I was too stupid to understand. And we never learned them by heart; I regret that. All I know is 'Jabberwocky', which is fun to recite but hardly high culture.

In history, after fabulous projects on Romans and The Middle Ages, I ended up studying The Industrial Revolution for my O Level. 1750-1900. It was interesting enough – the functional detail of road-builders, steam engines and innovations in loom technology were mixed in with factory acts, poor laws, William Wilberforce and the abolition of slavery. It was all good stuff – except for the opportunity cost. I never once studied WWI or WWII; never studied Vietnam or any 20th Century history at all. I never studied the history of any other nation. These seem to be pretty big gaps for secondary education. But, hey – if you want to know about Hargreaves' spinning jenny or legendary road-builder, Blind Jack of Knaresborough – I've got that covered. The stand-out topic was The Chartists which resonated with contemporary politics. We weren't explicitly seeking relevance but it was there and that helped us to take it seriously.

30 years at the chalkface

I rather fell into teaching by accident. Primarily, doing my teacher training was just a stalling tactic to maintain my student existence and keep playing in my band. However, once in, I was hooked. I've had the privilege of working in a range of wonderful schools that all seemed extraordinary to me while I was there. The elements of the Learning Rainforest were never explicit but, certainly, each school provides material to reinforce the metaphor.

Winstanley College in Wigan in England's North West gave me my first real job back in 1987. I taught physics and maths to Advanced Level in a school of 900 16- to 19-year-olds. I learned how to explain concepts to a class and how to ask questions to probe their understanding; how to use all kinds of exciting physics apparatus; how to set expectations for students' work ethic and study habits; how to teach students who were smarter than me and how to manage a student's self-esteem when they kept getting the answers wrong and began to lose hope.

As a teacher, I learned that success came from balancing rigour with enthusiasm, some awe and wonder and lots of basic human warmth and kindness. I was certainly capable of cracking the whip, pushing students to do things properly at every stage. But I also wanted to have some fun. I can remember pushing the limits on practical demonstrations – notably with our induction coils that sent a metal ring flying high up to the vaulted ceiling. It has always mattered to me that students share my fascination with physical phenomena or my joy in producing a neat maths solution. Obviously I made mistakes – some of which led to horrible electric shocks from the high-voltage power supply – but, to my great joy, my students got great results. It was immensely rewarding.

I also learned about my emotional range. A few years ago I received this comment on my blog:

Tom, I was in your Physics class for your 1st job...will never forget you throwing my ring binder full of notes plus 2 other students notes in the bin because we had drawn willies all over each other's work....you went nuts, we were terrified/ embarrassed...sorry. I did get a 1st and PhD in the end though.
Posted by Glyn[7]

I replied with a retrospective apology. Glyn subsequently wrote to tell me that, after several years working in finance, he did a stint of voluntary work in a secondary school and, suitably inspired, has now started out as a teacher. He told me he could still remember our lessons 25 years later – and not just for my tantrums. I couldn't be happier about that.

Moving to central London, I spent seven years at Holland Park School in the 1990s; the one-time 'flagship comprehensive' of the 1960s. Here, being a subject specialist seemed less critical than the general skills of holding attention and keeping order. It was a school firmly driven by progressive ideals about inclusion and challenging prejudice. For the first time I got a sense that this was important work; that teaching matters; that you can really make a difference to a young person's life.

I met my wife there; that sense of mission was important to us both – and still is. However, we used to joke about it being 90% ethos, 10% achievement. It felt good to be part of that community of people but any success was hard-won. Behaviour management was a massive challenge with some classes and, in the absence of any school-wide systems, you had to work on your feet to create a learning environment in your own lessons. Nearly all of the teaching was in mixed ability groups, including in maths. That was an interesting challenge. We followed an individualised learning scheme called SMILE[8]. Essentially this involved spending every lesson with a queue of students at my desk asking for

---

7. teacherhead.com/2014/02/10/miscellany-of-memorable-moments/
8. Secondary Mathematics Individualised Learning Experiment: www.stem.org.uk/resources/ collection/2765/smile-cards

help or getting their latest activity cards signed off; there was no whole-class teaching as such. It wasn't really teaching; it was administering a system where students basically taught themselves.

More generally, Holland Park in the '90s was deep-end teaching for anyone new; learning to meet the needs of students who couldn't speak any English and multiple students with severe emotional difficulties all mixed in with a small group of affluent middle-class children whose parents subscribed to the ideal of a comprehensive school education. The diversity of the school population in social and cultural terms was matched by the range of learning needs; the gulf between students could be extreme.

Happily, the departmental leadership culture was rather *laissez-faire* which created a vacuum for us to fill as young teachers. We used to joke about our boss's 'hands-off management style' but we loved it; we could try different ideas, challenge the prevailing orthodoxy and generally have a good time. More by accident than by design, I probably learned more there than anywhere else. Our team was driven by a determination that standards could be so much higher if we simply lifted our expectations and injected some rigour and drive.

Professional Development didn't have the status that is does now and there was no internet on which to search out ideas and resources. Computers slowly worked their way into our working practices but the bigger tech revolution was seeing chalkboards replaced by whiteboards – which was actually quite significant. Fortuitously, amid the joyful chaos of daily life there, we were lucky enough to encounter the fabulous CASE project[9] – Cognitive Acceleration in Science Education – a programme devised by researchers at nearby King's College London. This was my first taste of evidence-informed pedagogy; it had a profound effect on my thinking as a science teacher. CASE made us consider the nature and sequence of the questions we asked and of the practical problems we asked students to solve. Special 'Thinking Lessons' were interspersed with regular lessons to support the programme and started to influence how I taught all of my lessons.

The next move was to Alexandra Park School in North London. It was incredibly exciting – setting up a new school from scratch as Deputy Head, with an inspiring Headteacher, Rosslyn Hudson, to guide us. 9/9/99 was the day it opened, taking the mast from Alexandra Palace – the site of the first public television broadcasts in 1936 – as its logo. That radiating beacon was symbolic of the high-achieving school we wanted to create. From our fabulous

---

9. CASE via King's College London kcl.ac.uk Past Projects

Millennium Show onwards, we had high hopes. (*You should see the place now[10] – it's an exceptional school. I like to think we sowed the seeds ... but I can't claim any credit for what happened after I left*).

At APS I learned about planning a curriculum and about creating a shared culture around teaching and learning. As the school and staff grew year on year, we spent a lot of time thinking about effective pedagogy, the behaviour ethos, the role of homework, the use and limitations of technology, the concept of emotional intelligence. Sadly, we also fell prey to the educational virus of learning styles. I can still remember the training. We believed the hype and duly collected data on our students' visual, auditory and kinaesthetic learning styles. Total bunkum.

Fortunately, this VAK sideshow didn't do too much damage. There were much stronger ideas coming through. During the late 1990s and early 2000s I encountered the ideas of two great educational thinkers who have influenced me and thousands of others ever since. The first was Bill Rogers and his brilliant work on positive behaviour management[11] – a subject I cover in Chapter 7. Bill's video series changed my experience of teaching significantly. He saved me from being an unhinged shouter and gave me the tools to manage my classes and my own emotions in the face of significant challenges working in tough schools. The key was focusing on some specific strategies that I could practise and get better at. My Bill Rogers Top 10 blog[12] is a runaway leader compared to all the others I've written with over 250,000 views. For a long time it was the first thing that came up from a Google search on Behaviour Management.

The second was Dylan Wiliam. It's hard to overstate the impact Dylan Wiliam has had on our profession – and certainly on me as a teacher. From his seminal 'Inside the Black Box' pamphlet[13], written with Paul Black, to his influential work on formative assessment through the 2000s, Dylan Wiliam has injected an intelligent, accessible analysis of the processes of teaching and learning in real-world classrooms that has been transformational. He understands teachers incredibly well and has been able to cut through a lot of the noise that surrounds us to spell out some very powerful ideas about assessment, feedback and curriculum design – as they apply to the contexts we actually encounter.

Beyond the specifics of what he has said and written, possibly Dylan Wiliam's greatest contribution has been simply to communicate the idea that the quality

---

10. www.alexandrapark.school/news/aps-news/640-aps-students-triumph-in-pisa-tests
11. www.billrogers.com.au
12. www.teacherhead.com/2013/01/06/behaviour-management-a-bill-rogers-top-10/
13. Black, P. and Wiliam, D. (1998)

of teaching is something that can and should be improved and that our professional practice should be informed by evidence; by a rational examination of what happens in those complex teacher-student interactions.

Under the banner of Assessment for Learning (AfL), (leaving aside the issue of the distorting misappropriation by the English government whereby AfL became aligned with data gathering) Dylan Wiliam has spearheaded a shift in our professional culture. We now ask questions about embedded assumptions – such as the value of grading student work – and we accept the premise that teachers can improve through well-designed professional development activities. He hasn't been alone of course – but his influence has been huge.

To continue my professional journey, I left London with my family for an adventure in Indonesia, teaching at the sumptuous British International School in Jakarta for three years. Again, working in a new context, my eyes were opened to different possibilities. There were two main features of this experience that have shaped my subsequent thinking. Firstly, it was the experience of delivering the International Baccalaureate, as a teacher and school leader. It's an exceptional curriculum in my view, combining rigour and depth with breadth. The Creativity, Activity, Service programme and Theory of Knowledge components ensure that strong core values and critical thinking are interwoven with the subject content; the curriculum whole really is greater than the sum of its component parts. I loved it.

Secondly, it was the work ethic of the students. The blend of European, Australian and South-East Asian students was wonderful and, between the staff, students and parents, we fostered a work ethic that was quite breathtaking. I'd never seen anything like it. It meant that you could teach to a high level and trust students to engage with modes of teaching that I had never imagined were possible.

The experience of teaching such highly motivated students influenced my decision to take the job at King Edward VI Grammar School on our return to the UK. I would never have imagined working in a totally selective school before but something about KEGS caught my eye: it claimed to be a 'Research-Engaged Learning Community'. I wanted to know what it would be like to work in a school where that was a reality.

In my six years there I learned a great deal more about teaching, free from the preoccupying necessity of running a tight behaviour management regime and supported by some superb traditions built around student leadership. The professional learning culture I inherited and continued to develop was fabulous.

In our traditional, privileged setting – one I've previously described as like an Oxbridge college for kids – we were able to experiment with pedagogical ideas and engage students in the most sophisticated forms of student-led learning I've ever seen. This included whole programmes of computing and digital learning where senior students literally designed and taught the whole course to junior students (see Chapter 9, P7). Most of the best lessons I've ever seen were at KEGS.

Every teacher was engaged in an action research project of one form or another and many were supported by outreach staff[14] from Cambridge University to pursue this in more depth. We ran an annual celebration of our research work that was a genuine highlight of the year. As teachers became more tuned in to various ideas about research methodology, it became more common to hear people express their doubts; we became less inclined to trumpet the success of our endeavours – it was more a case of exploring our findings and making tentative conclusions based on the evidence of impact, if we could find it. That shift highlighted a stronger tendency towards developing evidence-informed practice amongst the staff. In addition to engaging in research, we wanted people to engage *with* research – arguably a more important pursuit and it was gratifying to see the development of this aspect of staff professional culture.

Finally, my teaching journey took me to Highbury Grove School in Islington. In sharp contrast to KEGS, HGS had around 70% of students classified as disadvantaged with the fully comprehensive diversity that I had first encountered at Holland Park. I learned so much as a teacher there, teaching maths and science to middle-ability groups. The range of student mindsets I encountered was amazing – fascinating and challenging in equal measure. I learned about the different mental models students work with in maths and the very different motivating forces that drive them. The power of peer dynamics and social context were major factors in our deliberations. We also explored lots of curriculum ideas – oracy, teaching for recall, effective modes of formative assessment, Ron Berger's ideas about excellence, and the importance of explicit knowledge and cultural capital. It's a fabulous school and I met some fabulous teachers and students there.

Prior to joining Highbury Grove School, there was a resurgence in public debate about our national and curriculum and the importance of core knowledge. This was informed by the work of E D Hirsch, the views of politicians such as the British Education Secretary Michael Gove and commentators such as Daisy

---

14. CamSTAR www.camstar.org.uk

Christodoulou and her famous book *Seven Myths*[15]. At the time I found that this debate was excessively polarising and I couldn't accept the knowledge-based curriculum drive as readily as perhaps I might have. We will explore these issues in Chapter 2. However, I then began reading the fabulous book *Trivium 21c* by Martin Robinson[16], with its sub-title 'preparing young people for the future with lessons from the past'. Martin provides readers with a fascinating account of the history of education in Britain and the three arts of the Trivium: grammar, dialectic and rhetoric. In seeking to identify the features of the education he would want for his then six-year old daughter, he sets out a case for a modern world version of the ancient Trivium:

> When I look at the three arts of the Trivium, I wonder why it was beyond the wit of my school to give me this grounding, and why it shouldn't be the grounding for a great education now. Surely there is nothing that could stop the trivium from being the foundation of schooling for my daughter in the 21st century?

Martin's notion that all children should become 'philosopher kids' was particularly striking:

> I want my daughter to be out in the global agora exchanging ideas, dialogue, argument, products, noises, and silences, in public and individual spaces, through dynamic, inter-personal and extra-personal communication, made possible by the technology of the electronic age, the architecture of our cities, and the maturity of our institutions and traditions.

In *Trivium 21c*, there is a place for a strong focus on grammar – our core knowledge – but also on various other crucial elements of a rounded education. Arriving at HGS, I felt that the ideas in *Trivium 21c* were completely relevant to a diverse inner city community of children. As I set out in more detail in Chapter 3, the emphasis on knowledge and cultural capital and the explicit teaching of rhetoric are clearly very powerful and important components of a great education. Working with staff across all subjects, we found that these ideas resonated and influenced some superb work on oracy and specifying the knowledge requirements in the curriculum.

That brings me to the present. I'm currently working as a travelling trainer, speaker and consultant. The journey continues. I'm meeting teachers and school leaders all over the UK and in various parts of the world, talking to

---

15. Christodoulou, D. (2013)
16. Robinson, M. (2013)

them about teaching and learning in their contexts and getting a sense of the challenges they face. From a Year 1 class to the test bays in college plumbing workshops, an English classroom, a drama studio or chemistry lab, teachers are wrestling with the same issues. They're working out their priorities for what their students should learn, how to set up the teaching and learning process for maximum impact and how they'll know if they've succeeded.

There are no certainties but there is a lot of wisdom to be found on which to base our judgements. One thing I know for sure is that there are great teachers everywhere. Passionate, committed, brilliant people working incredibly hard to carve out a path for their students to achieve success and fulfilment. Without doubt, one of the biggest influences on my thinking has been seeing great teachers teaching.

Great Teaching: Great Teachers

What is 'great teaching'? It's the phrase I find I use most often to describe the kind of teaching we're all aspiring to deliver, free from any associations with official accountability measures. It doesn't have the dubious hubris of 'outstanding teaching' or the functional dryness of 'effective teaching'. Great teaching is essentially the kind of teaching that great teachers do. Perhaps it is easier to capture a sense of what they might be like. This blog post is one of my very first:

BLOG: What makes a great teacher?
Over the last 30 years I've worked with hundreds of different teachers and had the privilege of watching thousands of lessons in the schools I've worked in and supported. My children have had quite a few teachers now and I have their perspective too. Without doubt, it is fair to say that teacher quality covers a range but right at the top of the pile, some teachers are simply exceptional. These are the teachers everyone raves about; you'd love them to teach your children; they inspire, enthuse, make learning accessible and challenging and get great results as well. At KEGS (one of my previous schools), they become 'legends'. For me, they are the profession's superstars; the people I look up to and strive to emulate.

I may never be an exceptional teacher – but I'd like to be better! So, as a new term approaches, I've been thinking about the very best teachers I've known. At first, they are all seem so idiosyncratic in their approach; uniquely charismatic and impossible to copy. But, if we are aspiring to join them, is there anything that they have in common that we can learn from and put into practice in our own lessons?

Well, actually, yes. There is lots of academic research in this area, but based purely on my subjective evaluations, here is my list:

1) They are drivers: Almost above all else, I'd say this is the key characteristic. They are standards-setters, never happy with mediocre work or sloppy thinking; always pushing every child to go further, to aim higher. This manifests itself through classroom dialogue, the inherent challenge in lessons, routinely giving challenging and engaging homework and so on. They are relentless in pursuit of excellence and their language with students is infused with this sense of urgency and drive: come on, there is another level; you can do it. Some have a glass half-empty demeanour; for some the glass is always nearly full ... but the effect is the same.

2) They nurture student-teacher relationships based on genuine mutual respect, where there is no argument about expected standards of behaviour. They achieve this in different ways – sometimes through the gravitas of maturity and experience; sometimes through amazing warm, interpersonal interactions with every child – but they create an environment where learning always thrives and there is a sense of the teacher and their students enjoying each other's company. Their rapport with students is palpably warm, friendly and trusting.

3) They take joy in going off-piste ... using deep subject expertise to go beyond the syllabus, inspiring students with their passion and their capacity to make connections and to tell stories or give examples that bring it all alive. At the same time, they take exams really seriously; it is not one or the other. Exams are not the be all and end all – they include all the 'fun stuff' as well – but if you want an A*, you'd be in safe hands.

4) They celebrate the intrinsic reward and motivating power of learning and achieving and use this to great effect. To varying degrees, they have the ability to explain complex concepts in ways that make sense; they ask good questions and give really good feedback; they are usually experts in the use of assessment for learning (even if they don't always call it that); however it is done, students feel that they are learning; they know where they stand and feel confident about the process. This is reward and motivation enough.

5) They are principled about people, about learning and work with integrity. This means that they do things for the right reasons – usually self-effacing and not the 'big ego' type. They are learners, happy to explore new ideas to develop their practice, but always in a way that captures the

spirit; they are not slaves to the tick box or the inspection crib sheet; they embrace change with integrity, with passion – or not at all.

It is obviously hard to capture – and some of the idiosyncrasy gets lost in the generalisation. But if we adopt the right attitudes and embrace the challenge, I don't think it is unrealistic to meet these standards. The hard part is to manage them all. Crucially, even the greatest teachers are not at their optimum day in, day out … but their routine core practice is so strong that they never fall too far from their peak.

Re-reading that early blog post it still feels right, taking account of the teachers I've encountered since. However, I would like to add another key factor, one that drives much of the thinking in this book:

6) **They design the curriculum based on a deep understanding of the learning process.** Great teachers design lesson activities, resources, assessments and feedback to maximise the opportunity for each of their students to understand concepts, develop skills and deepen their knowledge whilst also fuelling their motivation and seeking to support their broader development as well-rounded individuals.

I use the word 'design' very deliberately. It's a concept that I encountered in discussions with Joe Hallgarten and others at the Royal Society of Arts when I was invited to contribute to their 2014 'Licensed to Create' publication[17]. According to Joe Hallgarten, design is a form of creativity that suggests *deliberate, planned innovation built on a foundation of research-informed professional wisdom.* This informs all classroom interactions and responsive decisions. In the hands of great teachers, their professional wisdom can seem intuitive – an almost innate quality. There is research to support the idea that we have some innate capabilities as teachers[18]. However, wisdom can also be developed and enhanced through professional learning and practice.

If you are a teacher anything like me, you will share the experience that lessons rarely go according to plan. Real life is complicated! *Real teachers* are usually struggling to establish a healthy work-life balance; they are doing things somewhat on the fly in the turbulence of everyday school life; they are doing their best to cope with numerous demands on their time; they're riding the wave of perpetual educational change and wrestling with the imperfections and complexities of the teaching-learning process.

17. Licensed to create: Ten essays on improving teacher quality, RSA, 2014.
18. Didau, D. and Rose, N. (2016), p21

But all real teachers can aspire to be great teachers by engaging in professional learning processes that include sustained deliberate practice of new methods[19]. Learning that leads to better routines and habits, working smarter, not harder.

Real Classrooms: Real Students

My previous book was aimed at teachers of science at the very beginning of their career. That first 'I love teaching...' line ends with: 'I especially love teaching science.' This is true. I have also enjoyed teaching maths, sex education and religious education – but science is my specialism. Actually, teaching physics is my true home. To me, that is important because, as I will explore in this book, I don't believe we are teachers in some generic nebulous sense; we are teachers of specific knowledge and skills – very often a collection of knowledge, skills and ideas that have strong roots in traditional subject disciplines (like mathematics or history) or apply to specific contexts (like learning to abseil or play the piano).

Of course, knowledge doesn't exist in isolation; we can and should make connections between subject disciplines in various ways. You might also have multiple areas of knowledge that you can teach. But with that in mind, I would like to encourage readers to have some specific material in mind as you consider the ideas in this book. This will help to make it relevant to you in your context.

However, whilst the content matters a great deal, we are not simply teachers of our subjects; above all else we are teachers of our subjects *to our students*. This is the crux of being a teacher; it's not about us – it's about them. It's not about what we think we're teaching – it's about what they are actually learning. So, again, I think it will help to make this book useful (as well as, hopefully, interesting) if you have some real students in mind.

You will probably know hundreds of young people you could imagine as we explore the ideas in this book. But to give us some common ground, let's meet some of them. These pen-portraits are all based on actual people I have taught in real schools with the normal precautionary edits to protect their identities. Here are some of the wonderful specimens growing in our lush Learning Rainforest:

Sabrina is supremely clever and conscientious. She will do everything you ask, neatly and quickly and seems to grasp new ideas easily. She's a certain top grade candidate. She reads for fun at every opportunity. She's highly articulate with an active interest in politics. There's always a question about whether you're stretching her enough or perhaps putting on too much pressure.

19. Deans for Impact (2015). *The Science of Learning.* Austin, TX: Deans for Impact.

Jack never wants to write anything down but asks questions all the time. He is intuitive and enthusiastic, always puts his hand up, even if he doesn't really know the answer for sure. His book is a mess but he manages to do comparatively well on tests. He loves basketball and is really good at it. He's also extremely imaginative in art lessons.

Daisy is a lively engaging student but she thinks she is rubbish at science and maths. She is always checking to see what other people have done, lacking confidence in her own work. She is stressed by competitive answer calling and hangs back when questions are offered to the whole class; she will take a back seat during practical work if given the choice.

Sam is often disengaged – if he's allowed to be. He defaults to chatting, swinging back on his chair and fidgeting. He takes a long time to draw a table or to get organised for writing, even if he has remembered his basic equipment. His best work is reasonable but it takes a lot to coax it out of him. His main passion is science – especially anything to do with space.

Mo speaks English as an additional language but is very intelligent and is very good at maths. At times it is hard to separate problems with his cognitive understanding from his confidence with English. He loves computers and talks about going to university, following in his sister's footsteps. She is usually the person with him at parents' evenings.

Tamara is quiet. She joins in when encouraged, does most of the work, always performs averagely well when the class does a test and never causes trouble. She's in the Drama Club where people see a different side of her. Beyond that she spends hours a week on social media on her phone and never reads at home.

Luca is an exceptional student. He is socially quite awkward but scrupulously polite. His parents think he might have Asperger's Syndrome. He is miles ahead of all of his peers in the class with extraordinary powers of recall and the ability to explain complicated ideas far beyond anything covered in the course.

Shaniqua comes over as quite a troubled young person; she is popular amongst her peers but finds all learning processes incredibly difficult; she has developed a range of work avoidance strategies to mask her low literacy and lack of knowledge; she can be extremely defiant when challenged over minor infringements. She has fixed mindset attitudes and does not believe she will ever succeed.

Harun is a fabulous pianist and all-round talent. He can be a bit cocky but teachers like him because he always has interesting and perceptive comments and usually does extremely well in assessments. He's articulate and charming and is determined to study medicine at university.

Louisa is a quirky student who is hugely intelligent and conscientious but reacts negatively to the routines and constraints of school life. She likes to be argumentative and pushes the boundaries of school rules fairly regularly at the same time as delivering excellent work. She's superb at French and excels in maths and English.

Johnny has difficulties processing verbal instructions and is behind his peers with reading. He needs some support to access mainstream lesson materials and teachers have to check that he has understood any verbal instructions in lessons. He doesn't have anyone at home who can help him with homework when he gets stuck.

All the various learner-characteristics will be found in limitless permutations and in varying numbers in any one class. Constructing a curriculum and teaching lessons such that Sabrina, Jack, Daisy, Sam, Mo, Tamara, Luca, Shaniqua, Harun, Louisa and Johnny all thrive is the daily challenge.

This is the world of *real classrooms*. Imagine having all of those wonderful characters in your class at the same time. There are so many details to what you need to get right in order for each of those individuals to succeed. The culture and routines you establish will be critical; teachers have a big role to play in creating a classroom culture but there will be lots of other factors that feed into it from the whole school, families, the peer group. The curriculum that you deliver will overlap in complicated ways with each of the students who will each have different levels and ranges of prior knowledge.

As Graham Nuthall describes so vividly in *The Hidden Lives of Learners*[20], each of those students will learn a unique set of knowledge and skills within each of your lessons with them – and that will always be slightly different to the knowledge and skills you are hoping to teach them. All of this complexity is the source of the challenge of teaching but also the joy of it. No two lessons are ever the same and every class you ever teach engages with you in a different way.

This leads me back to the Learning Rainforest metaphor. Here I want to develop the idea to consider some of the wider cultural aspects of school life – the environment in which teachers have to grow and flourish themselves.

Rainforest Thinking?

The purpose of extending the metaphor is to explore how we think about our jobs as teachers and the organisations we work in. It is also to help us think about our purpose – the end product of all our endeavours as professionals –

20. Nuthall, G. (2007)

and the means of reaching our goals. Are we more concerned with students reaching specific standards in subject disciplines or with developing them as rounded individuals? Can we have both without unacceptable trade-offs? Can we create a culture that allows students to feel trusted and valued as individuals whilst also enforcing the rules and eradicating defiance and disruption?

Teachers usually place a high premium on their autonomy within an environment that can sometimes impose a rigid institutionalised professional existence. We want to feel free to express ourselves; to make choices and to not feel confined. However, at the same time we also complain about reinventing the wheel all too often and moan about chaotic systems or a lack of direction from our leaders. There is also the dimension of teaching as art and science: whilst we value our autonomy and the opportunity to be designers, we should be willing to accept that evidence-informed practice is the goal of our professional development which means that an 'anything goes' approach can't be justified.

If our job as teachers is to nurture our students into wonderful human specimens – our philosopher kids – as well as we can, are we talking about running a plantation or managing a rainforest?

First of all, let's consider **the characteristics of a plantation**:

The natural environment is heavily managed with interventions of all kinds to protect against pests and disease. There is a very specific view of what the desired outcomes are. Anything that grows outside clearly defined parameters is weeded out. It is important for all specimens to reach certain minimum standards but there is little or no room for diversity. This tendency towards a monoculture with a narrow gene pool halts natural evolution and increases vulnerability to long term or sudden environmental change. There is uniformity, conformity and an emphasis on control. The plantation managers are typically risk averse and, where improvements are needed, have a predisposition to seek out tried and tested methods with predictable outcomes. However, in the absence of sudden change, the products are consistently of high quality against a range of metrics of size and health.

How does Plantation Thinking manifest itself in schools?

- School culture is dominated by the notion that there is a right way to do things and that, consequently, schools or teachers should be doing things in a certain way; this requires controls and accountability measures. Teachers might be expected to deliver lessons that conform to a prescribed set of requirements, *eg* learning objectives must be written on the board, there must be a starter and a plenary, there must be a timed lesson plan; the scheme of learning is non-negotiable.

- School leaders are driven, to a great extent, by compliance with standards set by external bodies and accountability regimes; anything that is perceived to fall outside the accepted framework is avoided or dismissed as superfluous – or a luxury that can't be afforded.

- The curriculum and learning are heavily driven by what can be easily examined. Students have limited scope to make choices or direct their own learning – in case they make bad choices which is too risky. A high proportion of learning activities and experiences are standard, regardless of students' personal needs or interests – or even those of the teachers.

- Professional learning is standardised to ensure no-one falls through the net; there are lots of whole-staff meetings and compulsory workshops.

- Data has very high status, often beyond the limits of validity, with much less value placed on intangible or qualitative outcomes. A quasi-scientific methodology and belief system are imposed on assessment processes such that linear input-output correlations are devised and numerical data sets are given meaning as absolute measures of attainment and progress (see Chapter 5 for more on assessment).

- Interventions with students are heavily focused on short-term gains prior to examinations, with an emphasis on getting over the line set by the accountability measures.

- Any new ideas or initiatives that are believed to be beneficial are elevated to the status of a rule or become a standard requirement so, for example, everyone must have an interactive whiteboard, stick to the homework timetable, use traffic lights in their marking and stick rigidly to the behaviour code.

Depending on your mindset, some of this will sound horribly claustrophobic and restricting – but it might also just sound sensible and necessary for some contexts. Before we explore the validity of the characterisation, let's think about the alternative. What would the equivalent rainforest culture feel like? Let's revisit it, this time thinking about teachers, not students:

There is enormous variety in the range of trees and plants that are thriving in the environment; it is lush, exotic, awe-inspiring, unpredictable, non-linear, evolving, daunting. Each specimen is magnificent in its own right with different organisms occupying their niche in an environment that is self-nourishing. Without the need for artificial interventions, the soil is fertile and the process of evolution is continuous. Whilst each plant has distinctive features and unique requirements, they all co-exist in an equilibrium that develops organically over time in response to changing conditions. But, it is not cosy or safe; this environment is harsh at times. Not everything thrives unaided and, occasionally, invasive specimens inhibit the growth of others. However, as a result, the plants that flourish are very robust with extensive roots or they are nimble and adapt to change with ease.

In a school context, Rainforest Thinking suggests the following:

- The dominant mindset of leaders is to nurture the individual talents of staff and students, providing nourishment and creating a culture that is motivational and rewarding to operate in but not to control or micromanage the processes or predetermine the outcomes. There is a high-trust/high-challenge culture.

- Teachers and leaders recognise that the learning process is complex and, to a large extent, unknowable on an individual basis. Different learners can and do learn in all manner of ways. As a consequence, it is better to try a range of approaches; some will work better than others, but it is not possible to know which in advance. There is, therefore, great variety in the approaches adopted over time.

- Where teachers are thriving, delivering excellent lessons and securing student outcomes, there is a high level of autonomy. Maverick or eccentric approaches are certainly tolerated; they are actually celebrated – provided that they can be shown to deliver.

- Data is recognised as providing a rough guide to some aspects of learning – in a complex and non-linear fashion. Much of what matters is not measurable and value is placed on teacher knowledge that derives from interpersonal interactions and observations.

- It is understood that there is no 'right way' for most things we do in schools. There is still a recognition that there are aspects of bad practice – things that rarely or never seem to work – but, in the main, all kinds of teaching approaches can be effective in different contexts. The effectiveness research that promotes certain approaches is evaluated in context and is understood as suggesting an average general pattern with fuzzy edges, not an absolute truth.

- Organisational structures never operate in a linear, hierarchical manner. People exchange ideas in a dynamic, organic manner and each person has their own personal values, goals and priorities that align to a varying degree with the stated school values, goals and priorities. In the Rainforest, this is expected and valued.

- Professional development is highly personalised – on the basis that it is counterproductive and demotivating to impose a uniform model on every teacher. Training sessions are offered as options; coaching and mentoring are deployed to those that need or want it and the whole thrust of Performance Management is to nurture self-driven reflection and professional learning – not to satisfy external accountability pressures.

- Classroom learning is sometimes characterised by an experimental approach. Teachers try out new ideas all the time, do not expect standard responses and create a culture in which students can select from a wide range of possible options – for example in the pace of their learning, the sequence of tasks or the mode of response. Importantly, despite the rich variety and openness of the Rainforest, it isn't a case of 'anything goes'. Only learning and teaching that are effective survive...there has to be quality and rigour in whatever shape or form the learning takes. There is nothing soft or safe about it.

- Technology and other resources are seen as one of many options; no one textbook or computer device is the absolute solution or issued as standard. In the Rainforest, the approach is to make resources available as and when they are needed – by those that want to use them.

- Learning and achievement are recognised in the widest possible sense. It is understood that learners will have all kinds of talents and skills, personal goals and interests and in the Rainforest, these all have value. The curriculum has embedded within it a layer of learning that makes teachers and students focus on dispositional, attitudinal development that enables them to self-nourish their intellectual and emotional lives.

In writing this, I'm aware that the analogy is laced with a bias towards the Rainforest. However, I'm also painfully aware that this hasn't necessarily always worked for me as a teacher or school leader. When I worked in a selective school with highly motivated students and a very stable teaching staff, I used to be pretty certain that moving from plantation to rainforest was absolutely the right idea. In other more challenging contexts, I've had some moments of doubt. Is it too idealistic? In truth there are several benefits to plantation thinking: mainly it provides a safety-net that seeks to ensure that every child gets a solid curriculum experience and is able to reach certain standards. Whilst there is no single successful model for teaching, there are certainly some ideas that are universally true; our brains all work in similar ways and this ought to inform the way we teach. There is evidence about effective teaching, learning and assessment that all teachers should use to inform their practice. There is also huge power in having strong alignment across teachers in a school around some core principles – about ethos, curriculum and pedagogy. Sometimes that alignment needs to be engineered – not merely wished for.

There is also the reality that not all teachers are ready to perform at the required standards right away and, across our schools, there will be students who are being 'set free' to underperform; where mediocre work is accepted routinely and where behaviour standards impede learning. It's a classic leadership challenge: how to create a high-trust culture where autonomy-seeking expert teachers can thrive, when, amongst your staff, there are people who need a lot more direction and structure – and even, ultimately, intervention.

Another dilemma is that, whilst seeking to ensure that curriculum resources and planning meet certain standards, the desire to control this with tight prescription of schemes of work can ultimately lead to teachers becoming de-skilled in curriculum and pedagogical innovation. On the other hand, as with students, freedom to innovate can lead to teachers without enough expert knowledge or experience, sinking unsupported or simply creating crap. It happens. Quality assurance isn't a necessary evil; it's simply necessary.

We also need to consider the down-side of the Rainforest: *Not everything survives ... and occasionally vines creep and strangle the life out of other specimens.* Is it acceptable if we are leaving a student's learning to chance – dependent on the whims and capabilities of their particular teachers? Obviously not. Could it be that in some school contexts we just get away with trying out weird and wonderful teaching strategies – because the students will learn anyway? This doesn't make it good practice. 'It didn't do any harm' isn't sufficient to justify a teaching strategy.

Clearly, even if we want the high-level autonomy that Rainforest thinking promises, we need to mediate the full-blown wild experience to factor-in some safeguards. There must be a happy medium between the cultivated constraints of the plantation and the freedoms of the forest. Let's imagine a plantation that is set free a little, where some corners are left to run wild. Is that enough? Or is it more a case of bringing a degree of management to the rainforest? (Still with me?) At some point these two things will meet; there will be a metaphorical ecosystem that gives us the optimal combination of both worlds.

My inclination is to suggest that a managed rainforest is the most appropriate metaphor for the system we should seek and the mindset we need to adopt for great teaching. It's the most aspirational; where idealism is not lost – it is just made real; where lush diversity is still the goal, provided core standards are met. In the managed rainforest, teachers and leaders are the rangers, walking the forest floor, making sure that anyone floundering is nurtured without imposing restrictions on the others. At the same time, if anything is having a negative impact – an ineffective teacher, a dubious pedagogical practice, a disruptive student, a bureaucratic policy – action is taken to remove or resolve the issue, leaving the rest of forest to reach its climax form – in all its lush glory.

This is my preference because, given the power of our accountability systems, schools generally condition us to be Plantation Thinkers anyway; this is how we are forced to think by the pressures exerted upon us. Perhaps it is only by becoming better Rainforest Thinkers that we can face those pressures. We always need to take account of the management element to ensure that the conditions in our classrooms allow every student to grow, learn and flourish[21]. But that's not enough to sustain a career. School cultures need to feel liberating, invigorating and inspiring. That is what it should feel like to be a great teacher, a designer of great learning. It's also how the learners themselves should feel – but if the teachers don't, their students never will. So let's focus on ourselves to begin with.

Of course, as with all these dichotomies, it may not be about choosing one pole as being inherently better or more appropriate than the other overall; it can be about choosing the right approach at the right time and place. The leadership concepts of 'tight' and 'loose' can be very helpful. When things are new, insecure or contain weaknesses, leaders should exert more control, keep things tight. When you want to move to another level, to achieve excellence, you need to let things go; to develop more distributed leadership and give people more autonomy.

This is also the plantation-to-rainforest pattern for our students. Where you have weaker learners with low levels of prior attainment, a more standardised, controlled plantation approach is likely to benefit many of them. Where your learners are more sophisticated, with deeper knowledge – and as this develops over time – you can let them go a bit more and develop the rainforest canopy in ever more diverse ways.

Context and aspirations

To conclude this chapter, reflecting on my personal journey as a teacher, it's certainly true that in every new situation I have had to adjust and adapt my teaching. The context we work in has a major bearing on our priorities and our sense of what works. It can also shape our vision for what might be possible, limiting it or opening new doors. Working at KEGS and BIS Jakarta and seeing our vision for Alexandra Park School come into being taught me a great deal. Once you have met students with an extraordinary work ethic or students who

---

21. 'Where Children Grow, Learn and Flourish' is actually the motto of the Surrey-based academy trust, Glyn Learning Foundation www.glfschools.org

can dazzle you with their insights and imagination, students who respond to being trusted and challenged and challenge you back in return, you see possibilities for learning that you can never unsee.

With that insight, when teaching in more challenging contexts, where social deprivation and other community dynamics and pressures might make the need for control and standardisation more important for many students, without question, the Learning Rainforest is still the goal; that is still the aspiration. For example, silent corridors and rigid discipline might be a means to an end at a certain point in time but they are surely never the goal. Ultimately, you want students to develop the self-discipline, maturity and powers of self-regulation to thrive in a high-trust environment where these controls are no longer necessary.

If we are serious about giving students in any context as good an education as they would get anywhere else, at some point we need to make the transition from plantation thinking to rainforest thinking in the right way and at the right time. Largely that's a leadership challenge but individual teachers will have an important role to play.

Readers of this book will work in a vast range of contexts but my hope is that what follows resonates with teachers anywhere because we largely share the same aspirations for our students. Ultimately, the Learning Rainforest is for everyone.

THE PROGRESSIVE TRADITIONAL DEBATE AND THE TRIVIUM

" HOWEVER WE DEFINE THE OPPOSING POLES OF TRADITIONAL AND PROGRESSIVE PEDAGOGY, THEY BOTH HAVE A VITAL ROLE IN A CHILD'S EDUCATION. I AM NOT SUGGESTING THAT THERE IS NO DISTINCTION.

" IT'S IMPORTANT TO UNDERSTAND THE TRADITIONAL Vs PROGRESSIVE DEBATE – BUT IT IS ALSO POSSIBLE TO AGREE WITH POSITIONS ON BOTH SIDES.

" IF YOU ASSUME CLAXTON'S 'BELOW THE LINE' THINKING GOES HAND IN HAND WITH A STRONG BEDROCK OF TRADITIONAL KNOWLEDGE-RICH CURRICULUM DESIGN, IT MAKES SENSE; EDUCATING 'THE WHOLE CHILD' TRANSCENDS THE PROG-TRAD DIVIDE.

" THERE ARE LOADED CRITIQUES FROM BOTH SIDES THAT I RECOIL FROM INCLUDING SIR KEN ROBINSON'S NOTION OF SCHOOLS 'STRIP MINING' CHILDREN'S MINDS OR THE IDEA THAT STUDENTS CANNOT MAKE CHOICES ABOUT THEIR LEARNING OR THAT ANY COLLABORATIVE LEARNING MUST BE WEAK.

" THERE'S ALWAYS A RISK IN DOWN PLAYING KNOWLEDGE; IN THE LEARNING TREE METAPHOR, KNOWLEDGE IS ALWAYS CORE.

" HYMAN'S 'HEAD, HAND AND HEART' AND THE IDEA OF A TRIVIUM FOR THE 21ST CENTURY- GRAMMAR, DIALECTIC AND RHETORIC- RESONATE WITH THE RAIN FOREST METAPHOR.

" EACH SPECIMEN IS ONE OF THE 'PHILOSOPHER KIDS' 'OUT IN THE GLOBAL AGORA'.

> *'We need to educate all young people to be philosopher kids, to be part of the philosopher crowds, finding their way through the global village.'*

Martin Robinson, Trivium 21c[22]

For most of my career I was 'doing teaching' without properly engaging in the central debates that might have actually shaped my philosophy of teaching and my ideas about the purpose of education without me realising. It is possible to sustain a career in teaching in that way but I think it's so much better to consider the arguments explicitly.

Two key interrelated debates about teaching could be described as 'knowledge vs skills' and 'progressive vs traditional'. The knowledge-skills debate is arguably a particular theme within the broader progressive-traditional debate so the arguments on both sides often align. Sometimes these debates focus on pedagogy and sometimes on curriculum but, as I discuss in the next chapter, they overlap significantly. The 'what' and 'how' often align with different people's views within the debate.

As with so many areas of debate in public life, defining opposing views as polar opposites is potentially crude and simplistic but can also be helpful in seeking to clarify what the fundamental differences are. There is often a parallel search for the middle ground – or at least an attempt to assert that there is a continuum along which different people might place themselves between the poles. In that context, the murky grey reality makes attempts to force a black vs white dichotomy seem inappropriate or even false. Here, whether the tendency to seek out the grey is valid is part of the debate itself.

To give a flavour for some of the debate, here are some excerpts from articles and blogs in 2017. *Times* columnist Caitlin Moran wrote this provocative article[23] about what she would do if she ran the English education system. It could all be tongue in cheek – but these are certainly views held by people in the world of education:

> My plan is very straightforward, and rests on two facts: (1) the 21st-century job market requires basically nothing of what is taught in 21st-century schools, and (2) everyone has a smartphone....

22. Robinson, M. (2013)
23. Moran, C. (2017) www.thetimes.co.uk/article/caitlin-moran-why-i-should-be-education-secretary-9llh939r2

If education were really geared to supply you with a skill set that gave you power and value in the 21st-century economy, it would not be based around sitting on a chair from 9am-4pm, being told what to do – the perfect framework for creating obedient 19th-century clerks. It would, instead, be geared around the small, crucial presumption that you should play an active part in your own education: learning to set your own targets; devising your own schedules.

Imagine if, at the start of every term, you were told what your projects were – cells; ratios; Larkin – and then it was down to you how and when you completed them.

If I need to know the properties of halogens, I just google them. As does everyone not currently doing GCSEs or A levels. Quite why, of all the demographics in the world, millions of resolutely unscientific, anxious 16-year-olds in the middle of berserk emotional growth issues have to commit them to memory is baffling.

This was a response from Carl Hendrick, Director of Research at Wellington College, on his excellent Chronotope blog[24]:

This kind of pseudo-futurist ... philosophy is often found in self-made individuals who eschewed school to admirably forge a successful career in the communications industry. Fine for those outliers but unconscionable to advocate that for the vast majority of children from less privileged backgrounds for whom good A level results can be life changing.

Behind these ... views lies a dangerous conceit; namely that the purpose of education is to merely get you a job, and not just any job, but a job that doesn't exist yet. These phantasmic jobs often focus on alliterative groupings such as "collaboration, creativity and connectivity" ... and are positioned in opposition with the cruelty of 20th century education which apparently was some kind of mass conspiracy* designed to create a global village of the damned. (despite the phenomenal success of 20th century education in raising global literacy levels, for example.)

*Carl is referring here to this article by George Monbiot: 'In an age of robots, schools are teaching our children to be redundant'[25]:

24. Hendrick, C. (2017) www.chronotopeblog.com/2017/04/29/education-is-an-end-in-itself-not-a-preparation-for-the-workplace/
25. Monbiot, G. (2017) www.theguardian.com/commentisfree/2017/feb/15/robots-schools-teaching-children-redundant-testing-learn-future

In the future, if you want a job, you must be as unlike a machine as possible: creative, critical and socially skilled. So why are children being taught to behave like machines? ... Children learn best when teaching aligns with their natural exuberance, energy and curiosity. So why are they dragooned into rows and made to sit still while they are stuffed with facts? ... We succeed in adulthood through collaboration. So why is collaboration in tests and exams called cheating?

Governments claim to want to reduce the number of children being excluded from school. So why are their curriculums and tests so narrow that they alienate any child whose mind does not work in a particular way? ... The best teachers use their character, creativity and inspiration to trigger children's instinct to learn. So why are character, creativity and inspiration suppressed by a stifling regime of micromanagement?

Carl concludes his piece by saying:

Of course we should prepare students for an uncertain future, but if we adopt the techno-evangelist disruptive model and view education as merely a utilitarian enterprise for 21st century workplace then we truly will enact a "factory model" of schooling and furthermore, we will diminish the gift of knowledge for its own sake. Students should study Shakespeare not because of what job it might get them but because it's an anthropological guidebook that tells them how to live.

This kind of debate is an ongoing theme on social media, at education conferences and in the press. I used to think it was tedious; that the traditional-progressive distinction was a false dichotomy to be dismissed or side-stepped. Progressives vs Traditionalists acting out The North vs The South or Roundheads vs Cavaliers didn't feel like a good characterisation of my experience of education. My thought was: I don't get this. I don't understand the heightened righteousness of each position; it's not how I relate to my job as a teacher and school leader. Although I've shifted my position in recent years towards a more explicitly traditional view of teaching, I'm still far more comfortable in the murky middle road, in Third Way territory. This is largely because people on both sides of the debate say things I agree with and disagree with.

However, I now realise that the debate has actually influenced how I think about teaching and the curriculum in quite a fundamental way; it's been important to engage with what people are saying in order to clarify in my own mind what the purpose of what we're doing at school really is. I once gave a presentation entitled 'Walking the Traditional-Progressive Line; why it pays to have a foot in both camps'. This is where I first used a Pedagogy Tree metaphor to illustrate my middle-ground position.

My general argument is that, however we define the opposing poles of traditional and progressive pedagogy, they both have a vital role in a child's education. I am not suggesting that there is no distinction. I've probably been wrong in talking about a false dichotomy because there are certainly definable elements of each disposition that are distinct. Even if they overlap, the two camps are real and distinctive enough.

Here is my own gathering of the usual associations and clichés that define the elements of traditional and progressive education. 'Sage on the stage' is one of the more cringe-inducing; others are more neutral and prosaic. I've added the student- vs teacher-centred label because that is often how the whole debate is characterised:

Progressive: Student-Centred		Traditional: Teacher-Centred	
Experiential learning	Group work	Expert Knowledge delivered by teacher	Direct instruction
Personalisation	Discovery/Enquiry	Students receive knowledge	Guided instruction
Choice	Project-based learning		Teacher at the front
The guide on the side	Role play	Probing questioning	Didactic
Relationships	Co-construction	Rigour and Challenge	Facts and Testing
Resilience, Reciprocity	Empathetic writing	The sage on the stage	Formal assessment
Teacher as facilitator	Desks in groups	Teacher in authority	Rote learning and recall
Trust and openness.	Woolly, soft	Power and control	Desks in rows
21st-Century skills	Cooperation not compliance	19th Century Factory model	Gradgrindian
Creativity			Compliance is necessary

Reading this you might detect your own natural responses to some words. You'll read some as positive descriptors of the kind of teaching and learning experience you think children should have; you'll read others as negative, even pejorative. You might also feel irritated that certain words are in one list and not the other, as if your words have been appropriated by the other side. It's that sense that I could happily give value to things from both sides that has made we want to find a middle way.

Occasionally you find these opposing views very clearly expressed. It's a red-hot debate in the US. For example, on the website for Wingra School in Madison, Wisconsin, there is a full section on their progressive educational philosophy[26]. Here you will find the idea expressed that traditional education leads to a sense that 'school is a task to be endured' whereas progressive education means 'school is a challenging and fun part of life'.

High Tech High in San Diego is something of a beacon for advocates of project-based learning and explicit progressive ideas about the purposes of education. A graphic[27] promoted by one of their leaders illustrates their thinking through a series of student and teacher 'shifts' within an overall shift from Compliance (Old School) to Innovation (21st Century). This is characterised as moving from 'collecting dots' to 'connecting dots'; a move from 'factory schooling' with a goal of a homogenised, compliant workforce to 21st-century schooling with the goal of creating knowledgeable adaptable people who can work with others to innovate in the new economy.

Student shifts include *passive to active, consuming to producing, memorising to processing, isolation to collaboration, rigid to fluid, answering to asking.* Teacher shifts include *telling to listening, presenter to facilitator, scarcity to abundance, mass production to mass customisation.*

This is classic progressive rhetoric – and I find myself recoiling from it. I'm sure it's a fabulous school to visit but isn't this just a lot of clichéd caricatures? Although they express a desire for knowledgeable people to emerge, this rhetoric seems to demonise lots of really good processes for actually enabling students to acquire knowledge such as expert teachers 'telling' and students then memorising. I suspect that High Tech High projects are actually much more teacher-led than this sounds with plenty of teacher-telling. But how have we got to a place where these things are ever portrayed so negatively? Great teachers, well ... they teach! That's uncontroversial in my book.

In contrast to High Tech High, some of the reaction against a curriculum called CSCOPE, introduced in several schools in Texas, is staunchly anti-progressive. This table is an excerpt from a document produced by education campaigner Jeanine McGregor[28] which is very clear in its view. I've included a lot of detail because it shows how many areas of teaching the dichotomy is seen to reach into:

---

26. www.wingraschool.org/who/progressive.htm
27. Dr Kaleb Rashad pinned tweet: How are we moving learning from COMPLIANCE to INNOVATION? Posted 20/2/16. Accessed 29/8/17
28. www.senate.state.tx.us/cmtes/83/c530/0131-JeanineMcGregor.pdf

	Traditional (Classical)	Project Based Learning CSCOPE
General description	Conservative Capitalist (Individualist) Textbooks/Vetted Material Realism Logical (Productive)	Liberal/Radical/Progressive Socialist (Collectivistic) Textbooks Out/Unvetted Material Relativism/Social Constructivism Emotional (Social)
Teacher's Role	Academic instructor, source of knowledge, and authority figure	Facilitator, counselor, and mentor
Instruction	Direct instruction (vetted material) by teacher in homogeneous groups	Self-directed learning, discovery learning, and cooperative work in heterogeneous groups
Student's Role	learn what the teacher teaches focus on intellectual, factual learning (experts respected)	discover what they learn act as peer mediators, tutors and counselors focus on learning, feelings, and opinions (experts questioned)
Curriculum	focus on academic areas with facts, ideas, skills, methods based on research	balance academic and social concerns concerned with student's 'higher order thinking' without basic knowledge validated first often based on unproven fads or theories
Reading	Phonics	Whole-language
Mathematics	Direct instruction of math concepts prefers 'drill and skill'	Interactive and discovery learning – 'fuzzy' math rejects memorisation
Social Studies	Focus on American heritage, national sovereignty, and cross-cultural studies	Focus on diversity, multiculturalism, and global citizenship
Outcomes	Emphasis on academic skills in traditional core areas / measured objectively	Emphasis on the 'whole child' approach that blends psychological, social and cultural well-being of the child / measured subjectively

There's no attempt to present this as an objective evaluation; the loaded anti-progressive language is clear: fads and fuzzy math are lined up with an anti-phonics approach to reading and what she calls the 4Ps: 'posters, portfolios, projects, PowerPoint'. Even 'Experts are questioned' carries a tone of disdain. Heaven forbid! It later suggests that 'grades are inflated so all students succeed'; the final blow to the credibility of CSCOPE. Note how they go as far as attaching political labels so that this becomes Liberal/Radical/Socialist v Capitalist/ Conservative. For me, that's starting to lose the plot.

When you put 'whole child' in quotes, it means you don't accept the concept; when you suggest outcomes that are 'measured subjectively' are inferior, it's placing a lot of faith in some pretty shaky assessment practices. Again, I recoil from this. Of course we are educating the whole child; learning is not something that happens independent of the people doing the learning. As we'll see further on, relationships are key to even basic educational processes such as giving feedback.

Usually I find that arguments in support of traditionalist perspectives misfire when they overstate their case, leaving no room for nuance or for blending different forms of learning; there's too much plantation, not enough rainforest. Given all the unknowns and complexities surrounding learning processes, this can sometimes feel like a misjudgement: too rigid, too absolute; over-zealous. I also find that attempts to blame progressive ideals for the failures of our education system are too crude[29]. My experience is that most teaching you see walking around schools is very traditional. Most of the weak practice I have encountered has not been where groovy progressives are wasting time with pointless group work and ineffective discovery activities (although I have seen this too!); it has been teachers trying to teach in a traditional, direct manner but not having the skills to do it well.

Compliant behaviour: Good or bad?

This debate is another core element of the progressive-traditional divide. Again, I find myself conflicted. Having worked in some tough schools where teachers could face some very challenging, defiant behaviour that definitely impacted negatively on learning, I'm uncomfortable with the idea that compliance is inherently negative. But this discussion can become a bit of a semantic minefield; one that is rather important. Compliance to a set of reasonable rules sounds sensible and neutral to me – a necessary element of running social institutions where the behaviours of individuals have an effect on the collective. However the idea of 'compliant children' has other connotations.

Ever since my children were born, I've been imposing a regime on them; moulding them into little Sherringtons with a clear sense of the boundaries and

---

29. teacherhead.com/2013/08/05/a-perspective-on-seven-myths/

a strong set of values and attitudes that my wife and I share and want to pass on. I'd call this parenting. That's not incompatible with them growing up into well-loved, autonomous, creative, adaptable people with minds of their own. In fact, I'd argue that it's a necessary prerequisite. Of course, there comes a time to let go ... but this thing of romanticising non-conformity and non-compliance is hugely problematic. At times it feels like the indulgence of privileged people who already have cultural capital in abundance... (more of which later.)

However, I do also recognise that producing 'compliant children' isn't what schools aim to achieve. I don't think my children are compliant. To be compliant suggests something more than just being someone who follows the rules; it suggests being inherently submissive, excessively passive and possibly even afraid of those in authority rather than having a relationship with them. As with parenting, there is a crucial period during adolescence when children explore their boundaries; they learn to talk to adults – and even to argue with them – and learn that they have rights as well as responsibilities and that actions have consequences. This feels like a necessary and natural part of the journey to adulthood and parents have to learn to navigate this territory by giving their children an appropriate degree of leeway. To me there is clear daylight between the act of *compliance* and the state of *being compliant*.

Ideally we want students to cooperate with us voluntarily but in many contexts there is an authority relationship that is necessary to safeguard the learning and wellbeing of all members of a class. Teachers are in authority in the classroom; it's part of their duty to ensure that they are (see Chapter 7, **C6 Foster Relationships: positive, caring and defined**). I think that's uncontroversial yet there is plenty of debate around the idea of obedience, authority, teacher power and the extent to which students are controlled.

For example, there are schools where children are required to walk the corridors in single file in total silence; they are not trusted to walk and talk freely like the students at the traditional grammar school up the road or the more progressive comprehensive next door where behaviour standards are also regarded as being good. In all three situations it's possible for the children to feel happy, relaxed, loved and cared for but I understand why silent corridors might be a level of control too much for some people; that's not something my own children needed and it's not my idea of necessary compliance. The context will be crucial but the point I'm making is that there are degrees of compliance; it's not black and white.

***

The wider progressive-traditional debate is played out through the work of significant educational philosophers, the work of contemporary academics and the headline philosophies and practices of numerous schools. Here are some of the protagonists:

	Progressive	Traditional
Academics, writers and commentators	Guy Claxton *et al*: Ruby, Building Learning Power Alfie Kohn Sir Ken Robinson: Creative Schools and The Element George Monbiot	ED Hirsch Cultural Literacy: What Every American Needs to Know Doug Lemov: Teach Like A Champion Dan Wilingham: Why don't kids like school? Daisy Christodoulou: Seven Myths Robert Peal: Progressively Worse
Founding figures	Paulo Friere: Pedagogy of the Oppressed John Dewey "Education is the process of living and is not meant to be the preparation of future living", (Dewey, 1897) Jean Jacques Rousseau	Matthew Arnold: Culture and Anarchy GK Chesterton
Schools	RSA Opening Minds Curriculum High Tech High Steiner and Montessori Schools Holland Park School in the 80s and 90s	Michaela, London West London Free School Uncommon Schools in Boston and NYC King Edward VI Grammar School

Claxton: Below the line learning – Developing dispositions

One of the people that champions of contemporary progressive education often refer to is Professor Guy Claxton – even though he himself regards the progressive-traditional debate as something of a 'Punch and Judy' show[30]. He is known for the development of the Building Learning Power concept which was highly influential in English schools after the publication of the BLP book in 2002: *Building Learning Power: Helping Young People Become Better Learners*[31]. The ideas are communicated through the construct of 4Rs: Resilience; Resourcefulness; Reflectiveness and Reciprocity – the last of which includes collaboration and empathy, the capacity to work with others. An evaluation

---

30. Claxton comment made at Bryanstone Festival session, June 2017.
31. Claxton, G. (2002)

of their work in these schools is reported in a follow-up book *The Learning Powered School*[32] by Claxton *et al* in 2011.

For a time during the late 2000s, if felt like BLP was *the* thing in English education. A lot of teachers and school leaders warmed to the idea that we should be trying to develop students' dispositions as well as teaching them knowledge. Some schools have adopted BLP as the central driver of their school ethos whilst many more make reference to it, with laminated posters promoting the 4Rs dotted around their classrooms.

The problem I found with this kind of approach was that in some schools the dispositions were presented in abstract, removed from any learning content. As much as the authors assert that this is meant to complement a knowledge-rich curriculum, too often it becomes interpreted as 'instead'. I've attended conferences and Headteachers' meetings where BLP has been cited as an antidote to the straitjacket of the knowledge-heavy national curriculum. I've been to a school where they had off-timetable BLP days – including 'resilience workshops' which had no knowledge base at all. I once observed a history lesson where a teacher started by holding up his Resilience poster, announcing that 'today we will be building up our resilience'. There was some discussion about the idea of resilience but nothing in the content of the lesson required students to actually be resilient.

However, I'm happy to accept that a good idea can be misinterpreted or implemented really badly. When I listen to Guy Claxton talk, he always makes a lot of sense to me. He has told me directly that he's always viewed BLP as meaning 'both dispositions and knowledge' not 'or' – and yet his stance that knowledge itself isn't all there is to worry about is often portrayed as 'anti-knowledge', which is unhelpful.

This is an excerpt from a contribution he made to a 'Redesigning Schooling' event in 2013[33].

> There are always things in every lesson going on below the line: and what goes on below the line is important. Most educational discourse revolves around what's above the line; flat education with two dimensions of what shall we teach and how will we know if they've learnt it; curriculum and assessment...

> But ... what skills of learning are being invited, practised, strengthened? What skills ... attitudes and identity as a learner are being required? And

32. Claxton, G. *et al* (2011)
33. Claxton, G. talking at SSAT Redesigning Schooling Symposium London March 2013

what conceptions of knowledge? Either knowledge is fixed true and abstract or negotiable and present? Even though you're only 13 you can begin to play a candidate role in the investigation, the enquiry, the appraisal of what you're reading rather than the (unquestioning) acceptance of it.

Which wider learning habits (are needed) to build a disposition that asks skeptical, intelligent and respectful questions about knowledge claims? For the people working in the digital world this is a fundamental life skill for the 21st-century. Getting knowledge is easy; appraising knowledge is tricky.

Once you face up to the moral questions you can't opt out of it; which of the these things below the line is my school busy cultivating and which might they be neglecting and which are the things we might say young people should develop in order to flourish in the 21st-century?'

If you assume that this thinking goes hand-in-hand with a strong bedrock of traditional teacher-led knowledge-rich pedagogy, then it all makes sense. It's only problematic if you interpret it as a relegation of knowledge. In suggesting knowledge claims might be questioned, that need not suggest that you become wishy-washy about the provenance of most things you teach. If you take 'getting knowledge is easy' to mean 'you can just google it', that's a huge mistake. Claxton doesn't mean that. I agree that, if you are consciously, deliberately thinking about developing dispositions – below the line – then it's more likely that you'll succeed than if you just hope they emerge organically.

However, 'getting knowledge is easy' is potentially problematic because too often it isn't easy at all. For some learners, appraising knowledge is a luxury; surely you can't appraise knowledge you don't have. For many learners, filling the gaps in their knowledge base that might allow them later to ask questions about knowledge claims might be an absolute priority. Even at a reasonably advanced level it is perfectly sensible, for example, to get to grips with Newtonian mechanics and the Bohr model of an atom, before learning that quantum physics changes everything and that, yes, atoms can exist in multiple states simultaneously and 'action at a distance' is a real thing. It's not sensible to debate the veracity of claims about climate change until we really understand the science of global warming. It's better to have a good understanding of the chronology of key events in WWI before students are asked to evaluate different theories of causation.

There is a risk that, in asserting that knowledge isn't enough in itself, knowledge is downplayed. In the Learning Tree metaphor, knowledge is always core. There is no shortcut, no bypass, no 'instead'. I also support the view that any emphasis on 21st-century learning is problematic. Obviously that is the time in which we live – but, as Daisy Christodoulou tackles well in *Seven Myths*[34], there is nothing inherently different about learning now compared to learning centuries ago. For example, I've got no time at all for the idea that children learning in rows of desks, much as they did in Victorian/Dickensian times, is problematic. It's just a really very sensible way to arrange a space so a teacher can make eye contact with every student and engage in the dialogue required for great teaching and learning to happen. Technology and the internet and modern ways of living do not change this – and our brains work the same way they always have.

If dispositions are represented in the lush canopy of the rainforest, knowledge in the trunk and branches remains absolutely central. But more than that, knowledge is actually the means by which many dispositions are developed. You can't simply urge students into being resilient by endlessly repeating a mantra. However, by attacking some challenging maths problems, finishing a complex piece of art, completing an extended piece of writing or undertaking a 30-mile hike in the rain – all without giving up, despite crises of confidence along the way – our students might actually develop the resilience levels we are seeking.

Resilience – alongside many other dispositions – has context; it relates to a domain. It makes much more sense to focus on the substance of the learning activities through which dispositions will develop because, in doing so, we're more likely to succeed. The same argument applies to creativity, character and many other highly valued but wildly over-generalised educational outputs.

Sir Ken Robinson and the quest to rescue creativity

Another central arena for the progressive-traditional debate is the question of how we teach for creativity and innovation. It is uncontroversial that for us to solve humanity's problems, to create the conditions for a sustainable future and also to maximise the cultural richness of our lives, we need to develop our collective capacity to be creative and innovative. It also follows fairly obviously that our education system should contribute to this process. Creativity and innovation, to my mind, manifest themselves in two arenas:

Arts and Culture: our capacity to express ideas through art forms of all kinds including literature, music, art, theatre and design. This can be about composition and performance. It is also about creative approaches to interpreting our history and the selection of lines of enquiry in academic research.

---

34. Christodoulou, D. (2013)

Problem-solving: our capacity to develop our understanding of scientific and technical problems, or social and political problems, and generating solutions.

In both areas, there is demand for us to do better – whether you are driven by a hard-headed desire to put your nation at the cutting edge of industrial technology for economic purposes or by a more 'you can say that I'm a dreamer' ambition to create a society where people are able to express themselves more fully as rounded individuals with ideas and talents of all kinds.

Sir Ken Robinson is a key protagonist in the debate about the best way to teach for creativity. In his famous TED talk 'Do schools kill creativity?'[35] from 2006, Sir Ken essentially argues that, yes, they do. He suggests that creativity should be given the same status as literacy in schools and that, currently, our schools damage our capacity for creative thinking: He says that 'if you're not prepared to be wrong, you'll never come up with anything original', and schools are too busy focusing on being right:

> I believe our only hope for the future is to adopt a new conception of human ecology, one in which we start to reconstitute our conception of the richness of human capacity. Our education system has mined our minds in the way that we strip-mine the earth: for a particular commodity. And for the future, it won't serve us. We have to rethink the fundamental principles on which we're educating our children.

Elsewhere[36], he argues for a radical change in our approach to education, encouraging divergent thinking as a building block of creativity.

For sure, Sir Ken is always thought-provoking – even if, like me, you feel that our declining capacity to suggest a range of uses for a paper clip is more to do with our capacity to process and evaluate ideas before we volunteer them for serious consideration, than a fundamental loss of the power of imagination.

But the question remains – does the prevailing culture in our accountability driven system allow space and time for creativity to flourish? SKR's position is that our current model of knowledge-based, teacher-led, classroom-located learning is inadequate and needs to be broken up to be replaced. He is much less clear about what the replacement would be. There are some schools here and there that meet his criteria but it is not clear that they could be scaled up to a national system or succeed beyond the specific context in which they are located.

---

35. Robinson, K. TED Talk 'Do schools kill creativity?' www.ted.com/talks/ken_robinson_says_schools_kill_creativity
36. Robinson, K. RSA Animate Changing Education Paradigms 2010

In response to another Ken Robinson talk at a Bush Foundation 'Power and Possibility of Individualised Learning' event in the US[37], once again bemoaning the state of our education system, Carl Hendrick suggests this is 'teacher bashing'. He had this to say in the *TES*[38]:

> Robinson says that children lose interest the deeper they get into school. I can relate to this, because when I was 14 I pretty much lost interest in school, but it had nothing to do with school and everything to do with the fact that I was 14. As Rob Coe reminds us, learning happens when children have to 'think hard' and this is anathema to most teenagers. Robinson wants to see kids being given more freedom and choice to do things that are more closely aligned with their own interests. Well, the more freedom and choice I had in school, the less I wanted to do things that would ultimately give me more freedom and choice later on in my life. As an avid reader, I didn't want to study Shakespeare at school but wanted to read science fiction and contemporary poetry. It took me a university degree in English to realise that my understanding of contemporary culture would be spectacularly enriched by studying Shakespeare, not diminished by it.

> ... The notion that children can only learn things through the prism of their own interests and that to ask them to consider things outside of that is somehow beating a love of learning out of them is demeaning, not just to teachers but to students themselves. Possibly the greatest thing a teacher can do is to introduce students to wondrous worlds beyond the limited borders of their own experience, to allow them to see the previously unseen and to make new and enriching connections that were hitherto unavailable to them.

I completely agree with Carl here and I find that the characterisation of schools as strip-mining our children's minds doesn't ring true. That said, there is certainly merit in the idea that, somewhere in the curriculum, students ought to have time and space in which they can be creative. However, rather than this being an unstructured, open-ended process, there are plenty of advocates of a more traditional approach to developing creativity. The argument is that, in order to have creative ideas, students need to 'stand on the shoulders of giants' – in art, in technology, literature, science, mathematics, dance. New ideas that are considered to have real value tend to emerge from the knowledge and understanding of what has gone before – not from a naive discovery.

---

37. June 2017, Minneapolis
38. Hendrick, C. (2017) www.tes.com/news/school-news/breaking-views/ken-robinson-a-teacher-basher-schools-must-stop-listening-his

The challenge for teachers is to design opportunities for students to build on their knowledge in creative ways at an appropriate point where their knowledge is deep enough for this to be a meaningful process with some rigour and substance. Creative thinking can be regarded as an ingredient of successful problem-solving in maths and science – although the likelihood is that this sense of creativity will stem from the recall of successful methods that students have encountered in related problems, rather than inventing new approaches. Creativity is embedded in certain subjects by their nature; subjects where students compose, design, devise, write creatively, build or make. Alternatively, there is scope to set up one-off projects and creative processes within or between subjects, where this is genuinely adding something. There are ample opportunities for this to happen, built around a knowledge-rich curriculum as I set out in Chapter 9.

In every case, this does not represent some kind of unshackling from the torture of learning facts. In my experience, strong creative processes in schools always emerge from strong knowledge foundations.

***

The difficulty I have with critiques from both sides of these debates is that I feel I'm continually being asked to make a false choice. When people protest against the weight given to tests in our accountability culture, they often end up sweeping away quite sensible practices around learning facts and taking tests. For example, in her foreword to *World Class*[39] – which is an excellent collection of essays – Carol Dweck says:

> Who will be better prepared for the unknown jobs of the future – students who know how to memorise facts and take tests or students who know how to wrestle with hard problems and figure out how to solve them?

Much as I am a huge admirer of Carol Dweck, I find this kind of statement rather exasperating. It's an entirely false choice (and there is that 'unknown jobs' meme again). There is no 'or'. I'll return to this in Chapters 4 and 5 when we look at memory, testing and assessment in general.

In England, new free schools that have opened since 2010 have given educationalists the opportunity to create new schools based on very clear principles. Michaela school in Brent has a strong identity as a school promoting a traditional philosophy – as well as lots of highly innovative practices, around classroom management, reading, curriculum planning, assessment and

---

39. Dweck, C. Foreword to James, D. and Warwick I. (2017)

reducing staff workload, as documented in their book *Battle Hymn of the Tiger Teachers*[40]. Here are some quotes from their website:

> At Michaela, we believe all pupils, whatever their background, have a right to access the best that has been said and thought. This includes a variety of writers, from all parts of the world, and thinkers from all the ages. The curriculum ensures that pupils are knowledgeable enough about the world around them to transform it in the future.
>
> The education provided at Michaela is broadly traditional and academically rigorous. We expect our pupils to be polite and obedient. We encourage competition and allow our pupils to win and lose. We believe that knowledge about the world is central to our pupils' success. Only when they have acquired this knowledge will they be ready to lead and participate as full citizens.
>
> We want our pupils to be compassionate, considerate and kind, always looking after those who haven't been given the same opportunities
>
> Rather than canteen provision, pupils at Michaela sit at tables, eating together and engaging in conversation. Children serve food to their classmates, clear each other's plates and eat the food that they are given. At Michaela we believe that school should develop the whole child. The dining experience at Michaela helps to do exactly that, teaching restraint, respect for others, and ensuring that bullying does not take place in our dining halls.

I have visited the school and I can attest to the fact that it has a very friendly, warm, loving ethos as well as being characterised by strict discipline. Teachers teach in a very direct way and students are drilled in the habit of self-quizzing for strong recall of the knowledge they encounter. Although the approach is very distinctive, attracting both arch-critics and devoted admirers, without question there is a blend of character development and knowledge acquisition at work and it's impossible to argue with the standards of work students are reaching. 'Below the line' learning is happening at Michaela, albeit not as explicitly as Guy Claxton would advocate.

Another free school, School 21 in Newham, East London, has attracted a lot of interest because of their commitment to oracy and project-based learning where students are given opportunities to make 'beautiful, meaningful work'[41].

---

40. Birbalsingh, K. (ed.) (2016)
41. School 21 website www.school21.org.uk

However, it is a common mistake to pit School 21 against Michaela as if they are polar opposites. In fact, they have far more in common than they have differences. Both schools make explicit references to educating 'the whole child' and to the 'learning the best that has been thought' quote from Matthew Arnold (see Chapter 3).

In an essay written in 2017[42], Peter Hyman, Head of School 21, sets out his vision for education; the kind of education he is trying to deliver in his school:

THE EDUCATION OF HEAD, HEART AND HAND (Selected excerpt)

The 21st century demands so much more in terms of agile thinking than the old tramlines of education, which will leave young people floundering.

We need a different course – an education for head, heart and hand.

- An academic education (head) that gives people in-depth knowledge of key concepts and ways of thinking in science, maths and design, as well as history and culture. This knowledge should be empowering knowledge, knowledge that draws on 'the best that has been thought and said' from the past, as the cultural critic Matthew Arnold advocated, but importantly it should be shaped and applied to the needs of the present and future.

- A character education (heart) that provides the experiences and situations from which young people can develop a set of ethical underpinnings, well- honed character traits of resilience, kindness and tolerance, and a subtle, open mind.

- A can-do education (hand) that nurtures creativity and problem-solving, that gives young people the chance to respond to client briefs, to understand design thinking, to apply knowledge and conceptual understanding to new situations – to be able to make and do and produce work through craftsmanship that is of genuine value beyond the classroom.

To achieve this multi-dimensional education will require fundamental changes in the way schools are run. A revolution in curriculum planning, timetabling, the role of the teacher and, perhaps most of all, our attitude to young people.

---

42. Hyman, P. (2017) 'Success in the 21st Century: The education of head, heart and hand' www.ippr.org/read/success-in-the-21st-century#

Perhaps, the 'tramlines' are the same as the constraints that Sir Ken Robinson bemoans continually. However, here we have a coherent vision for the way forward. Rather than perpetuating a clash between progressive and traditional ideas, School 21 shows that, whilst the two philosophies might be inherently in opposition, they can coexist – they are intrinsically linked facets of excellent learning and an excellent education overall. They might even be considered to exist in a symbiotic relationship. In practice, students at School 21 only do some of their learning through projects. Within these projects, there is clear knowledge content. A lot of lessons are traditional teacher-led knowledge-driven lessons albeit that there is a strand of oracy woven into their approach to teaching and learning.

This approach seems to echo the Learning Rainforest metaphor. 'Head, heart and hand' certainly puts knowledge at the core in a traditional manner with multiple, structural opportunities for a diverse canopy of learning possibilities to be built around it. The nurturing culture is unquestionably providing the environment for all of this to take root and flourish. Comparing Michaela and School 21, the debate seems to be whether focusing more extensively on knowledge acquisition ultimately leads to stronger emergent 'whole child' outcomes or whether schools should be engineering more of the canopy directly. This is not an either-or debate and it is likely to be highly context-specific, as my school leadership experience would suggest.

Trivium 21c – 'Preparing young people for the future with lessons from the past'

A major influence in my thinking about schools, curriculum and teaching has been the ideas contained in *Trivium 21c* by Martin Robinson[43]. It remains very firmly my all-time favourite book about education. When I first read it, I wondered 'could this be the answer?'[44] It has been a joy to subsequently meet and work with Martin.

His book is framed partly as a quest to conceive of the ideal education he would want for his daughter. In surveying the landscape of progressive and traditional philosophies and their origins, Martin arrives at the Trivium as providing the way forward. As Martin explains in great detail, the Trivium of Grammar, Dialectic and Rhetoric formed the basis of a classical education from Ancient Greece up to Shakespeare's time at school and beyond. He argues that in the 21st Century, it remains a powerful framework for formulating ideas about learning, the curriculum and pedagogy:

---

43. Robinson, M. (2013)
44. teacherhead.com/2014/01/17/trivium-21st-c-could-this-be-the-answer/

The three ways of the Trivium – knowing, questioning and communicating – had come together as the basis of a great education. This is what I want for my daughter. I want her to know about things and how to do things. I want her to be able to question, both to find out more and also to realise that some things aren't known, can't be known, or aren't fully understood. I want her to communicate about things she has discovered, surmised, or created in the way of an open hand to the world. Finally, I want all this to have a purpose, which can be summed up by the phrase 'a good life'.

At my previous school, we embraced these ideas to guide and inspire us, working with Martin to formulate our Trivium in practice. As part of this work, he wrote these short sketches of the key concepts for us:

Grammar: Knowledge, Skills, tradition, authority, discipline, hierarchy, the 'culture', what makes this art unique? The relationship between the 'master' and her apprentice is central with the teacher as expert and the pupil as needing to know. The body of knowledge: the 'best' that has been thought, said and done. Connecting ideas, the importance of the whole narrative, and also how the subject connects with others, beyond its own confines.

Dialectic: Exploration, critical thinking, analysis, philosophical enquiry, thought, reasoning, creative, scientific and mathematical thinking, encouraging dialogue, debate, argument, questioning, the individual pupil gradually coming into view and finding themselves flourishing through practice and self-discipline. Humour, wit and playfulness. Authentic experience.

Rhetoric: Communication, turning outwards to the world, persuasion, product, performance, community, relationships, caring, love, responsibility. Writing, speech, challenge to exist and 'be' in a public space, giving of yourself to others. Parenting, leading, emotionally controlled and mature, thoughtful, empathetic, – ethos, pathos and logos.

In practice this meant that we tried to create the conditions in our schemes of learning and lesson planning where the Trivium elements came alive with more familiar associations for communication with students and parents. Our simplest distillation of the Trivium was expressed in our Framework for Teaching and Learning as shown below. With the Trivium in mind, we started to be much more focused on specifying knowledge with strong direct instruction; we also developed a strand of oracy that we wanted to weave into everything.

Grammar = Knowledge

- The direct transmission of knowledge and explicit teacher instruction

- Retention and recall: teaching for memory; learning by heart; low stakes testing; knowledge for its own sake; repetition and practice

- Explicit teaching to build cultural capital; explicit teaching of subject-specific terminology and the skill of -reading different texts

Dialectic = Exploration

- Opportunities to debate, question and challenge

- Opportunities for hands-on authentic experience and experimentation

- Opportunities for enquiry, analysis, critical evaluation and problem-solving

Rhetoric = Communication

- A strong emphasis on structured speech events to share and debate ideas with others

- Opportunities to perform, to make things and to showcase the products of learning

- Opportunities to contribute to the discourse about the values shared in the school and the wider community

Crucially, the three elements do not need to be delivered in a crude linear sequence. They overlap and coexist. However, by highlighting them it made it much clearer how to build some units of work. For example, it gives value to doing some science experiments purely as dialectic – a hands-on authentic experience; it suggests that acting out a poem, to feel the words as you say them, is a valuable element of learning what it means. It also made us question whether students had sufficient mastery of the grammar before they could hold a debate. It also gave value to oral communication at a time when the exam system was taking oral exams out, with a risk that oracy would be downgraded.

At various points in *Trivium 21c*, Martin refers to the concept of philosopher kids. It was this that, to some extent, provided the greatest inspiration for staff. Again, we asked Martin to write something for us that pulled the ideas together:

- We believe that children need to feel they are on an adventure in the pursuit of wisdom through which they develop as lovers of learning in all its rich variety. We believe in the importance of knowing, exploring and communicating; we believe in building a strong community where every member of the school bears responsibility for the strength of our institution.

- Plato talked about the need for Philosopher Kings and Queens; we wish to enable our pupils to become 'Philosopher Kids'. Philosopher Kids are curious to know, question, and they can lead as well as follow. Philosopher Kids like to feel, to think, and are notable for their eloquence and ability to take part in the 'great conversation' through which they make a contribution to our common life.

- Philosopher Kids engage thoughtfully in dialogue and argument, they appreciate and make beautiful things, they are confident when grappling with difficult ideas, they love music and also seek out space for quiet reflection and contemplation.

- We challenge all our pupils to become cultural polymaths, true 'renaissance people', able to flourish both as individuals as well as realise that they have an important role to play in enabling their family, friends and community to flourish as well.

These are lofty ideas that are much easier to write than to deliver in practice. However, I do feel it is important to raise our sights and aim for high ideals. The ideas in *Trivium 21c* resonate loudly with Peter Hyman's 'head, hand and heart' and breathe life into the Learning Rainforest with each specimen, one of the philosopher kids. As in the Rainforest, the cornerstone is grammar, knowledge. But it is not an end in itself. Knowledge needs to be questioned and debated – the dialectic is essential for a rich learning experience which in turn helps still more knowledge to develop by making things, feeling things, experiencing things. And finally, knowledge needs to find expression through rhetoric if we are to engage in debate and deepen our understanding. All of these elements of dialectic and rhetoric in the Trivium form parts of the Rainforest canopy supported by the trunks of grammar. That works for me; it's the same idea in essence.

As we will see in Chapters 4 and 5, once we've taken account of the learning from research and considered the role of assessment, I think there is a route through this debate that makes sense and does manage to extract value from the different positions. Trivium-driven thinking supports this viewpoint. Whilst traditional and progressive ideas might be inherently in opposition, at least in their origins, and the differences are real, there is a symbiotic relationship between them; they are always in tension with each other without one succumbing to the other. It's a question of emphasising and sequencing teaching modes and enacted curriculum experiences at different points in the learning process and in the curriculum overall.

THE CURRICULUM DEBATE

> WE WANT OUR CHILDREN TO HAVE IT ALL: KNOWLEDGE AND UNDERSTANDING ACROSS MULTIPLE DOMAINS; A RANGE OF PRACTICAL AND INTELLECTUAL SKILLS AND A RANGE OF CHARACTER TRAITS-RENAISSANCE PEOPLE.

> THE CORE KNOWLEDGE DEBATE IS VITAL-WHAT KNOWLEDGE SHOULD ALL STUDENTS HAVE? ANY SELECTION HAS CULTURAL BIAS- SO WHAT DO WE INCLUDE AND EXCLUDE?

> CULTURAL CAPITAL NEEDS TO BE TAUGHT DELIBERATELY-AND SHOULD INCLUDE EXPERIENCES LIKE CONCERTS, PLAYS, WALKING IN MOUNTAINS, VISITING MUSEUMS AND ENGAGING IN CURRENT AFFAIRS.

> WHAT WE TEACH AND HOW WE TEACH ARE INTERLINKED IN THE ENACTED CURRICULUM.

> CURRICULUM IS SPECIFIED IN DIFFERENT WAYS BUT THERE IS ALWAYS SOME ROOM FOR TEACHER INPUT - OFTEN A LOT OF FREEDOM TO CHOOSE THE BOOKS AND HISTORICAL PERIODS THAT STUDENTS STUDY.

> BEYOND TEACHING 'THE BEST THAT'S BEEN THOUGHT AND SAID' WE'RE TRYING TO GIVE STUDENTS THE KNOWLEDGE TO ENGAGE IN 'THE CONVERSATION OF MANKIND.'

'Culture – a pursuit of our total perfection by means of getting to know, on all the matters which most concern us, the best which has been thought and said in the world, and, through this knowledge, turning a stream of fresh and free thought upon our stock notions and habits.'

Matthew Arnold[45]

What should students learn?

Having argued for a central role for knowledge in a broader, Trivium-inspired curriculum, the question about what children should actually learn at school remains. It's a huge question – and one that I'm sure we don't engage with enough. I'd argue that great teachers should know why they are teaching what they teach; better still they should be involved in the debate about what defines the content of the subjects they teach. In devising a curriculum from scratch we would probably find some common agreement around a basic list: the essentials of mathematics, how to read, basic grammar in our mother tongue. But beyond some subject headings, what else would we agree on in any detail?

Here are 20 questions for you:

1. What is the capital of Equatorial Guinea?

2. In which year was Rome supposedly founded by Romulus and Remus?

3. List the prime numbers between 101 and 201.

4. In which classic novel would you find Clara Peggotty?

5. What is the key molecular structural difference between a gel and a foam?

6. Which Battalion in the Crimean War suffered the greatest losses?

7. What were the key reforms sought by the English Anti-Corn Law League formed in 1838?

8. Who contested Super Bowl II in 1968 and what was the score?

9. How far away is Proxima Centauri in astronomical units? How do we know?

---

45. Arnold, M. (1869) *Culture and Anarchy: An Essay in Political and Social Criticism.* Oxford: Project Gutenberg.

10. Describe the relationship between the central characters in Cormac McCarthy's *The Road*.

11. Translate into English: *Omnia vincit amor; et nos cedamus amori.*

12. Name five leaders of sub-Saharan African nations, past or present.

13. What is the keyboard shortcut for a screenshot on an iMac?

14. What are the structural characteristics of the 2nd movement of Mahler's 1st Symphony in D Major?

15. What is the maximum collision energy now delivered by the Large Hadron Collider?

16. What was the outcome of the Tet Offensive?

17. Name three 19th-Century British Prime Ministers and US Presidents

18. What's the difference between a viral and a bacterial infection?

19. Complete the quotation: 'Now is the winter of our discontent...' What is its significance?

20. What is the common name for Rembrandt's *The Militia Company of Captain Frans Banning Cocq?*

How did you get on? I would be surprised if anyone knows all the answers without having to look something up. This eclectic collection of knowledge-based questions spans a wide range of subject domains, each of which is vast. Is our goal to accumulate as much of this knowledge as possible? Is that what makes somebody an educated person? Or, at least, is our goal to give students enough of a knowledge foundation for these questions to make enough sense so they can research the answers?

Alternatively, perhaps we should express our ideas about what students should learn as a set of skills:

Students should be able to:

1. Swim 50m.

2. Write a letter to their local representative arguing their case for a cause they are passionate about.

3. Compare the language features used to create emotional effects in two different poems.

4. Evaluate the relative merits of siting a nuclear power station or a wind farm in a particular location.

5. Recite a Shakespeare soliloquy from memory.

6. Make a pie (Or program a Raspberry Pi?!).

7. Challenge homophobia, sexism and racism amongst a group of their peers if they witness it.

8. Engage in an informed debate about the ethical and moral implications of assisted suicide.

9. Evaluate the evidential value of a Russian propaganda poster from 1917.

10. Fill in a tax return and keep track of a set of financial accounts.

11. Use simultaneous equations to find the intersection of two straight-line graphs.

12. Hold a conversation in a foreign language.

13. Complete a 20km hike using a map and compass, including a night of camping.

14. Sustain a regular commitment to supporting a local community project.

15. Compose a piece of music or produce an original piece of art – of real quality.

16. Organise and deliver a speech or group presentation.

17. Complete an extended project or depth study on a specific area of the curriculum.

18. Evaluate the merits of the arguments put forward by politicians during election campaigns.

19. Filter the bias and sensationalism to identity the factual content in a news report.

20. Give first aid to someone who has fainted.

Can you do all of those things? Is this a better way to capture our goals as teachers – the things we can do rather than the things we know? Or are these 'skills' just a different way to express forms of knowledge? In either case, what would be on a list that most of us would agree on? Does everyone have their own personal list that would be rigorous enough to be valued?

Or is our primary goal to develop students' personal attributes? A recent review of the curriculum in Wales has led to the publication of the Successful Futures report,[46] which suggests that the main purpose of the curriculum is to develop four 'capacities'. This is captured as follows:

The purposes of the curriculum in Wales should be that children and young people develop as:

- ambitious, capable learners, ready to learn throughout their lives.

- enterprising, creative contributors, ready to play a full part in life and work.

- ethical, informed citizens of Wales and the world.

- healthy, confident individuals, ready to lead fulfilling lives as valued members of society.

It is hard to argue that developing all of these capacities is what we would want for children – just replace Wales with wherever you live.

So, as teachers, we are presented with multiple, parallel sets of ideas about what we're trying to do. There is the content – the knowledge and understanding that we want students to accumulate over time; there are the skills we want them to acquire and then there is also this wider sense of developing our students as rounded individuals. We want it all. Renaissance people; philosopher kids.

With those wide aims in mind, one of our central challenges as teachers is to break down the grand thinking into a curriculum we can work with in practice: before we start thinking about how to teach, it's important to think about what to teach. This applies not only to the selection of whole subject areas but also the details of each one; the specific component facts, concepts and skills that we want students to learn.

One of the shifts I have made in my thinking over the years has been to move away from thinking about pedagogy in a generic sense. I've recognised that many of the issues teachers face stem from not giving the curriculum content enough thought – the micro details of what, exactly, they are trying to teach and why. Pedagogy has some generic components but the skills of teaching always have a content-driven context.

We also have to be very careful about wishing generic 'thinking skills' into existence. You can't develop students' capacity for critical thinking in isolation from a knowledge domain – say science, history or literature. Students develop

---

46. Successful Futures: gov.wales/docs/dcells/publications/150225-successful-futures-en.pdf

the critical thinking through developing ever-deeper knowledge of these subjects, building more sophisticated schema that allow them to evaluate new information in that domain. There is not an absolute barrier between domains – there are parallel logical reasoning processes that relate to multiple disciplines – but in general, that's how it works: detailed knowledge is the basis for skills which tend not to be as generic as people often suggest.

However, to complicate things a little, in truth, you can't really fully separate what you teach from how you teach it. Tim Oates has suggested that 'curriculum' has multiple meanings[47]:

Intended curriculum: the required knowledge, skills and understanding that might be written down in the specification for a unit of study.

Enacted curriculum: the curriculum that students actually experience as delivered by their teachers, each teacher applying their own filter, adding or subtracting content, deploying a unique combination of learning tasks and resources.

Assessed curriculum: the knowledge, skills and understanding that students encounter in their assessments – normally a subset of a much wider curriculum.

Learned curriculum: the knowledge, skills and understanding that students are left with at a later time. (As referenced earlier, Nuthall's work suggests that this will be unique to each student in any class.)

It's helpful to bear these distinctions in mind when discussing the content of what we teach. The enacted curriculum – the way it is delivered and experienced in any given classroom – may vary significantly even between colleagues sharing the same schemes of work, especially if they have different ideas about the way students should learn. Increasingly I find that it's more useful to consider 'pedagogy' as a component of what we mean when we say 'curriculum'.

For example, you could teach history by asking students to read about some key historical characters and their situation and asking them to engage in role-play based on a script; you could ask them to embed as much historical knowledge in the script as possible. On the other hand, you could try to cover the same material by telling students the whole story in more of a lecture style, discuss the meaning of some historical sources and get them to take some recall

---

47. Oates, T. (2015) from Cambridge Assessment talk 'A world without levels'.

tests and write a formal essay. Or, you could give the students a text to read that covers the material and ask them questions after a class-reading activity. Even if the three teachers here started with the same content outline, students' curriculum experience would be very different.

In another example, in science, students might watch a series of teacher demonstrations of an electrical circuit, learn the definition of electrical resistance as voltage divided by current (R = V/I) and then engage in some practice questions. Alternatively, they might be asked to explore a range of 'what happens' questions, working in pairs with their own set of circuit equipment, to see if they can see a pattern in the current values when voltage and resistances are altered. This could then lead to the equation R= V/I being explained more formally. Of course, students might do both of these things but one is more theoretical, the other more experiential.

An English teacher, seeking to teach students how to compare the linguistic devices used in two Sylvia Plath poems might take an analytical approach. After reading out the poems herself, the teacher might then invite students to follow a line-by-line comparison searching for specific identified features – thematic connotations or onomatopoeic word effects – before comparing their findings. Another teacher might ask students to work in pairs to give animated readings of each poem, using their voices to highlight the structural features of the text, emphasising the beat and key language features. This would lead to a written summary of their findings.

The point is that, in the detail, the enacted curriculum is a function of both the stated knowledge content requirements and the nature of the learning experience. Can we say who would have learned the most or whose learning is better? Clearly, the *learned curriculum* is likely to be very different even if we can't agree on criteria to judge 'most' or 'better'. One method might support the learning of more concrete factual knowledge whilst another might lead to learning some other skills that are less tangible, perhaps independent to the subject in hand. Some students might have their love of the subject fired up by one of these modes of learning but not the other.

The question then is which kind of learning we value. Our values come into play; it's not purely objective. Our choices will also depend on our understanding of how students learn. It's an interplay of values and science. Another reason to love teaching! Of course this comes with a great degree of responsibility. The likelihood is that your students will learn a certain part of the curriculum from you alone, the way you do it. In a very direct way, we're going to be imposing our values onto our students in the way we choose to teach.

What should we include in our intended curriculum?

Leaving the complexity of enactment aside, what scope do teachers have for shaping the intended curriculum within and around the parameters that might be set by our governing institutions? There is an important democratic debate to be had about who decides what students learn about and where teachers' expertise and values come into play. I think all teachers should develop an understanding of where their curriculum comes from and, wherever possible, contribute to the debate about what is in it.

Curriculum specifications

In the UK, very much of the curriculum for upper secondary students is determined by the specifications for national examinations – English and Welsh GCSEs and A levels for example. But who decides what goes in them? And how much freedom is there beyond what we're told to teach?

Whatever the official framework says, there is always another layer of discussion about the level of detail in what is prescribed. In practice, this varies hugely from country to country and from state to state. But wherever you may be, it is important to get a sense of the scope you have as a teacher to determine the curriculum you are going to teach – within your district, your school, your team, and ultimately in your classroom.

It is interesting to compare how the curriculum is defined in different systems. The International Baccalaureate is followed by over 4600 schools across every region of the world. The curriculum for the IB starts out with a strong mission statement[48]:

> The International Baccalaureate aims to develop inquiring, knowledgeable and caring young people who help to create a better and more peaceful world through intercultural understanding and respect.
>
> To this end the organization works with schools, governments and international organizations to develop challenging programmes of international education and rigorous assessment. These programmes encourage students across the world to become active, compassionate and lifelong learners who understand that other people, with their differences, can also be right.
>
> IB learners strive to become inquirers, knowledgeable, thinkers, communicators, principled, open minded, caring, risk-takers, balanced and reflective.

---

48. IB website www.ibo.org/benefits/why-the-ib-is-different/

These broad principles and the IB learner profile are rather wonderful in my view. I love the ambition behind the explicit goal of creating 'a better and more peaceful world'. Having worked in an IB school I know how all of this translates into a school context. The strong guiding principles follow through into the way the curriculum is prescribed. Each of the four programmes – Primary Years, Middle Years, Diploma and Career-related – are designed around the idea that their courses should be broad and balanced, conceptual and connected. All of this feeds into the relatively new suite of circles[49]:

This sets out the range of subjects that combine to make up the overall programme including the compulsory theory of knowledge component. Within each subject, teachers are given a detailed subject guide. In biology at Higher Level, for example, the range of units is specified – *eg* Unit 8 is metabolism, cell respiration and photosynthesis. 14 teaching hours are suggested for this unit. Within the unit, the specification goes into fine detail in specifying the content. Further exemplification is provided through the publication of sample questions.

---

49. Based on original www.ibo.org/globalassets/digital-tookit/logos-and-programme-models/ dp-model-en.png

In history, given the need for the curriculum to resonate with students from any part of the world, the content has a looser structure[50]:

Prescribed subjects

One of the following, using two case studies, each taken from a different region of the world:

1. Military leaders 2. Conquest and its impact 3. The move to global war 4. Rights and protest 5. Conflict and intervention

World history topics

Two of the following, using topic examples from more than one region of the world:

1. Society and economy (750–1400)

2. Causes and effects of medieval wars (750– 1500)

3. Dynasties and rulers (750–1500)

4. Societies in transition (1400–1700)

5. Early Modern states (1450–1789)

6. Causes and effects of Early Modern wars (1500–1750)

7. Origins, development and impact of industrialization (1750–2005)

8. Independence movements (1800–2000)

9. Evolution and development of democratic states (1848–2000)

10. Authoritarian states (20th century)

11. Causes and effects of 20th-century wars

12. The Cold War: Superpower tensions and rivalries (20th century)

Here, there is much greater flexibility to the extent that two history students could study a completely different curriculum, albeit with common concepts and themes. However, once you've chosen your periods, there is some tighter specification of the content. For example Unit 12, The Cold War, includes the study of the overthrow of the Allende regime in Chile in 1973 and the Soviet invasion of Afghanistan in 1979.

Overall, the IB has done a superb job in constructing a framework that starts with significant philosophical values-driven statements of intent before drilling

---

50. www.ibo.org/contentassets/5895a05412144fe890312bad52b17044/history-hl-2016-english-final-web.pdf

down into the layers of structural detail and knowledge specification.

In the UK, England, Scotland and Wales all have a different national curriculum; this is one of the areas of governance devolved to each country. In England, the Secretary of State for Education has ultimate responsibility for determining the curriculum – an enormous power and responsibility for one person who is not ever directly elected to do this job and seldom has any school experience beyond attending one as a child or as a parent, lived through their children's experience. Since 2012, changes to the English curriculum have provoked a wide-ranging debate about what should be included. Unlike the IB, the national curriculum in England is mainly just a collection of subjects. There is very little emphasis on interweaving themes or philosophical elements to knit it together into a coherent whole. This is what it says:

> The national curriculum[51] provides pupils with an introduction to the essential knowledge they need to be educated citizens. It introduces pupils to the best that has been thought and said, and helps engender an appreciation of human creativity and achievement.

> The national curriculum is just one element in the education of every child. There is time and space in the school day and in each week, term and year to range beyond the national curriculum specifications. The national curriculum provides an outline of core knowledge around which teachers can develop exciting and stimulating lessons to promote the development of pupils' knowledge, understanding and skills as part of the wider school

> The curriculum … satisfies the requirements … if it is a balanced and broadly based curriculum which

> • promotes the spiritual, moral, cultural, mental and physical development of pupils at the school and of society, and

> • prepares pupils at the school for the opportunities, responsibilities and experiences of later life.

There are several things to note from this. One is the explicit suggestion that the curriculum should form a preparation for 'opportunities, responsibilities and experiences of later life'. It is a means to an end; it has a purpose beyond the here and now. Whilst you might agree with this entirely, it's interesting to note how this directly contradicts the progressive ideas espoused by American

---

51. The National Curriculum documents www.gov.uk/government/publications/national-curriculum-in-england-framework-for-key-stages-1-to-4

philosopher John Dewey who said 'Education is the process of living and is not meant to be the preparation of future living' (Dewey, 1897)[52]. So, at the heart of the English national curriculum is a challenge to progressive thinking. However, the same argument is often made by traditionalists who bemoan the much-touted progressive mantra of preparing students for jobs of the future – or jobs that haven't been invented yet, as Carl Hendrick does in the exchange cited in Chapter 2. Third way, anyone?

Another feature of the national curriculum is the clear statement that the content of the specified curriculum is only a sub-set of a wider whole; teachers are explicitly encouraged to 'range beyond the specifications'. I can hear the chorus of 'Thank you, that would be lovely – if only we had the time'. In practice, there doesn't seem to be much room to explore beyond the specifications because of time pressures, but at least the intention is there. This point is often forgotten, but is there just too much specified content to make this a reality? The reference to 'exciting and stimulating lessons' is also interesting. The intended curriculum is only an outline of core knowledge requirements; in theory, the enacted curriculum is all to play for and the pedagogy is totally up for grabs.

However, perhaps the most interesting feature is the direct statement that the national curriculum 'introduces pupils to the best that has been thought and said'. Here, once again, we have a reference to a very specific vision for a traditional knowledge-driven curriculum that is gaining traction across schools in England. 'The best that has been thought and said' is a quotation from the essay Culture and Anarchy by Matthew Arnold, a 19th-century English poet, essayist and school inspector[53]. This phrase, quoted more fully at the start of the chapter, is often cited by politicians and commentators seeking to emphasise the importance of handing down knowledge and traditions from generation to generation. It's a phrase given prominence at Michaela and School 21 as we've already seen.

In fact, the statement had a rather wider meaning to its author. As Martin Robinson explains, 'this was education as cultural capital for all, cultivating character as well as intellect in order to help eradicate human misery ... Education in England continued to evolve shaped by Arnold's romantic and anti-utilitarian desire to ensure individuals are touched by the best that has been thought and said'[54].

52. Dewey, J. (1897) 'My pedagogic creed', *School Journal* 54, pp. 77–80. Retrieved on November 4, 2011 from dewey.pragmatism.org/creed.htm
53. Arnold, M. (1869) *ibid.*
54. Robinson, M. (2013) p81

The so-called Programmes of Study are designed to crystallise this idea of 'the best that has been thought and said' into something concrete for each subject discipline. As with the International Baccalaureate, there is a blend of specificity and freedom of choice. For example, here is an excerpt from the Programmes of Study[55] for English at Key Stage 3 (students aged 11-14):

Subject content: Reading

Pupils should be taught to:

- develop an appreciation and love of reading, and read increasingly challenging material independently through: reading a wide range of fiction and non-fiction, including in particular whole books, short stories, poems and plays with a wide coverage of genres, historical periods, forms and authors. The range will include high-quality works from:

  - English literature, both pre-1914 and contemporary, including prose, poetry and drama
  - Shakespeare (two plays)
  - seminal world literature

Very reasonably and sensibly, the curriculum is just a framework for the range of texts that students should engage with if they're going to learn the best that has been thought and said. Whilst there might be some agreement about what 'the canon of literature' might contain, there are no specific texts that all students must read and only Shakespeare is named – for obvious reasons, given his contribution to our culture. 'Seminal world literature' is wide open and the requirement to study pre-1914 literature provides enormous scope while still giving value to a period of literature that might otherwise be absent, giving way to the vast sway of contemporary fiction.

In an English department in a typical English school, there is going to have been a discussion – and hopefully a heated debate – about which exact texts should be taught. Should this be left to individual teachers to teach the books and plays they like – or should there be a consensus reached across the school so that all students get the same curriculum opportunities? Should the Head of a school have a say in which texts are studied or should this be delegated to the English specialists? These are debates that shape the curriculum experience of students in our schools.

---

55. www.gov.uk/government/uploads/system/uploads/attachment_data/file/244215/
SECONDARY_national_curriculum_-_English2.pdf

The degree of freedom for 11 to 14-year-olds is significant. However, this is slightly less real for 15 to 16-year-olds studying for GCSE exams. Here, the high-stakes nature of the tests tends to force schools to converge towards a narrow set of texts from the lists provided by the exam boards. This reached a peak in 2015 when, according to the former education secretary, Michael Gove, 90% of students were studying John Steinbeck's *Of Mice and Men*[56]. There's a whole generation of English citizens for whom George and Lennie are key figures in their reservoirs of cultural capital. More recently, following major curriculum changes, the vast stocks of OMAM books tend to be read by younger students whilst Orwell's *Animal Farm*, Shelley's *Frankenstein* and J B Priestley's *An Inspector Calls* dominate the GCSE courses.

There is obviously absolutely nothing inherently wrong with choosing to study any of these books – they're all extraordinary in their own way. The question is whether we should all tend to read the same books or whether it is more healthy for there to be greater diversity in the range of texts studied across the nation. There must be a trade-off between a common canon that helps to bind us through common cultural references and a diverse 'gene pool' of literature that is known and loved. Of course, the more books students read, the less pressure there is on any one of them to carry the load of cultural transmission.

It's here that I find the Learning Rainforest metaphor has value. We're not trying to create carbon-copy children with identical learning experiences. There is value in diversity. Provided that each of our learners' reading diet supports them in building up a strong trunk – rich with cultural significance, powerful knowledge[57] that will help them engage in national and global cultural life at a level of their choosing (not the level defined by the limitations of their education), finding joy and inspiration along the way – it doesn't matter precisely which books they read. It would be possible to devise hundreds and thousands of reading lists for children, each with equal value yet each one unique. It would also be possible to produce a list that was weak, limited and limiting. That's where great curriculum design comes in and where every English teacher's responsibility lies.

Things are slightly less contentious in geography.

Here, one section of the National Curriculum Programme of Study suggests that pupils should be taught:

---

56. www.theguardian.com/education/2014/may/25/mockingbird-mice-and-men-axed-michael-gove-gcse

57. Young, M. (2014) www.cambridgeassessment.org.uk/Images/166279-the-curriculum-and-the-entitlement-to-knowledge-prof-michael-young.pdf

Locational knowledge: to extend their locational knowledge and deepen their spatial awareness of the world's countries, using maps of the world to focus on Africa, Russia, Asia (including China and India), and the Middle East, focusing on their environmental regions, including polar and hot deserts, key physical and human characteristics, countries and major cities.

Place knowledge: to understand geographical similarities, differences and links between places through the study of the human and physical geography of a region in Africa and a region in Asia.

Teachers are given the scope to select the regions they are interested in or perhaps that have connections with the school community. There is a framework to ensure some breadth but significant flexibility to make choices.

In science, there is a different picture, largely because the content of a science curriculum is less open to debate. It's really a question of what you can cram in with some debate at the fringes regarding what is in and what is out. The core material is straightforward. For example, in biology we have this section:

Genetics and evolution: Inheritance, chromosomes, DNA and genes

- heredity as the process by which genetic information is transmitted from one generation to the next

- a simple model of chromosomes, genes and DNA in heredity, including the part played by Watson, Crick, Wilkins and Franklin in the development of the DNA model

- differences between species

- the variation between individuals within a species being continuous or discontinuous, to include measurement and graphical representation of variation

- the variation between species and between individuals of the same species meaning some organisms compete more successfully, which can drive natural selection

- changes in the environment which may leave individuals within a species, and some entire species, less well adapted to compete successfully and reproduce, which in turn may lead to extinction

- the importance of maintaining biodiversity and the use of gene banks to preserve hereditary material

The level of specification is much greater for science. However, even here there are lots of decisions to be made about the examples and contexts in which these ideas are explored. Usually, this is where textbooks come in handy because they will have made a set of choices for us. We don't have to follow their choices but we can if we want to.

Where there is a high level of subject knowledge required to design and shape a curriculum – and ensure it remains current given the pace of change with scientific thinking – it makes sense to defer to people with the appropriate expertise. The detailed curriculum specifications and related textbooks in science are hugely influenced by the work of associations such as the Institute of Physics or the Royal Society of Chemists, organisations that are regarded as the custodians of the body of knowledge that make up the subject disciplines. Once these experts have had their input, most teachers are happy to bow to their greater wisdom. That's controversial for some – I've always been happy to accept it.

Significantly, woven into the science curriculum are some very clear positions in relation to the nature of science. For example, there is no equivocation regarding the theory of evolution: it is a scientific fact on the same basis as all the laws of physics. There's no fudging; no room for intelligent design or young-Earth creationism as alternatives. A clear set of values is evident in the curriculum – values based on the well-established traditional, rationalist paradigm, built on testable scientific theories, supported by physical evidence.

As a final example, here is a section from the history curriculum for 11- to 14-year-olds in England. Here the national curriculum is expressed in terms of broad themes and periods:

- the development of Church, state and society in Britain, 1509-1745

- ideas, political power, industry and empire: Britain, 1745-1901

History teachers are free to make curriculum choices within these very broad areas. Here is how one school has planned their Year 8 curriculum:

Term 1	Term 2	Term 3
Making of the UK 1509-1745	**Slavery in the Americas**	**Campaigns for rights and freedoms –** **Slavery and the Suffragettes**
Life in 1509, Henry 8th, Reformation, How bloody was Mary?, Elizabeth 1st, Why did Elizabeth kill her cousin?, Spanish Armada, Causes of the civil war, Charles 1st, Roundheads vs Cavaliers, Execution, Cromwell, The Merry Monarch, Great Fire of London	Justice2History – Mali, Africa in the 18th Century, Why did Britain have an empire? Causation, evidence, change, significance, interpretation	Why was the slave trade abolished? Importance of the slave trade, Middle Passage, Arrival, Plantations, Slave resistance, Underground railroad, Abolition, Suffragettes – women's roles, WSPU, Tactics, Emily Davidson mystery, Militancy, The vote
Causation, evidence, change, significance, interpretation		Causation, evidence, change, significance, interpretation

Unlike the science curriculum, there is an almost overwhelming degree of freedom in history. From school to school, students could be studying a very different set of events. In practice, there is usually a consensus around the key elements that ought to be included for any given theme and period, at least at a level of detail that makes the curriculum workable and reasonably consistent across the country. But there's no straitjacket and teachers who want to go off-piste would appear to have ample room for doing so. Once again, the students' history education is very much in the hands of their teachers and the choices they make. It's Rainforest territory.

Core knowledge

In the US, the debate about what should be taught has been fuelled by the thinking of Eric Donald (E D) Hirsch. In his books *Cultural Literacy: What Every American Needs to Know* (1987), *The Knowledge Deficit* (2006) and *Why Knowledge Matters* (2016)[58], Hirsch makes the case that failures in our education systems often stem from a lack of attention given to developing students' 'cultural literacy' and the explicit teaching of knowledge. He makes a very persuasive case that students' difficulties with reading largely stem from their lack of knowledge rather than any deficits in reading and comprehension skills.

Taking his ideas further, Hirsch has established the Core Knowledge Foundation to promote the idea of a Core Knowledge curriculum for the US. It is non-statutory but over 1000 schools across the country have adopted the curriculum as the basis for what they teach.

---

58. Hirsch, E. D. (2016)

Significantly, for Hirsch, the drive for a knowledge-led curriculum is absolutely not about cultural elitism; it is driven by a commitment to social justice. Here is an excerpt from the Core Knowledge Website[59]:

> **Knowledge-Based Schooling: From Ideas to Practice**
>
> Both the realities of cognitive science and the ideals of social justice support the need for knowledge-based schooling. Cognitive science confirms these facts:
>
> Children can advance educationally only when they have the expected prior knowledge.
>
> They can become better readers only by building extensive knowledge of the world.
>
> They can become effective members of the wider society only by sharing the knowledge taken for granted by literate writers and speakers in that society.
>
> Social justice demands that we give all children equal access to important shared knowledge. Only by specifying the knowledge that all children should share can we guarantee equal access to that knowledge.

This last point is the key: the equity case for specifying core knowledge.

To give a flavour, this is how one part of the music curriculum is specified.

Grade	Sixth Grade	Seventh Grade	Eighth Grade
Music Content	• Classical music from Baroque to Romantic (Bach, Handel, Haydn, Mozart, Beethoven, Schubert, Chopin, Schumann)	• Classical Music: Romantics and Nationalists (Brahms, Berlioz, Liszt, Wagner, Dvorak, Grieg, Tchaikovsky) • American Musical Traditions (Blues and Jazz)	• Non-Western Music • Classical Music: Nationalists and Moderns • Vocal Music (Opera; American Musical Theater)

The rationale is clear, even if one might quibble about the specific selections. There's a balance to be struck between giving value to the canon; the classics – and recognising that any selection is omitting a massive array of alternatives. Any selection has a cultural, political bias – it is unavoidable. Without doubt selections of books, works of music and periods of history often over-emphasise

---

59. www.coreknowledge.org/our-approach/knowledge-based-schools/

the work of 'dead white men' rather than representing the work of people with a contemporary breadth and balance of genders, cultures and ethnicities.

The debate to be had – especially amongst any group of teachers and school leaders devising a curriculum – is how to balance the traditional subject canon, with its inherent biases, with a more esoteric mix of ancient and modern knowledge elements and contexts. The idea is that students ought to know something about Mozart and Tchaikovsky – whatever else they also know about. We might want European students to also know about African and South Asian musical styles – but that would be in addition to the classical romantics, not instead.

The Core Knowledge supporting materials for teachers take things further. Here is an excerpt from the teachers' guide to one of their 'Core Classics':[60]

> *Sir Arthur Conan Doyle's Selected Adventures of Sherlock Holmes*
>
> What makes a hero?
>
> Is Holmes a hero? Have students discuss what qualities they admire in their heroes. They should then discuss whether or not Holmes possesses these qualities, using examples from the text. Students may want to consider whether some of the flaws Watson acknowledges keep Holmes from becoming truly heroic in their eyes.
>
> Note: Holmes has been compared to the great heroes of epic fiction. He is a man of extraordinary, almost superhuman abilities fighting more or less alone against the forces of evil in order to protect his society. If students have studied any epic literature, you might draw this comparison.

There's a valiant attempt here to go beyond the intended curriculum to shaping the enacted curriculum through quite detailed guidance; they're not leaving anything to chance – albeit that no-one is forced to use it. Guidance is only guidance – but this is going to be really helpful as a starting point or as a basis for ensuring different teachers are giving students similar experiences.

The general point for teachers to take from this is to consider how your curriculum might be specified in your context. Is there enough structure, guidance and detail in the specification of what students should know? If there is too much, what would you do differently? If you have had to devise your own curriculum, how do you know you've made choices that can contribute to students' capacity to 'become effective members of wider society'?

---

60. https://3o83ip44005z3mk17t31679f-wpengine.netdna-ssl.com/wp-content/uploads/2017/01/Core-Classics-Sherlock-Holmes-Teacher-Guide.pdf

Cultural capital

As an extension of core knowledge, it is worth thinking more about the general concept of 'cultural literacy' or the idea of 'cultural capital' that was proposed and developed by French sociologist and intellectual Pierre Bourdieu[61] in the 1980s. Beyond the confines of our subject domains, a large part of the knowledge base that informs our daily lives – either empowering us or inhibiting us – is gained through socialisation, engagement with traditions within families and communities and exposure to language and cultural events and practices. Cultural capital can't simply be taught in a direct sense; it has to be acquired, which is much more subtle and difficult to control. In Trivium terms, not all grammar can be acquired through instruction. In Rainforest terms, a trunk can't grow without some leaves.

Each of our students will have a different range of components to their cultural capital that they can draw on in different situations. The content of the curriculum we are teaching will interact with their cultural capital in different ways, depending on how much the new learning resonates with their past experiences.

What might these things include? Here is a list of some bits and pieces of cultural capital that students in England might find they are expected to recognise and engage with in different situations. Some are places, experiences, some are people, fictional characters, references to food, history, film and television, a tone of voice ... it goes on:

- Scafell Pike. The White Cliffs of Dover. The Pennine Way.

- Brick Lane. Penny Lane. Soho.

- 'To boldly go where no man has gone before'; 'It's one small step for man'; 'We will fight on the beaches'.

- Elvis Presley, Frank Sinatra, Bette Midler, Nina Simone, Ella Fitzgerald, Simon and Garfunkel.

- Sunset on the beach; a log fire under the stars; walking through woodland leaves in your wellies.

- The grocer's daughter; the milk snatcher; the Iron Lady; 'the Lady's not for turning'.

- The silence of the public library on a Saturday. The Rosetta Stone. The Tate.

---

61. Bourdieu, P. (1986) 'The Forms of Capital' in *Handbook of Theory of Research for the Sociology of Education*

- 1066, 1966, 9/11, 7/7, November 5th.

- The grassy knoll, JFK, Jackie O, Malcolm X, MLK.

- MIT, Yale, SOAS, Balliol.

- Kurt Cobain, Ian Curtis, Jimi Hendrix, Jim Morrison, Amy Winehouse.

- *Madame Butterfly, Lark Ascending, Rhapsody in Blue*, ('Bohemian Rhapsody'!)

- Lamb Rogan Gosht, Peking duck, Foie gras, Rice and peas.

- The final ball of the over; it's a six, over the covers at deep backward square.

- It had a certain je ne sais quoi; joie de vivre.

- My dear friend, that's awfully kind; terribly thoughtful; you're an absolute treasure.

- I swear down, fam; that's bare nasty, innit, you get me.

- *Reservoir Dogs. The Godfather. Annie Hall. The Man with the Golden Gun*

- Walter Sickert; Ai Weiwei; Damien Hirst; Laurie Anderson; David Hockney.

Each one of us will have a different level of recognition for these different references. Many of these elements of knowledge are unlikely to find their way into a formal planned school curriculum but our students will encounter them and, at some point, they may be at a disadvantage if they have significant cultural capital deficits. Typically, students with the most advantages in their home environments are going to have the greatest access to cultural capital with the exponential accumulation that follows. The Matthew Effect[62] comes into play just as it does with literacy in general – the more you know, the more you can know. Disadvantaged students will need to rely much more on the diet they get from school. As teachers and school leaders, addressing this layer of inequality is part of the challenge of the job.

Of course, the only way to address a knowledge gap is to fill it; to use every opportunity to share our cultural capital; to make it explicit and to give our students opportunities to enrich their lives in a wide variety of ways. A great curriculum is more than just a set of traditional subject disciplines. It should also include trips to museums and galleries, to mountains, rivers and forests, to plays and concerts. It should include exposure to current affairs, recent political history, artists, film-makers and a range of foods and dialects.

---

62. The rich get richer and the poor get poorer

We can't necessarily do it all – of course not. But we can at least try to consciously build cultural capital through the curriculum we design in its very broadest sense, through the way we teach and through the way we interact with our students every day. In the Rainforest metaphor, all of this gives value to the varied diet of learning experiences we might find in the canopy – in the Mode B teaching we discuss in Part 2 – alongside the traditional teacher-led acquisition of core knowledge in the trunk.

Student voice and the Conversation of Mankind

There are those who worry about core knowledge thinking for fear that it amounts to a form of social control, an imposition of cultural hegemony that suppresses counter-cultures and minority voices. That's clearly a danger – but what's the alternative? Surely the best we can do for our students is to ensure that they have the greatest possible access to the cultural capital of the elites that have power to shape their lives – not to deny them access. That doesn't make sense at all. What we also need to do, however, is to make sure they have the tools to ask questions and to have their voices heard – which is where the Trivium is so powerful.

A question to consider is where students can or should ever choose what to learn. Can they shape their own curriculum? For the most part, I'm inclined to say 'no'. Why? Because it is unlikely that students will make choices that stretch them unless they already know a lot and have a sense of knowing what they don't know. One of the values in explicitly learning from experts or through subject disciplines with strong traditions is that they are able to set students off onto paths of learning that students would never choose because they don't know they are there.

However, as I will share in more depth in Part 2 when I explore Mode B teaching, when I was at KEGS I did see several examples of where student input was highly effective, if not essential. One was the process of teaching through co-construction where students and teachers led the learning together. If you asked a group of 11-year-olds what they should study about say Christianity or Islam, it was amazing what they would come up with. In computing, this was even more evident, because students often had greater expertise than teachers. We had older students teaching younger students a range of computing courses, based on student choice. It was 100% student-run with some background logistical support from staff.

I have often found that making choices doesn't come easy to students. In some subjects, compliant, conscientious children can be inhibited when presented with options for fear that they pick the wrong one. As part of a wider path toward engendering confidence with problem-solving and making creative choices, I do think students need to have these opportunities built into their curriculum. This is why art and drama are such powerful components of a curriculum; students have the space to build on their knowledge by making lots of choices and exploring very individual curriculum paths.

I've often been surprised how negative people can be about students' capacity to make good decisions about their learning. At KEGS, this happened all the time; students had a lot to say on nearly everything and it paid to listen. They had ideas about questions they wanted to explore in religious studies or artists they wanted to take inspiration from in art; they would bring in articles for discussion about new phenomena in physics or in economics, too new to be on the syllabus; they would have clear political standpoints that they wanted to explore and debate. In Chapter 9, 'Exploring the possibilities', I make reference to KEGS several times. It was a selective school with a phenomenal work ethic which made these things more possible. But there are KEGS-type students in every school.

However, to consider the Learning Tree again, you can't put students in a position to make meaningful choices if they don't have the knowledge-base required. It's not a binary decision, giving them choices or specifying everything; it's about choosing an appropriate point in a curriculum sequence when students' choices will be well-informed and can shape their learning in a significant way.

Ultimately, our goal is perhaps best captured by Michael Oakeshott in his idea of 'the Conversation of Mankind':

> As civilized human beings, we are the inheritors, neither of an inquiry about ourselves and the world, nor of an accumulating body of information, but of a conversation, begun in the primeval forests and extended and made more articulate in the course of centuries. It is a conversation which goes on both in public and within each of ourselves.[63]

This suggests that we're not simply trying to transmit a set body of knowledge – the best that has been thought and said. That's too limiting; it presupposes that there is a defined notion of 'the best' when actually the scope for what to include is too vast and subject to all kinds of political, social and cultural biases and traditions. Oakeshott is suggesting that, instead, we are actually giving our students as much knowledge as we can so that they can themselves

---

63. Oakeshott, M. (1962) 'The Voice of Poetry in the Conversation of Mankind' in *Rationalism in Politics and Other Essays*. London: Methuen.

engage in 'the conversation of Mankind'; so that they can have their say about what 'the best' might be and not simply accept a predetermined package without question. This, in essence, is what Martin Robinson captures with his 'philosopher kids'; and it's the philosophy that underpins the curriculum in the Learning Rainforest.

WHAT DOES THE RESEARCH SAY?

CHAPTER 4

> IT'S IMPORTANT TO DEVELOP AN UNDERSTANDING OF EDUCATIONAL RESEARCH; ITS SCOPE AND LIMITATIONS. IT'S NOT 'ANYTHING GOES' OR 'WHATEVER WORKS FOR ME'; THERE ARE STRONG MESSAGES THAT EMERGE FROM THE COMPLEXITY.

> THERE'S A CONSENSUS EMERGING FROM COGNITIVE SCIENCE AND EDUCATION RESEARCH IN GENERAL. I HAVE MADE THREE CATEGORIES:
>
> ■ CLIMATE: RELATIONSHIPS, EXPECTATIONS AND MINDSETS ALL PLAY AN IMPORTANT ROLE.
>
> ■ PRINCIPLES OF INSTRUCTION: PEDAGOGICAL CONTENT KNOWLEDGE, QUESTIONING, GUIDED AND INDEPENDENT PRACTICE AND EFFECTIVE FORMATIVE FEEDBACK.
>
> ■ MEMORY AND BUILDING KNOWLEDGE: IT'S IMPORTANT TO GIVE PRIORITY TO TEACHER-LED INSTRUCTION THAT EXPLICITLY BUILDS LONG-TERM MEMORY.

> THE IDEAS BEHIND THE LEARNING RAINFOREST METAPHOR APPEAR TO BE SUPPORTED BY THE EVIDENCE FROM RESEARCH.

'Awareness of the limits of our knowledge is also awareness of the fact that what we know may turn out to be wrong, or inexact. Only by keeping in mind that our beliefs may turn out to be wrong is it possible to free ourselves from wrong ideas, and to learn ... Science is born from this act of humility: not trusting blindly in our past knowledge and our intuition. Not believing what everyone says.

'The answers given by science... are not reliable because they are definitive. They are reliable because they are not definitive; because they are the best available today.'

Carlo Rovelli[64]

Following on from debates about curriculum content and the progressive-traditional axis, an important influence on my thinking and practice has been the findings from education research. This is very much Rainforest territory because there are so many variables at play. We want answers to a vast array of questions but good research requires patient exploration in particular conditions and, very often, the conclusions are more complex than we might hope. As my friend and colleague, Tom Andrew-Power, put it, 'How, practically, should a teacher engage with research, other than feeling loved, understood for a moment; starry eyed at the possibilities, deflated in practice?' Engaging with research requires teachers to understand something of the process so that we know what the possibilities are.

Over the last few years, there has been a slow but important coming together of ideas from the world of classroom practitioners and the world of academic research. Movements such as ResearchEd[65] in the UK, run by Tom Bennett, and a host of conference and festival events have been pivotal in giving a forum for this dialogue. From my perspective, Twitter has played a key role in providing a communication link to bridge what previously felt like a chasm. Teachers and researchers are talking to each other in ways that did not used to happen – albeit with a long way still to go before this feels like an integrated relationship for both groups of professionals.

It would be a mistake for me to try to present any of the research from the perspective of an expert on cognitive science or research methodology. There are

---

64. Rovelli, C. (2017)
65. researched.org.uk

already lots of excellent distillations of research findings that I couldn't possibly emulate. However, I am a consumer of research; a recipient; a beneficiary. On that basis I will try to share the ideas that have cut through and made sense in the contexts I've worked in to examine whether the Rainforest metaphor stacks up. Of course, it's not a theory of learning that needs any kind of proof; it's a loose metaphor to help us think about teaching and learning. But still, it ought to resonate with the evidence to some degree if it's going to have any value.

Before diving into the findings, I think it is worth exploring the nature of educational research itself. It's continually frustrating to me that so much of the discourse in our debates and in the reading of education research reduces teaching and learning effects to crude averages and sweeping assumptions, ignoring complexity and context. At the same time, it's equally frustrating that some people's response to this complexity is to reinforce a view that 'anything goes'; 'it's too hard to pin anything down so I'll be fine doing what I like.'

A more sensible position is to allow ourselves to embrace research evidence about effective teaching whilst also recognising its limits and being extremely cautious about definitions and contexts.

Do your homework: Reading research

In talks I give on this topic, I often use some of the findings from John Hattie's *Visible Learning*[66] study of meta-analyses to explore the pitfalls of interpreting the results from research at a superficial level. The ranking of effect sizes[67] that Hattie's team generates is updated every few years. The use of effect sizes is hotly debated – even absolutely refuted – because the nature of what is being measured and the ranges of the scales used have a major bearing on the results. However, leaving aside the actual scales and their relative sizes, Hattie's analysis provides a useful point of reference for some wide questions.

Within the Hattie framework, it is interesting to see for example that 'Drugs' appears as a label for an intervention, with an effect size of 0.32[68]. Drugs? 0.32? This is above Homework, at 0.29, but below Creativity at 0.35. Clearly the use of these apparently quite precise numbers is problematic. Even if we accept them, immediately Drugs = 0.32 leads to a whole host of questions: Which drugs? For which students? In what doses? Over how long? Measured in relation to which

---

66. Hattie, J. (2009)

67. An effect size measures the ratio of the change in a particular measure like a test score, before and after an intervention, to the spread in that measured. It gives some idea of impact but the numerical value depends on the scales used in the assessments and favours certain types of interventions over others.

68. From visible-learning.org

kind of learning tasks? The list of questions is endless. We all know that 'Drugs' can't mean one thing so we're not likely to take that ranking at face value. In turns out, if you read *Visible Learning*, that this relates to interventions for ADHD. Even with that insight, the same questions apply in querying whether a single effect size would be meaningful.

Similarly it is patently obvious that 'Creativity' can't be one thing; a definable teaching strategy. Neither is Homework. In one of my early blog posts I explored this in some detail. This was significant because John Hattie actually engaged with my post and left his own comment.

BLOG: Hattie on Homework

John Hattie's *Visible Learning* is an attempt to distil the key messages from the vast array of studies that have been undertaken across the world into all the different factors that lead to educational achievement. As you would hope and expect, the book contains details of the statistical methodology underpinning a meta-analysis and the whole notion of 'effect size' that drives the thinking in the book. There is a discussion about what is measurable and how effect size can be interpreted in different ways. The outcomes are interesting, suggesting a number of factors that are likely to make the greatest impact in classrooms and more widely in the lives of learners.

I was particularly interested to explore what Hattie says about homework. This stems from a difficulty I have when I hear or read, fairly often, that 'research shows that homework makes no difference'. It is cited as a hard fact in articles such as this one by Tim Lott in the *Guardian*: 'Why do we torment kids with homework?'[69] Even though Tim is talking about his six-year-old, and cites research that refers to 'younger kids', too often the sweeping generalisation is applied to all homework for all students. I think this is wrong.

All my instincts as a teacher (and a parent) tell me that homework is a vital element in the learning process; reinforcing the interaction between teacher and student, between home and school, and paving the way to students being independent autonomous learners. Am I biased? Yes. Is this based on hunches and personal experience? Of course. Is it backed up by research…? Well that is the question.

So, what does Hattie say about homework?

69. www.guardian.co.uk/lifeandstyle/2012/oct/20/tim-lott-man-about-house-homework

Helpfully he uses homework studies as an example of the overall process of meta-analyses, so there is plenty of material. In a key example, he describes a study of five meta-analyses that capture 161 separate studies involving over 100,000 students showing homework as having an overall effect size d=0.29. What does this mean? This is the best typical effect size across all the studies, suggesting:

- improving the rate of learning by 15% – or advancing children's learning by about a year

- 65% of effects were positive

- 35% of effects were negative

- average achievement exceeded 62% of the levels of students not given homework

Hattie then says that terms such as 'small, medium and large' need to be used with caution in respect of effect size. He is ambitious and won't accept comparison with 0.0 as a sign of a good strategy. He cites Cohen as suggesting with reason that 0.2 is small, 0.4 is medium and 0.6 is large and later argues himself that we need a hinge-point where d>0.4 is needed for an effect to be above average and d>0.6 to be considered excellent.

So what is this all saying? Homework, taken as an aggregated whole, shows an effect size of d=0.29 that is between small and medium? Oh … but wait … here comes an important detail. Turn the page: The studies show that the effect size at primary age is d=0.15 and for secondary students it is d=0.64! Well, now we are starting to make some sense. On this basis, homework for secondary students has an 'excellent' effect. I am left thinking that, with a difference so marked, surely it is nonsensical to aggregate these measures in the first place.

Hattie goes on to report that other factors make a difference to the result. For example, when what is measured is very precise (*eg* improving addition or phonics), a bigger effect is seen compared to when the outcome is more ephemeral. So, we need to be clear: what is measured has an impact on the scale of the effect. This means that we have to throw in all kinds of caveats about the validity of the process. There will be some forms of homework more likely to show an effect than others; it is not really sensible to lump all work that might be done in-between lessons into the catch-all 'homework' and then to talk about an absolute measure of impact. Hattie is at pains to point out that there will be great variations across the different studies that simply average out to the effect size on his barometers. Again, in truth, each study really needs to be looked at in detail. What kind of homework? What measure of attainment? What type of students? And so on. Are there so many variables that aggregating them together is more or less made meaningless? Well, I'd say so.

Nevertheless, d=0.64! That matches my predisposed bias so I should be happy, QED. Case closed. I'm right and all the nay-sayers are wrong!?

Maybe, but the detail, as always, is worth looking at. Hattie suggests that the reason for the difference between the d=0.15 at primary level at d=0.64 at secondary is that younger students can't undertake unsupported study as well, they can't filter out irrelevant information or avoid environmental distractions – and if they struggle, the overall effect can be negative.

At secondary level he suggests there is no evidence that prescribing homework develops time management skills and that the highest effects in secondary are associated with rote learning, practice or rehearsal of subject matter; more task-orientated homework has higher effects than deep learning and problem-solving. Overall, the more complex, open-ended and unstructured tasks are, the lower the effect sizes. Short, frequent homework closely monitored by teachers has more impact than their converse forms and effects are higher for higher ability students than lower ability students, higher for older rather than younger students. Finally, the evidence is that teacher involvement in homework is key to its success.

So, what Hattie actually says about homework is complex. There is no meaningful sense in which it could be stated that 'the research says X about homework' in a simple soundbite. There are some lessons to learn.

The more specific and precise the task is, the more likely it is to make an impact for all learners. Homework that is more open, more complex is more appropriate for able and older students. Teacher monitoring and involvement is key – so putting students in a position where their learning is too complex, extended or unstructured to be done unsupervised is not healthy. This is more likely for young children, hence the very low effect size for primary-age students.

All of this makes sense to me and none of it challenges my predisposition to be a committed advocate for homework. The key is to think about the micro-level issues, not to lose all of that in a ridiculous averaging process. Even at primary level, students are not all the same. Older, more able students in Years 5/6 may well benefit from homework where kids in Year 2 may not. Let's not lose the trees for the forest. Also, what Hattie shows is that educational inputs, processes and outcomes are all highly subjective human interactions. Expecting these things to be reduced sensibly into scientifically absolute measured truths is absurd. Ultimately, education is about values and attitudes and we need to see all research in that context.

And this is what John Hattie wrote in the comments:

Thanks for the courtesy of reading my work, and not tripping over headlines of those who don't bother. I knew when writing the section on homework that it could be misinterpreted (as has class size, streaming, finances, etc.) and tried my best to make the picture clear. Yes, homework is one influence where there is a critical moderator – there is a major difference between its effects in primary and secondary.

I like your summary but can I add one more critical comment …

Visible Learning is a literature review, therefore it says what HAS happened not what COULD happen. The message about the low effect in primary school means that there is a high probability that many homework practices may not be working. The key is that this highlights the importance for schools to now evaluate the effectiveness of its primary homework practice. And if it turns out to be like most other practices (low effect), then there is an invitation (indeed an imperative) to try an alternative set of practices re homework – and evaluate their impact on learning, involvement in learning, and increasing the students' (and parents') understanding about the language of learning.

I do NOT recommend abandoning homework, and I do provide some direction for effective homework policies (as you note), but most of all the invitation is to "Know thy impact".[70]

The point about the review looking backwards is critical. Hattie is averaging the effects that have happened in these particular studies, rather than identifying

---

70. teacherhead.com/2012/10/21/homework-what-does-the-hattie-research-actually-say/ comment-page-1/#comments

some fundamental truths. I'm stressing that point because I have heard a presentation from a school leader where he explained how he would praise his staff for using a high effect-size strategy, placing slips in their pigeon hole after an informal lesson observation with a note such as: *Well done, it was good to see you were using Self-questioning, Effect Size 0.64, Keep it up.* As if, in that lesson, that strategy was having that effect – because it always does. This is a kind of edu-madness, where someone is so thrilled to have something concrete, they've lost the point. They've lost the plot.

In the homework example, there is a lot of learning from the analysis – but the averaged numbers don't really tell the story. The research-methods debate about the validity of effect sizes in comparative research is important; it's questionable whether we should give any weight at all to the Hattie rankings given how problematic they are[71]. However, even for Hattie, the numbers are meant as broad-brush indicators. In any case, the meaning lies in the detail of the various different studies – to the point where the concept of 'homework' pretty much falls apart as a coherent definition. It depends on too many variables. The same must also apply to many other research findings.

A thousand questions and clarifications are needed before we could discuss something as broad as, say, 'group work'. For sure, some forms of group work are bound to be lame and ineffective. I once watched a pitiful 'Envoys and Experts' lesson involving groups of students whizzing around a class to share their facts about Henry VIII; less information was disseminated between students (never mind learned) in an hour than would be possible in five minutes of reading or teacher exposition.

To emphasise this point, 'group work' is not always an inherently good thing in itself; but nor is it fundamentally a bad thing. In situations where teachers want students to learn specific sets of knowledge with a degree of depth and complexity, group work is not going to be as effective as direct teacher instruction. Where there are gains to be had from students sharing their ideas, checking their fluency against a set of criteria or, for example, rehearsing some form of performance, group work can be necessary and very effective (see Part 2 Strategy **P5 Groups: Goals and roles**).

Where there is ambiguity in the research, it doesn't mean 'each to their own' or 'anything goes'. That would mean we're just guessing and we can do much better than that. This principle has resonance with the leading-edge of quantum gravity research as articulated beautifully by Carlo Rovelli:

---

71. This David Didau post with comment from Dylan Wiliam gives a flavour of the issues www. learningspy.co.uk/myths/things-know-effect-sizes/

If we are certain of nothing, how can we possibly rely on what science tells us? The answer is simple: Science is not reliable because it provides certainty. It is reliable because it provides us with the best answers we have at present ... It is precisely its openness, the fact that it constantly calls current knowledge into question, which guarantees that the answers it offers are the best so far available.[72]

We need to be very clear about this in our profession. Amongst our values-led debates about educational purposes, there will still be emerging and evolving truths from cognitive and social science that should guide us. In practice, in the context of group work, this means teachers that should evaluate whether a particular group-based activity is going to yield good learning outcomes for a particular set of students compared to some other strategy for a particular set of concepts and skills. Context will be critical; where you have a class full of sophisticated learners with lots of prior knowledge, you can do things a bit differently to where the opposite characteristics dominate.

Graham Nuthall explores this issue at length in his brilliant book *The Hidden Lives of Learners*[73]:

Teaching is about sensitivity and adaptation. It is about adjusting to the here-and-now circumstances of particular students ... Things that work one day may not work the next day. What can be done quickly with one group has to be taken very slowly with another group. What one student finds easy to understand may confuse another student ... As a teacher you make adaptations. You must. The important question is: what adaptations to make? You can do it by a kind of blind trial and error, but it would be much better if you knew what kinds of adaptations are needed, and why.

Another factor that Nuthall reports – as have Wiliam and others – is that teachers are not good at describing what they do. These two effects occur in studies: different teachers doing the same things in their lessons will describe them as being very different. Also, different teachers doing very different things in their lessons can describe them as being the same. For example you might be picking up on a wave of interest amongst teachers about explicit knowledge and providing your students with knowledge organisers. You might self-report that 'yes, I'm using knowledge organisers'. However, in the school or even classroom next door, you might see that it is the routine of daily review and self-quizzing that is yielding returns based on their knowledge organisers – something you

72. Rovelli, C. *ibid.*
73. Nuthall, G. (2007)

are not doing. You might think you are 'doing knowledge organisers' but your version is massively ineffective compared to the more intense approach next door. It's not good enough to assert that 'it works for me' – unless you have some evidence to support that based on students' long term learning.

'The spirit of AfL'

In true Rainforest style, interpreting findings from research is about balance; using informed professional wisdom to design a breadth of learning experiences, doing things in the right proportions in the moment and over time, to maximise particular students' outcomes based on their needs as learners.

For example, to contrast the large-scale meta-analysis approach used by Hattie, it's interesting to look at a study such as the work on formative assessment or Assessment for Learning (AfL) by Mary James *et al* in *Learning to How to Learn* (2007). In a study into 'learning to learn', there is a section dedicated to the research evidence. In one study reported by Bethan Marshall (Kings)[74] *et al*, 37 teachers were interviewed of whom 27 had lessons recorded on video and analysed. From this evidence, numerous conclusions were drawn including the idea that a few (20% – which is just a handful of actual people) showed 'the spirit of AfL' in their lessons whilst the others modelled a more rigid 'letter of AfL' approach. This is linked to various other attitudes and beliefs; those showing 'the spirit of AfL' not only are judged to have delivered more effective lessons but, on interview, are seen to be more likely to accept their responsibility for overcoming external pressures; they see themselves as the source of the solutions – referred to as holding 'incremental views of learning'.

Very significant conclusions are drawn from the research; there are some bold claims made based on a relatively small number of interviews and observations. These are discussed in the analysis as if they hold true for many more teachers than the data set allows. The values of the researchers are clear – their belief in the superiority of 'the spirit of AfL' is evident throughout. The issue of bias in teacher interpretation is something we always have to consider. For me, although there is a potential credibility gap given the sample size, their conclusion that, in teacher development, 'beliefs and practices need to be developed together' sounds sensible. It's worth thinking about. The more specific analysis regarding AfL really depends on whether you belief that 'the spirit of AfL' is inherently a positive attribute. There's a strong values component required to accept the findings.

---

74. Marshall, B. *et al* 'Learning how to learn in classroom' in James, M. *et al* (2007) *Improving Learning How to Learn*, Routledge.

This idea is reinforced by John Hattie in a recent video interview for The Educator TV in Australia about 'myths and distractions'[75]. He argues that the key to improving schools is not to isolate teaching strategies; it is to develop expert teachers who have the skills to gauge their impact and make adjustments, echoing the words of Nuthall. He suggests that they can't identify a neat top 10 of strategies because it always depends when you use them. *'We're developing a model called the Kenny Rogers model, because you've gotta know when to hold 'em and you gotta know when to play 'em.'* He argues that the skill of knowing when to use a strategy, when to stop and try something else is the central skill for teachers to develop. 'Some people think that there is one best way but that's just not the case.'

Of course, we have to be cautious about 'lucky pants' syndrome – a phrase I borrowed from a comment by teacher and blogger Greg Ashman in relation to my co-construction experiments at KEGS (see **P15 Sidekicks**). My students did well but he suggested that you might wear lucky pants during your exams but this does not account for any successes you might have. In other words, spurious causal attribution is a danger we face as we're heavily influenced by our biases. It is hard to accept that a strategy you have invested time in might not have worked or might not be the reason for success.

Possibly above all, beyond what you do, it is how well you do it. That might go without saying but I'd suggest that, where teaching is ineffective, it is very often less about the selection of strategies and more about problems with confidence, subject knowledge, the pitch of the content and expectations of students. Very occasionally, a really great teacher picks a duff strategy – but that's not going to kill anyone if, most of time, they are having a positive impact. And if we're scared of getting things wrong as teachers, we'll never take the risks needed to try out new ideas that will help us improve.

What does the research say?

One of the challenges for teachers is to find time to engage with all the research that has been done and to then make sense of it. Fortunately, there is a growing number of collections of research that different people have compiled in order to disseminate the ideas. There appears to be quite a lot of overlap between them showing that there is a consensus building around certain themes and ideas about how learning works.

It's important to stress that I'm only making reference to a certain set of research findings – those that have come to my attention in relation to general

---

75. John Hattie on The Educator TV vimeo.com/209826301

ideas about teaching. I'm well aware that there is other research regarding boys' and girls' education, children with special needs of various kinds, strategies for reading, teaching students in a second language and so on. I have not attempted an exhaustive summary.

Here is a list of some of the sources that I have found incredibly useful. Each of these sources is worth reading in detail.

- Education Endowment Fund Toolkit – a web-based tool linking to hundreds of studies ranked by cost and impact in terms of months of progress: educationendowmentfoundation.org.uk/resources/teaching-learning-toolkit/

- Barak Rosenshine's '10 Principles of instruction: Research-Based Strategies that all Teachers Should Know', *American Educator*, Spring 2012.

- Dylan Wiliam's '9 Things Every Teacher Should Know' – a *TES* article (2016) www.tes.com/us/news/breaking-views/9-things-every-teacher-should-know

- Dunlosky *et al* (2013) – 'Strengthening the Student Toolbox: Study Strategies to Boost Learning', a review of 10 learning strategies for *American Educator*, Fall 2013.

- The Learning Scientists website, where they identify six key strategies. www.learningscientists.org/downloadable-materials/

- John Hattie – *Visible Learning* (2009)

- Daniel T Willingham – *Why Don't Kids Like School* (2010), which is neatly summarised into nine key ideas.

- Professor Rob Coe *et al* (2014) 'What makes great teaching? Review of the underpinning research'. A paper for the Sutton Trust.

- Coe's Poor Proxies for learning – via his inaugural lecture as Professor at Durham University, Improving Education: A triumph of hope over experience (2013)[76]

- Review by James Ko *et al*, *Effective Teaching* (2014) for Education Development Trust

- American Psychological Association Top 20 Principles from Psychology for preK-12 teaching and learning (2015)

---

76. Coe, R. (2013) www.cem.org/attachments/publications/ImprovingEducation2013.pdf

- Robert Bjork: 'Desirable difficulties – varying conditions, spaced practice, interleaving, retrieval over testing' – featured in Bjork and Bjork (2011) 'Making things hard on yourself but in a good way'.[77]

- Carol Dweck: Growth *Mindset in Mindset: How you can fulfil your potential* (2008)

- Graham Nuthall – *The Hidden Lives of Learners* (2007)

- Robert Rosenthal's Pygmalion effect study (Video link[78])

- David Didau and Nick Rose – *What every teacher needs to know about Psychology* (2016) – Domains and schema, misconceptions

- John Sweller – Cognitive Load Theory[79]

In an attempt to pull all of this together, I have found that these research findings seem to fall into three general categories.

1. Classroom climate

Attitudes and beliefs

Behaviour and Relationships

2. Principles of instruction

Pedagogical content knowledge

Modes of questioning

The role of practice

Formative assessment

3. Memory

Knowledge and memory

Cognitive Load Theory

Metacognition

Retrieval Practice

---

77. Bjork, E. L. & Bjork, R. A. (2011). 'Making things hard on yourself, but in a good way: Creating desirable difficulties to enhance learning'. In M.A. Gernsbacher, *et al* (Ed) *Psychology and the real world: Essays illustrating fundamental contributions to society*, New York: Worth Publishers (p56-64).

78. www.youtube.com/watch?v=EjbL7zW-Wig

79. Nicely accessible via this Oliver Caviglioli graphics: teachinghow2s.com/docs/CLT_chapter_summaries.pdf

I've tried to summarise some of the key findings in each category.

1. Classroom climate

Classroom climate includes teacher attitudes, student-teacher relationships and behaviour management. An important precondition for effective learning is that classroom management – of time, space, resources and behaviour – is effective. This requires consistent reinforcement of some clear rules. (Coe *et al*, 2014)

> There is a 'need to create a classroom that is constantly demanding more, but still recognising students' self-worth'. (Coe)

> Teaching is about relationships, and these relationships are best when they involve mutual respect.

> When teachers start from the basic assumption that pupils in the class are people, then good things tend to follow. (Wiliam, 2016)

As we will see in Chapter 5, this also links into the effectiveness of feedback.

Carol Dweck's ideas about fostering growth mindsets and challenging fixed mindsets are a recurring theme:

> Positive climate involves 'attributing student success to effort rather than ability and valuing resilience to failure (grit)'. (Coe)

> Intelligence can be changed through sustained hard work. (Willingham)

However, a valuable insight from Yeager *et al*[80] is that it is important to consider the domain in which any mindset interventions are enacted. It is only in applying effort to a particular, more effective strategy that students improve and learn that effort pays off. Working harder in itself is not sufficient – especially if that energy is wasted on an ineffective learning strategy. The consequence of this can be to further embed a fixed mindset with a negative impact on achievement.

As an aside, I rather like Guy Claxton's suggestion that Eduardo Briceno's[81] concepts of learning and performance zones might be more useful than growth and fixed mindset. In a nutshell, 'the performance zone maximizes our immediate performance, while the learning zone maximizes our growth and our future performance'. We switch between these zones at the appropriate time, recognising that both are important and require different attitudes. This

---

80. Yeager, Walton and Cohen (2013)
81. Briceno, Eduardo: TED Talk 'How to get better at the things you care about' (2016)

is more realistic. Too many schools have undertaken a big 'Growth Mindset School' launch, supported by banners and laminated posters in classrooms, without necessarily being a growth mindset school.

There is evidence that the Pygmalion Effect is real, even if any impact on IQ is likely to be small[82]: if we think students are 'smarter' we are more likely to be nicer to them; we ask them more questions, we give them more time to answer and we expect more of them in terms of the quality of responses we'll accept. Students can literally do better on tests over time if their teachers think they are smarter than they might seem (Rosenthal). There are significant implications here for the power of teachers having high or low expectations of their students, especially if these expectations are sustained and the effects are allowed to accumulate over time. Group work is only likely to succeed in yielding better outcomes than teaching where students work individually, if students have group goals (*ie* working as a group, not just in a group) and individual accountability within the group whereby the group's success depends on each student's successful contribution (Slavin[83] – via Wiliam).

Peer dynamics play a big role in student motivation and their interaction with the learning process in a lesson. Nuthall identifies three worlds that students inhabit: the public world of the classroom, the semi-private world of their peer relationships and the private world of their own mind. There's a complex interplay between them that makes teacher-to-student transmission highly non-linear and unpredictable. Rainforest!

> It is assumed that learning is the more or less automatic result of engaging in classroom activities. If students do what the teacher expects of them, follow instructions carefully, complete all aspects of the tasks, then the students will learn what the teacher expects. Our research shows almost none of this is true. There are so many variables at play that the students learn or fail to learn substantially different things from the same tasks.[84]

Summary: Positive relationships, high expectations, mindsets, well designed/ supervised group and peer dynamics – all play a part in establishing a climate conducive for learning.

82. Jussim, L. and Harber, K.D. (2005) 'Teacher Expectations and Self-fulfilling Prophecies' *Personality and Social Psychology Review,* Vol.9, No. 2, p131-155 with thanks to Harry Fletcher-Wood.

83. Slavin, R. (2010) 'Co-operative learning: what makes group-work work?' *in The Nature of Learning: Using Research to Inspire Practice, OECD Publishing, Paris.*

84. Nuthall, G. (2007)

2. Principles of instruction

Rob Coe *et al*'s Sutton Trust paper suggests that both pedagogical content knowledge (PCK) and the quality of teacher instruction have significant impact on student outcomes. PCK includes teachers' subject knowledge, which must exist above a minimum to avoid major detrimental effects; it also includes their understanding of how students engage with a subject and the common misconceptions.

High quality instruction is reported on in numerous studies. This will include:

- sharing learning intentions so students and teachers know where they are heading and whether they've arrived

- asking frequent, probing questions as part of the instruction/exposition of ideas

- checking for student understanding including eliciting responses from all learners – not just relying on the answers of the high attainers

- obtaining a high success rate (suggested by Rosenshine to be around 80%) to optimise the balance between challenge and confidence-building

One of my favourite Teach Like a Champion strategies from Doug Lemov is the very first one in TLAC 2.0: Reject Self-report[85]. This suggests asking questions or setting tasks that require students to demonstrate their understanding, not merely asking them if they have 'got it'. I've seen teachers literally ask a whole class 'is everyone ok with that?' – before moving on after being met with an awkward silence.

Willingham suggests it is important that we recognise that children are more alike than different in terms of learning – aside from the issue of prior knowledge. The implication is that we should plan lessons around the content of what we teach, rather than let student differences drive decisions about how to teach. This makes differentiation a whole lot more meaningful, especially given that we cannot know each of their private worlds in great detail.

The role of practice is reported in several research summaries. Gladwell's 10,000 hours is overly generalised – we can master some skills much more quickly than others – but practice is key, even if success is not guaranteed. Rosenshine is clear that effective teachers ensure a smooth transition from instruction to independent practice; they guide practice for sufficient time, building confidence and checking for understanding. However, it is also necessary to

---

85. Lemov, D. (2015)

withdraw the guidance and include time for independent practice within an instructional sequence. Ko *et al* suggest that one key to success is for teachers to build on high quality instructional materials to make time for practice.

Feedback features in multiple studies and research compilations, scoring highly on the EEF toolkit and Hattie's Visible Learning effect size ranking. The nature of feedback is explored extensively by Dylan Wiliam. His often-repeated mantra is that the most reliable, most proven strategy for improving student outcomes is short-cycle 'minute by minute' formative assessment and feedback teachers give during lessons. Whilst feedback has many forms and contexts, 'the only thing that matters is what students do with it' (Wiliam, 2016). Chapter 5 is dedicated to the whole area of assessment and feedback.

Other specific instructional methods that show positive outcomes in studies are mastery learning – where students pursue specified objectives until they have been achieved (at 80% or above) before moving on, and reciprocal teaching – which is a bit like 'I teach it, you teach it back' – involving students in taking the teacher role to explain concepts to the teacher and other students.

Summary: Develop PCK and anticipate misconceptions, develop effective questioning methods, secure a high success rate, plan teaching based on content-based learning goals; guided and independent practice need time and formative feedback is central to any effective learning sequence.

3. Memory and building knowledge

A significant body of research from the field of cognitive psychology has focused on the nature of memory. It's impossible to capture the depth of it in a broad summary so I'm consciously only listing some key concepts that emerge without too much exploration.

Learning is a change in long-term memory. This means that we can't really assume our students have 'learned' something unless, at some point later, they can show that they can remember it. Crucially, this has implications for filtering out some of what Rob Coe calls 'poor proxies for learning' such as being engaged, being busy, listening or answering questions in a lesson. None of those things necessarily generate learning; we have to assess that later to see if learning has occurred. You can't 'see' learning in the here and now of a lesson.

Factual knowledge precedes skill. This is covered in detail by Willingham. It means that you can't think about, analyse, interpret, evaluate, juxtapose, critique or debate things unless you have factual knowledge on which to base those things. This suggests that students need to acquire knowledge as a precursor to attempting to engage in activities where those seemingly generic skills might be developed. They are not actually generic and cannot be learned in isolation from content; they emerge from a body of knowledge.

We understand new things in the context of things we already know; shallow knowledge comes before deep knowledge. This idea that new knowledge accumulates around prior knowledge is vital; the more you have, the more you can get. And you can't have too much knowledge. The implication is that knowledge acquisition needs high priority in a student's learning, especially for those with the least to start with. It also means that teachers need to consider how new learning sticks for each student; finding out what they already know that they can connect new learning to. Nuthall's research suggests that it typically takes three encounters with new concepts for a student to learn them: once to become aware of it; a second to make an association with prior knowledge; and a third from a different perspective, to embed the link and commit the knowledge to long-term memory. It's less precise than that but it makes sense as a rough guide.

The much-loved and often-quoted Bloom's Taxonomy that is so often represented as a pyramid with Knowledge at the base underneath Comprehension, Application, Analysis, Synthesis and Evaluation is actually a major misrepresentation of the ideas Benjamin Bloom and his colleagues published in 1956. Similarly the 'revised taxonomy' that places Creativity at the top of the pyramid is based on a misreading of the original concept. The intention was never to suggest a cumulative hierarchy; talk of 'higher order thinking skills' is misplaced and the common interpretation that knowledge recall is subordinate to creativity and the other processes is completely wrong. There is no Bloom's pyramid. Knowledge is the key driver for the other cognitive processes but, beyond that, each of them can operate independently. The triangular image has been popularised but is inaccurate and misleading. Education researcher Pedro De Bruyckere captures the issues superbly on his blog[86].

Kirschner and Sweller's work on Cognitive Load Theory is extensive and is explained in multiple sources[87]. Dylan Wiliam has suggested it is the most important theory in education for the last 40 years[88].

Some key points are:

- Our working memories are limited in capacity and this, in a basic model, serves as a bottleneck to building long-term memory. The implications

---

86. theeconomyofmeaning.com/2017/08/24/a-longer-piece-on-the-taxonomy-of-bloom/
87. This is covered comprehensively in Didau and Rose (2016), Chapter 4.
88. From Wisconsin Mathematics Council Ignite session: May 3rd, 2017, via @dylanwiliam twitter 5/6/17

are that new material should be presented in small steps and overload through distractions of various kinds should be avoided.

- Strategies such as dual coding, where images are used to illustrate ideas that are explained verbally, help because our brains can process speech and images simultaneously. However trying to listen to speech and read simultaneously causes overload and is less successful.

- There is a difference between the way novices and experts think. Experts are able to refer to extensive, complex schema in their long-term memories that they have built up over time. Once a part of a schema is retrieved, it brings the rest with it. Experts do not have to use much thinking power to solve problems because they can recall similar problems from their long-term memory. This means that a lot of advanced problem-solving requires more knowledge retrieval than might appear. In contrast, novices do not yet have these extensive schema; they may even have incorrect schema to break down. It is therefore more difficult to learn at the early stages and learners need to acquire a lot more knowledge across a domain including solutions to numerous possible problem types before they can become expert. The implication is that greater knowledge acquisition is often a higher priority for learning rather than say more practice with problem-solving, especially for less able students. You need to build the schema before you can use it.

Robert Bjork's ideas about 'desirable difficulties' emerge from research around optimising transfer of knowledge to long-term memory. The same ideas are echoed in several other studies including those reported by Dunlosky, The Learning Scientists and Rosenshine. Essentially, to maximise long-term retention – *ie* 'learning' – several strategies are effective, albeit not necessarily natural or easy. As Wiliam puts it, 'learning requires forgetting'.

- Retrieval practice is required for students to become proficient in retrieving knowledge; the more they practise retrieving specific knowledge, the easier and more secure it becomes.

- Practice testing: repeated low-stakes testing where students need to retrieve knowledge has a greater impact on long-term memory than re-reading or having material re-taught.

- Spaced practice: retrieval should be spaced over time, for example using what Rosenshine calls Daily, Weekly and Monthly Review. This is more effective than testing immediately after learning – and then leaving a massive gap.

- Interleaving: concepts from different domains should be mixed together and tested in a varied or even an unpredictable fashion. This is more difficult in the short term but more effective in the long term.

- Varied practice: Bjork suggests that variety in the rhythm and content of practice, whilst reducing short-term performance, helps to build long-term performance as it forces us to strengthen our retrieval of information in different contexts.

Memory is the residue of thought. This is one of Willingham's most powerful findings, encapsulated in a neat sentence. This means that, unless we have to think about the information we are handling, we do not necessarily learn it. Simply transferring information from a textbook to an exercise book without the need to think about meaning or context or using that information to answer a question – will not require thinking and therefore will not be learned.

Metacognition and modelling are strongly rated in several studies. This is the process of demonstrating to students how to think through problems and then using concrete examples and walking through model answers, teaching students good thinking strategies within a particular context. This could be applied in solving mathematical problems or approaching an essay or creative task. It is important for students to make links back and forth between general/abstract ideas and specific, concrete examples.

Self-explanation and the related process of elaboration is regarded as a strong feature of good teaching; it's one of the six main strategies promoted by the Learning Scientists. This is where students are trained to explore ideas by asking themselves questions, make links to other ideas to consider how and why they are connected, how and why models work and so on. It's about making this process explicit, teaching students to use it and giving them opportunities to practise.

Summary: Teachers should teach explicitly for building knowledge in long-term memory; plan appropriate cycles of high-frequency, low-stakes, spaced and interleaved review and put knowledge content at the forefront of curriculum planning, broken down into appropriately small steps. Metacognition and elaboration are helpful strategies for building stronger schema.

Weak practice
Several studies include reference to teaching methods that do not produce strong results in research. Suggestions from Ko *et al* and Coe *et al* include:

- Inconsistent expectations for different learners that are lower for disadvantaged students

- An emphasis on supervising and communicating about routines at the expense of teaching the content

- Low levels of teacher-student interactions – *eg* insufficient questioning or checking for understanding

- Low levels of student involvement in their work (high-level engagement does not necessarily lead to learning but low engagement is not likely to)

- Student perceptions of their teachers as not caring, unhelpful, under-appreciative of the importance of learning and their work

- More frequent use of negative criticism and feedback

- Using praise lavishly – as this is often unrelated to the application of effort or learning from mistakes and can reinforce fixed mindsets or lead to reduced effort on subsequent tasks

- Allowing learners to discover key ideas for themselves (compared to instruction methods); there is a place for discovery (see Chapter 9, **P3 Play detective**) but for most knowledge areas, it's much less effective than being taught explicitly

- Encouraging re-reading and highlighting to memorise key ideas; this can emphasise familiarity instead of understanding. It's better to test for understanding instead

- Addressing issues of confidence and low aspirations before trying to teach content; building knowledge and skill will foster confidence – it's that way around

- Presenting information to learners in their preferred learning style (learning styles do not exist). No study would ever show that, say, 'visual learners' taught visually would perform better than if they were taught normally without reference to this supposed preference

- Ensuring learners are always active, rather than listening attentively, if you want them to remember

Once again, I recognise that this is all generic. However, it's important to note that, whilst beyond the scope of this book, there are multiple studies that focus on specific subjects including a lot of work on teaching maths and improving literacy. In science, for example, an important study by Millar and Abrahams into the effectiveness of science experiments[89] is a must-read for science teachers. Here they suggest that, whilst practical work will always have a key

---

89. Millar, R. *et al* (2009) www.gettingpractical.org.uk/documents/RobinSSR.pdf

role in science teaching, much of the current practice is ineffective in achieving the purpose of securing deeper understanding. They argue that the key is to identify clear objectives for any practical activity, to develop an informed analysis of the conceptual learning demands of tasks and then to make sure students are guided to think about how their actions and data relate to the concepts. Planning highly effective practical work is more important than simply doing more of it.

It could be that teacher-led demonstrations of certain phenomena are more effective than some hands-on student practicals; it could also be that some experiments are planned purely for their experiential value, not their merits in relation to making accurate measurements. The key is to be sure of the purposes and not to mix them up.

Implications for teaching in the Learning Rainforest

In my view, the survey of current educational research findings lends significant weight to the three elements of the rainforest analogy. Findings about the role of relationships, peer dynamics, mindsets, expectations of students and classroom climate in general, suggest that it is certainly important to invest in these elements in any school and classroom. Establishing rich, nourishing conditions for growth is essential; they are prerequisites for successful learning.

The large body of evidence from cognitive science tells us that building knowledge is crucial to taking learners on the journey from novice to expert. This is a technical business where effective instructional methods are vital. Effective teacher-led instruction and teaching for long-term memory are strongly evidenced in the research. Strong knowledge-rich trunks and branches are fundamental to building deeper, wider schema that then inform creative processes and problem-solving.

Finally, there's no doubt that varied practice and opportunities for challenge reinforce the knowledge acquisition process. In the right sequence and proportion, a wide range of learning experiences can be used to elicit evidence of student understanding in order to support effective feedback and to adjust teaching inputs. Multiple learning modes can provide students with opportunities to reinforce their conceptual understanding whilst also supporting the development of various dispositions.

Overall, in my view, perhaps the most important conclusion from research is that teacher-led instruction designed explicitly to build knowledge in long-term memory is at the core of successful learning. There is no canopy in the lush rainforest, without strong trunks and branches. This is critical in planning effective schemes of work and delivering great lessons in real classrooms.

However, at the same time as assimilating research findings into our reservoirs of wisdom, there is a need to continually keep the research in perspective. There is a huge risk in becoming excessively reductive and linear, overly blinded by the reassurance of science-like research findings, when the processes we are dealing with are much more organic, unpredictable and non-linear. Real life is more rainforest than plantation. For example, even though research might lead us to believe that knowledge-rich teacher-led instruction is hugely powerful, it's a mistake to assume that this mode of teaching must replace all else. It's much more subtle than that.

Sometimes teachers talk about this in terms of opportunity cost: if Strategy X is better than Strategy Y, every minute spent on Y is an opportunity cost when you could be doing more of X. However, as with the multiple chemical compounds that we require for healthy living, it is often the way they work in combination that delivers the benefits. Very few studies are done exploring how a Strategy X and others W, Y and Z interact and what the optimum combination might be. It's just too hard to control all the variables to conduct studies of this type. The implication is that even if we accept that, say, direct instruction beats discovery learning for most factual content, it might be that there is an optimum level of discovery learning, even if very small, that could be woven into a total curriculum experience that leads to the best long-term outcomes.

Add to this the very important issue of our fundamental values about the kind of education we want our children to have. It might be that we don't want to use Strategy Y because it 'works'. We simply want students to experience that kind of learning for its own sake. This could be reading aloud or designing experiments or taking part in a roleplay or making a model. These things might not, in themselves, yield superior measurable learning outcomes in terms of long-term memory – they might simply create valuable experiential memories of their own. They are part of the dialectic of the Trivium – the experience; the journey.

The counter-risk is that people will seize on the last two paragraphs as a cue to cast all the research aside and do what they like just because they want to. This is obviously foolish. The great responsibility we have as teachers – as well as the joy and privilege – is to find the balance; to synthesise our values, our experience and our research-informed wisdom into a coherent set of ideas that allow us to design and deliver in practice the education we believe in in theory; to put our philosophy into action. That requires a blend of art and science – to make our curriculum and teaching as effective as possible in doing what we want them to whilst also allowing ourselves to be surprised by alternative forms of excellence that we didn't expect or control.

HOW DOES ASSESSMENT WORK?

CHAPTER 5

> WE NEED A REAL PARADIGM SHIFT AWAY FROM MACRO SUMMATIVE DATA TRACKING TOWARDS AUTHENTIC FORMATIVE ASSESSMENT.

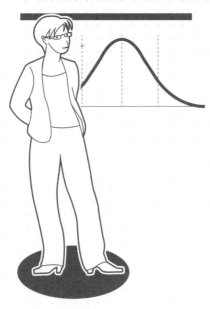

> STANDARDS ARE ALWAYS DETERMINED BY REFERENCE TO THE BELL CURVE WHETHER WE LIKE IT OR NOT.

> "DEFINING THE BUTTERFLIES" IS THE GOAL IN EVERY CONTEXT. WHAT DOES EXCELLENCE LOOK LIKE AND HOW DO WE COMMUNICATE THAT TO STUDENTS?

> LOW STAKES HIGH-FREQUENCY TESTING IS A POWERFUL FORM OF FORMATIVE ASSESSMENT.

> AUTHENTIC ASSESSMENT HAS DIFFERENT FORMS IN DIFFERENT SUBJECT DISCIPLINES. IMPOSING A GENERAL GRADE SYSTEM LOSES THE INFORMATION THAT SUPPORTS ACTUAL IMPROVEMENT.

> 'RESPONSIVE TEACHING' REQUIRES USING STRATEGIES THAT ELICIT INFORMATION ABOUT WHAT STUDENTS HAVE LEARNED AND GIVING THEM FEEDBACK THAT MOVES THEM FORWARD.

> *'We have to remember that what we observe is not nature herself, but nature exposed to our method of questioning.'*

Werner Heisenberg[90]

This statement by Heisenberg relates to his work in the field of quantum physics which led to the development of his famous Uncertainty Principle in the 1920s and '30s. It is not possible to determine both the momentum and position of a particle with absolute certainty at any given time; this uncertainty is an inherent feature of the quantum universe and goes beyond being merely an observer effect whereby the process of measurement interferes with the process in hand.

However, the spirit of the quotation resonates loudly with so much of our thinking about assessment in education; just replace 'nature' with 'learning'. In recent years I have explored this issue in numerous blogs with titles such as 'The Data Delusion' and 'The Assessment Uncertainty Principle' – ideas I'll return to in this chapter.

So many teachers around the world are operating in conditions straight from the plantation where the value given to the assessment of student outcomes in the form of measures, grades and qualifications has been elevated to such a great height, with such high-stakes consequences for success or failure, that the fundamental principles of assessment have been distorted beyond all meaning. If we're going to create conditions for everyone to thrive in the Learning Rainforest, we need to put that right.

At a basic level, assessment is simply any process by which we can gauge the quality of students' learning via the proxy of some form of performance, using a set of criteria that determine the range of what we regard as standards relevant to the learning in hand. We then decide to use the assessment information to contribute to the learning process itself – feedback – or we use it communicate our findings to anyone with an interest. We might well do both. As it is often complicated and cumbersome to communicate the details of what someone has achieved, we have invented a host of numerical and alphabetical systems to try to serve as scales – to keep things simple. And this is where the problems begin.

The current prevailing assessment paradigm is dominated by what one might call 'macro summative attainment tracking'. This has reigned supreme in England for the last 15 years or possibly more and is common around the

---

90. Heisenberg, W. (1958) *Physics and Philosophy: The Revolution in Modern Science.*

world. The focus has been on trying to represent students' attainment across all disciplines in terms of generic ladders of grades and levels, occasionally supported by rubrics and descriptors, so that attainment and progress can be tracked. The value given to data tracking has been a driving force in educational management thinking; the idea that summative macro data is a requirement for driving up standards is widely held.

Elements of this paradigm include the following:

- Confusing bell-curve ranking with absolute standards and presenting one as the other alongside the false assertion that grades, by themselves, communicate information about learning.

- The illusion of 'progress' as something than can be measured via reference to bell-curve grades or data points in general; the very idea that 'progress' in learning has a measurable size, ludicrous as it is, is still widely held onto.

- The target-grade culture: the idea that, by setting systematic attainment targets to aim at, in the language of summative grades, students will learn more because students and their teachers will 'do better'.

- The attempt to use summative tests formatively. This is very common with students sitting endless mock tests and using 'exam-style questions' prematurely. This is akin to getting students to play a whole piano piece over and over before they've learned their scales or endlessly practising match situations in sport without drilling on basic skills.

- Schools' cultures around book marking where how the marking looks (to parents, inspectors, school leaders) has been more important than what it achieves with an appallingly low impact to workload ratio. Most marking is wasted and yet is often the cause of major teacher overload.

- Massive centralised data-tracking machinery where learning is represented in data form: schools across the world have got sprawling colour-coded spreadsheets where numbers and grades are entered for the purposes of tracking students' performance. Tracking may have its purposes in terms of describing where students are on a crudely defined flight path, but unless this feeds back into different actions in the classroom you can stare at the numbers and grades all day long and no child learns anything more as a result.

The trouble with macro data-tracking is that the journey from the spreadsheet to the classroom is circuitous at best, and normally doesn't happen at all. All we are doing is generating data that might tell a story about relative student performance – it might, at best, give a picture of where students are – but it does nothing to take them further. This is because the grades themselves do not actually tell us much at all about what students know or can do at a level that is actionable.

If we are going to break out of this paradigm, to engineer a paradigm shift, we need to build a better one that is more fully focused on students' learning, building the knowledge structure that is so necessary in creating the lush canopy in our Learning Rainforest. To do this we need to agree on some key principles and explore some misconceptions about assessment, adopting a mentality that mirrors a shift from Plantation Thinking to Rainforest Thinking.

5.1 Assessment, standards and the bell curve

There are lots of well-worn clichés in educational discourse around assessment and testing that are problematic; often challenged for the wrong reasons. It's worth exploring them.

'Weighing the pig doesn't make it fatter.'

If we are talking about the assessment data we collect for tracking purposes then yes, this analogy works – but only if the data does not feed into any programme that might adjust the conditions that determine what the pig eats and how it lives. As with the literal pig-weighing scenario, educational assessment data has no intrinsic value in relation to improving the quality or depth of student learning; that would only be true if we use it to inform our understanding of how the teaching and learning process might need to change. So, of course, if we do use assessment data formatively as part of a feedback loop, then the pig might well get fatter because we weighed it and learned something. The question – which we'll return to – is: what might that kind of data or information look like?

However, as we now know from cognitive science – for example from Bjork's work on desirable difficulties referenced in Chapter 4 – the process of testing can in fact strengthen retrieval and improve our retention of knowledge in our long-term memory. In that context, the act of weighing our pig is actually going to make it fatter; regardless of the measures we use, testing that supports retrieval of knowledge we've already encountered can support deeper learning. Too often, people talk in damning terms about testing when it is really the value placed on test outcomes and the way they are used that are the problem.

If tests are low-stakes, the very act of being tested has a positive learning effect. We need to bear this in mind. If we are going to be serious about building a strong knowledge structure for all the specimens in the Learning Rainforest, we need to embrace testing as a positive tool in our armoury. Tests are good! This is especially true if the curriculum being tested is quite tightly defined so that the test scores are raw marks that reveal some specific information about what the teacher might need to work on in order to push his or her students further.

One of my provocations to schools leaders is to consider the scale of the data machinery that they create. A favourite Heath Robinson drawing depicts a complex arrangement of cogs, levers, pulleys and string that supposedly facilitate the process of peeling potatoes one by one. The alternative? You could just use a peeler. I enjoyed the response to this 'thought experiment' that I once posed on Twitter. Try it:

Your entire assessment database is wiped (Oops!). How long before this has an impact on a single student?

Or try this: Ask your colleague teachers to write down the names of their students who they feel are excelling and those who need some special attention to get them back on track. Compare this with the data. How did they do? When you factor in assessment error and the time taken to produce the spreadsheet, teachers' knowledge of their students probably stacks up pretty well. For sure it will be more nuanced than the crude data representations. So, let's be sure not to equate 'assessment' with 'data'. That's missing by a mile.

'Raising the Bar.'

With the classic high-jump metaphor the suggestion is that, by making assessments more challenging, we will also be raising standards of attainment automatically. As with the real high-jump, this could work in situations where our learners were always capable of achieving higher standards but expectations were too low – or, if, by raising expectations, learners become more motivated and consequently strive to succeed at a higher level. I've known plenty of situations where that is true – and it echoes with the Pygmalion effect mentioned in Chapter 4.

However, if a student is already struggling to jump over the bar, despite a high level of motivation and effort, then raising it is unlikely to lead to greater success. Harder exams don't, in themselves, raise standards. They tend to have the effect of stretching out the distribution of scores but they don't make anyone a better learner unless other effects come into play. You need to be very sure that the low expectations effect is the key reason for underperformance before making the learning more difficult, especially as, as discussed in relation to mindsets, a high initial success rate is needed to build confidence and generate a growth mindset in any given situation.

'The exam factory'; 'teaching to the test.'

These are often part of the well-rehearsed rhetoric from those who protest against the dominance of examination outcomes over our school system. As we discussed in Chapters 2 and 3, there is a lot more to a 'great education' than accumulating examinable knowledge. If a school is an 'exam factory', the suggestion is that exam results matter more than they should, that decisions are taken that might yield stronger examination results but might not necessarily provide students with the full 'philosopher kid' experience.

At a more granular level, within each class, 'teaching to the test' is almost always offered as a critique of the effect high-stakes testing has on the enacted curriculum. Instead of a test sampling a wider curriculum, the curriculum is confined to overlap closely with the possible content of any test. It's clearly the wrong way around.

However, the danger of both of these high frequency edu-memes is that they overly diminish the positive or at least necessary role that assessments, examinations and testing play in our education system. Do we want to have well-respected qualifications that indicate a level of mastery in a particular field? Do we think awarding qualifications should be based on examinations and other formal assessments? Are they a reasonable means of gaining a measure of students' learning – their capacity to deliver in Briceño's Performance Zone? Do we want our public examinations to be well-regarded as a valid, reliable indicator that certain standards have been met, carrying a degree of public confidence, recognition and prestige? Do we think it is fair for learners to be able to be set tests that are reasonably predictable within a range, so that they can prepare adequately? Is that not fair?

As ever, there is a degree of balance required, especially in the context of an education system where socio-economic disadvantage plays such a big role. We can't allow our justified concerns about the excessive status of exam outcomes to perpetuate inequalities by approaching exams for disadvantaged children with any less rigour than the more privileged school up the road. As Headteacher John Tomsett says, sometimes the best pastoral care we can give a disadvantaged child is a good set of exam results[91]. In the real world they live in, this is their ticket to opportunity. Which leads me to the last of these statements:

---

91. Tomsett, J. (2014) johntomsett.com/2014/07/20/this-much-i-know-about-what-year-7-pupils-mums-really-worry-about-and-why-your-keepy-uppy-skills-really-matter/

'We value what we measure when we should measure what we value.'

In terms of public examinations, this is clearly true. We should reflect on the value we place on examination results relative to all the other elements that constitute 'a good education'. Exams don't capture the extent to which young people contribute to their communities; their capacity for moral leadership; their commitment to artistic and sporting excellence; the empathy and support they give to people living in poverty across the world or their willingness to tackle prejudice.

Exams don't provide a measure of how effectively someone works in a team; their ability to take initiative or to respond calmly in a crisis; their ability to undertake a long-term in-depth study; their skills in dealing with people from different backgrounds or their powers of persuasion or to be thoughtful, kind and tolerant. Obviously enough, exams only measure what can be measured in exams.

Meanwhile, as a society, we place considerable value on all the other attributes. In the ideal world, our diverse, thriving rainforest education would encompass a system that takes greater account of this bigger picture and allows young people to show more clearly what strengths they have and the full extent of their personal achievements. I'm currently working with people from across the education sector in England to devise a qualifications framework that gives greater weight to these other dimensions – The National Baccalaureate for England[92]. Taking inspiration from the International Baccalaureate, our model places academic learning at the core whilst also giving credit for aspects of learning that are not included in exams but that employers and colleges value. It's a grassroots initiative which means it takes time to build – but I am convinced that its time will come.

In the meantime, it is vital that we continue to remind ourselves that, however important exams and qualifications are, they only tell a part of the story of learning and achievement for any student and for any school. This does not mean we should start to engineer arbitrary measures for student qualities and characteristics – to turn qualitative evaluations into data. The folly – the horror! – of trying to measure children's character as they move up the Resilience Scale or the Collaborative Learning Index. If you ever find yourself down that blind alley, turn around and run. It's a dead end. We don't need to turn everything into data in order to give it value.

---

92. National Baccalaureate Trust www.natbacctrust.org

Absolute standards vs relative standards

At the heart of our problematic relationship with assessment lie two contradictions. One is that tension we've just explored between the assessed curriculum and the broad curriculum we value. We might all recognise that formal assessment is an important element in the big picture and accept that only part of our curriculum can be assessed in a reliable manner; at the same time we are determined to give value to the learning experience in all its diverse glory, going far beyond what can be measured in tests. It's not an easy balance to strike in a climate of hyper-accountability where data is king.

The other key tension is our desire to give all of our learners the opportunity to succeed, whilst also holding a strong desire to establish standards that must be met at various points along every student's educational pathway. Here we need to clarify what we mean by standards; we need to face the reality that absolute standards are very difficult to isolate from a deep-seated devotion to a bell-curve distribution where, in essence, learners are in competition with each other.

The bell curve

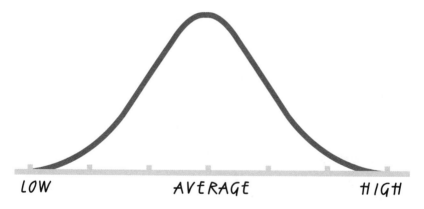

LOW   AVERAGE   HIGH

Of course we should also acknowledge the limitations a bell-curve philosophy imposes on us. 'Shock!! HALF of all students are BELOW AVERAGE!!'. 'ONLY 2% of students are good enough to get the top 2% grades!!' Some politicians and newspaper editors don't seem to understand that these data scandals are a joke. Perversely, if things go too well, we're still in trouble. There is a fairly profound schizophrenia that leads to people jumping up and down about standards slipping because too many people gain the highest grades. This is 'proof' that standards are falling. Grade inflation undermines public confidence in standards. It's a deeply held principle that accolades of any kind are cheapened if they appear to be freely attainable.

However, before we get our tinfoil hats out looking for injustice, let's examine our own sense of what we mean by standards. What about marking an essay? We can all acknowledge that marking extended writing is a messy business. We can give an impression mark using some criteria; we can count up some definable features – we can give a score out of 30 referencing some exemplars. All of this is complex and, in truth, there is no one correct mark for something as complex as an essay or any form of composition.

Try getting two or three people to agree the mark or grade on ten pieces of work. Then scale that up to 2000 markers across the country and see the scale of the issue. What is a boundary for a B-grade? How do you measure it? How consistent are we from one person to another or even as individuals, from one day to the next? It's hard just to agree with yourself over the space of a few hours of marking.

On a comprehension paper, if the marks vary from one year to another, how do we know whether it was a hard paper or a less successful cohort of students? We need reference points and these generally arise from the cohort. It is a safer bet that each cohort of students has a similar ability profile year on year than that the tests we set each year are of the same standard – especially on a national scale.

Let's look at something that should be purely objective and absolute. The high-jump. Imagine 1000 children being asked to do the high-jump, giving them a few attempts to get their personal best. There is no limit imposed on them. Imagine Jane goes home and tells Dad, 'I jumped 120 cm today'. He's delighted of course…at first. But then, after a moment, he asks, 'Was that good? How high did everyone else jump?'.

It's the obvious question. Without any reference point, 120 cm means little. It could be very high, average or very low. Dad needs to know what the background profile is in order to gauge his child's achievement. 190 cm is an exceptional jump because of how it compares to everyone else. 50 cm is a low standard for high jump – but only because almost anyone could jump this high. Of course we can talk about progress, about personal bests, personal triumphs, the impact of disability and so on, but every child will also want to know where they stand along the line before their personal achievement makes sense.

The same is true of piano exams. In various instrumental grading systems such as ABRSM[93], grades 1-8 are chosen at intervals of difficulty that span the typical range of human ability at playing the piano. It would be daft to set Grade 1 so high, no-one could pass, or so low that anyone could pass. It represents a fair challenge – a standard – for beginners. This is uncontroversial. Even within the cohort of Grade 1 entrants, there is a range. A bell curve. Some fail, some pass, some get Merit and some get Distinction. These measures are defined with reference to a background spread of ability within what is possible given the pieces and scales (the curriculum) set for Grade 1. There is a good sense of piano exams being absolute standards, but every aspect has an origin in relative standards. The success and stability of ABRSM exams lies in the extent and quality of the moderation processes that the examiners are required to undertake.

We might like the idea of fixed benchmarks that anyone can meet but, in practice, do we really?

- Elif can spell 'accommodation'.

- Sam can multiply any three digit number by any other.

- Ruby can explain the formation of Durdle Door in Dorset.

- Eleanor can write a coherent paragraph analysing Othello's character flaws.

- Joshua can work out the nth term of a linear sequence.

- Daisy can state which of two compounds is formed via ionic bonding.

Naturally enough, it turns out that some perfectly sound explanations of Durdle Door or analyses of Othello's flaws are much more sophisticated than others; the seemingly straightforward assertion that someone 'can do' something is often far too simplistic. It might be true that Samir can define 'connotation'; he might be able to think of a connotation for the word 'red' used in a poem. But, given various alternatives, could he determine which connotation from a set of plausible alternatives is the most appropriate in the context of the imagery intended by the poet?

Whilst 'can do' statements appear to be absolute, if they are used to set standards, they are no use unless we know how difficult they are. So, we ask thousands of children questions that tease out whether they can do these things and see what we get. If lots of children can do something, we say it is easier

---

93. Associated Board of the Royal Schools of Music www.abrsm.org

than something only a few children can do. Absolute standards only fully gain meaning in reference to a cohort; that's an inherent feature of our sense of 'difficulty'.

The paradox we face is that we want all children to be able to succeed; we're uncomfortable with the idea that there are only ever a limited number of positions on the achievement scale that we might consider 'excellent' or even a pass. And yet, at the same time, a *de facto* competitive, comparative process underpins nearly all our attempts to define standards.

The solutions might lie in giving more value to every position along the scale. When my son took piano exams, in passing Grade 1 and all the grades up to Grade 5 – by which time he'd had enough! – he did not feel that he failed Grade 8. He started out at the bottom end of the bell curve and made his way along at his own pace. The structure of assessment built confidence at each step whilst remaining challenging continually. He always knew where he stood but the system still allowed him to feel that he was succeeding.

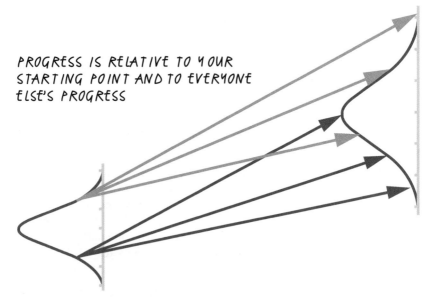

PROGRESS IS RELATIVE TO YOUR STARTING POINT AND TO EVERYONE ELSE'S PROGRESS

If only our public examinations were like this. In England we have the frustrating situation where, on a scale of 1-9 in our 16+ GCSE exams, 9 is reserved only for the top 2% or so; only grades 4-9 are deemed by the government to be 'good grades' so that grades 1-3, by extension, are regarded as 'bad grades'. Approximately 30% of students must get bad grades by definition; it's locked into the grade-award mechanism, a hard-wired technicality. The assumption is that a student with a Grade 1 has simply failed; there is no positive value at all given to the elements of knowledge that they do have; all we know is that they've performed less well compared to 90%+ of their cohort.

Another way to harness the bell curve is to use it to focus on progress. Given that some students will continually struggle to match the standards of their peers, we can at least look to see how much progress they make. Quantifying this is problematic but, using comparative measures of various kinds, we can establish how well students are doing compared to their relative starting points. It could be that a low attainer makes excellent progress compared to their peers – as illustrated in the diagram. Similarly, we can identify whether a higher attainer continues to make progress or whether their attainment level is masking a drop-off in their progress. In terms of identifying success stories and students causing concern, relative progress is as secure a concept as fixed benchmarks, given how difficult benchmarks are to pin down.

The data delusion and the assessment uncertainty principle

As well as the constraints of the bell curve, I think teachers and leaders should give greater weight to the inherent limitations of awarding marks and grades to pieces of learning. Grading is such a massively flawed process but it still holds sway across the world, protecting an illusion of certainty and precision that isn't actually there. It still astonishes me that across the US, the Grade Point Average system retains such high status when there is so little benchmarking. There are no robust mechanisms at play to make sure that a GPA of 3.3 for a student from School A has the same value in terms of standards of learning as the same score for a student from School B.

Grading works as long as we are clear that they are essentially impressionistic; broad distribution markers with fuzzy overlapping edges. If Elif, James, Hassan and Louisa all write essays about *Of Mice and Men*, a range of markers might not agree the marks for each one because it depends how each marker interprets the criteria. However, they could probably agree on the rank order for the four essays. With the help of some graded exemplars, they might even agree where the essays fall within broad standards that could be labelled A, B, C.

But, let's look at a grade boundary scenario. What if Elif's score in a set of assessments made of several questions is 31/60 and Louisa's is 32/60 , where 32 is the pass/fail boundary? The assumption that Louisa has 'more knowledge' or is 'better at writing' than Elif is highly dubious. It really depends on which questions they got right and which fairly arbitrary criteria are being used to award marks. Even if they had the same score, they could have a very different range of knowledge about *Of Mice and Men* and the process of writing in the appropriate style. The score itself tells nothing about what each of them has learned. This is true of all data outcomes from assessments; as we move from marks to total scores to grades, we're getting further and further away from knowing any single detail about what students know.

Importantly, it's also a fact that, with a different combination of equally plausible mark weightings for different parts of the assessment, Elif and Louisa could reverse their scores. And yet that cliff-edge – where 32 is a Pass and 31 is a Fail – could have real-life consequences for those students. There's an element of arbitrariness in the mix that doesn't have enough recognition. I'm especially sceptical about A-/B+ grading. A former colleague told me that his university tutor would award grades such as $B^{\alpha\beta}$ as distinct from $B^{\beta\alpha}$. The tutor was adamant that she could apply those grades consistently for a history essay. The truth is that it's a delusion to believe that anyone's judgement of grades has anything close to that level of precision and reliability.

I've always loved this story: A colleague at KEGS was challenged by a parent at parents' evening: *Why is this essay only worth a B?* The teacher looked at it and then proceeded to explain how he'd applied the assessment criteria, leading to a B being the best fit. The parent wasn't happy. *'I still think it's worth an A'.* There was a heated debate. The parent felt the teacher wasn't giving his son the credit he deserved. After a while, the teacher, very wise but slightly weary, said 'OK'. He took the essay back, got out his pen and wrote 'A' on the top before handing it to the parent. 'There you are'. Had this changed the quality of the essay? No. Did it change the true value of the essay? No. Did it change the teacher's judgement of the actual standard? No. It was a Pyrrhic victory for the parent – who knew this all too well.

I love this because it shows how precarious and shallow the whole notion of grading can become. What is an A? How can we be sure? Who is it for? Most importantly, we should be asking – what does a grade or score tell us about what students know and can do so that we can help them to improve? Imagine coaching a tennis player to improve their technique. How much use would it be to tell them that their serve deserved a B+?

5.2 Formative and summative assessment

In the rainforest, growth actually happens at a cellular level, not at the level of trunks, branches and leaves. That's just what we can see; what we can measure as an overall effect. The same is true of learning; it only happens in the detail of what students know and understand and the things they can do. In order to get past the limiting bell-curve grading issues, a part of the solution is to focus less on the graded representations and more on the actual elements of what is being learned.

There are three sets of ideas that I want to explore here:

- Daisy Christodoulou's ideas about separating formative and summative modes of assessment to suit their different purposes

- The idea of formative assessment as expressed by Dylan Wiliam and others – what he now calls 'responsive teaching' – and the role of feedback within that

- The idea of authentic assessment, which prioritises meaningful measurement appropriate to subject disciplines over the need to provide comparable grading measures

Making Good Progress

In her excellent book *Making Good Progress*[94], Daisy Christodoulou performs a thorough dissection of prevailing assessment practice. Drawing extensively on ideas from cognitive science and core knowledge advocates such as E D Hirsch, she makes a compelling case that we are often using the wrong forms of assessment for the purposes we seek. This has some significant consequences for the breadth and depth of our curriculum, our understanding of standards and the tools we use to raise them. She concludes by setting out exactly what the features of effective formative and summative assessment should be.

Formative assessment should be geared towards 'identifying consequences'. This kind of assessment is all about providing information that can directly feed back into the teaching process. To be effective, assessments need to have the following features. They should be:

- Specific: focused on quite narrow content domains so that precise gaps can be identified for future teaching and further practice. Knowledge organisers or personal learning checklists are excellent for helping students to know exactly what they are meant to have learned for any particular micro-test.

- Frequent: building on the idea of regular retrieval practice to develop long-term memory and recall taken from cognitive science (as in Rosenshine's Principles of Instruction featured in Chapter 4).

- Repetitive: to ensure skills and retrieval are actively practised in a focused manner – as happens in sport with skill drills or with rehearsing

94. Christodoulou, D. (2016)

a performance where you repeat small elements over and over before assembling the final piece.

- Recorded as raw marks: to ensure the information is kept as close to the details of the original assessment as possible, without being morphed into a bell-curved grade or standardised score.

Summative assessment should be aimed at 'creating a shared meaning'. Here, we need to be sure that our data on assessment has meaning beyond the context of a single classroom so that standards can be compared between classes, subjects and schools. To be effective, summative assessments need the following features:

- Standard conditions: the time, availability of supporting resources, the same kind of questions (obviously enough!).

- Scaled scores: comparing raw scores across different tests is unhelpful because the level of difficulty can vary between tests; they need to be standardised in a form that allows comparisons to be made.

- Sampling a large curriculum domain: to ensure that a broad curriculum is maintained and is included in the sampling process that characterises any test design.

- Infrequent: to ensure that teachers have maximum time for teaching, covering a broad curriculum and engaging in more formative assessment. Lots of large-scale summative tests get in the way of the learning process and we don't need that many to provide the tracking information we really need.

Within the area of summative assessment, Christodoulou is keen to stress that different subjects require different specific forms of assessment – as I explore a little further on.

All of this makes perfect sense to me. It has significant implications for the decisions teachers make when planning their assessments. In the Learning Rainforest, the end result will be a sensible blend of formative and summative assessment depending on what is being studied, where students are in their learning and what their particular needs are. Crucially, we need to be clear of the purpose and if we really want students to improve we need to be sure that actions are taken as a consequence of the assessment, whatever form it takes. In practice things like knowledge organisers (see **C15 Specify the knowledge**), planned drills (C18) and regular retrieval practice (K18) are going to be helpful elements in a teacher's Rainforest assessment kitbag.

If these become embedded features of our practice, they allow us to gauge how well students are doing in terms of how much they actually know about specific topics and how well they can perform specific skills. Assessment is much more powerful when it is formulated purely in terms of what students know and can do in the absence of any proxy grading system or before details are lost in the context of a complex multi-level task or synoptic test. Can you capture all the details or learning in your markbook or data system? No. But why do you need to?

Dylan Wiliam: Responsive teaching and feedback

As I described in the introductory chapter, a major influence on me and many others during my career has been Dylan Wiliam. When *Inside the Black Box*[95] by Wiliam and Black came out in 1998, the ideas seemed absolutely radical – and yet so logical. One of them was the idea of comments-only marking. It required a major mindshift for teachers to ditch grades in order to give formative feedback via marking comments that students would actually read – instead of simply reading the grade and nothing more as their research indicated.

Dylan Wiliam has continued to be a strong influence and recently, in his conference talks and writing, he has a very clear message. Wiliam suggests that, from all the research studies there have been, formative assessment practice encompassing effective feedback is our best bet for raising standards. He says he wishes he had used the term 'responsive teaching' in the very beginning instead of 'assessment for learning' as this conveys the essence of the concept less ambiguously.

For Wiliam, it is short-cycle, 'minute-by-minute' feedback that is of particular significance – not the long arc feedback that students might get via marking in books. Short-cycle 'in the moment' feedback – in tight feedback loops – requires teachers to continually engage students in activities that tell them where they are and then, absolutely crucially, to adjust their teaching in response so that students' learning is advanced. This is responsive teaching.

In *Embedding Formative Assessment*[96] Wiliam provides numerous examples of how this works in practice under five main headings – his five strategies. Four of the strategies are:

- Clarifying, understanding, and sharing learning intentions, *eg* devising success criteria for an open-ended task or a successful piece of writing

- Engineering effective classroom discussions, tasks and activities that elicit evidence of learning, *eg* whole-class response methods of questioning

95. Black, P. and Wiliam, D. (1998)
96. Wiliam, D. (2011)

- Activating students as learning resources for one another, *eg* class critique, peer assessment, peer to peer instruction

- Activating students as owners of their own learning, *eg* self-quizzing, self-assessment against mark schemes or criteria.

The fifth strategy is 'providing feedback that move learners forward'. Wiliam explores the nature of feedback extensively in his books and conference sessions. Feedback has been the subject of multiple research studies but it is complex. Feedback can have negative impacts, demotivating students or lulling them into setting lower expectations for their achievement if they reach goals too easily. Also, feedback can be ignored. Given that it can all go wrong, Wiliam seems to suggest that good feedback has some particularly important elements:

Primarily, there needs to be trust and good teacher-student relationships. *'In the end, it all comes down to the relationship between the teacher and the student'*[97]. This is so that teachers know their students well enough to judge how best to give them the feedback they will respond to; it is also so that students will listen and respond to the feedback they are given, making the effort needed to effect a change in their performance. In the absence of relationships, these things are much less likely to happen. There's something rather wonderful – and intuitively commonsensical – about this finding: at the bottom of all the technical analysis of feedback, we get down to the need for good relationships. When we're establishing the conditions in our rainforest, relationships based on trust and respect are not just a fluffy feel-good element of a happy classroom: they are a hard-edged necessity for effective formative assessment; for effective responsive teaching; for building knowledge.

In addition to the technical elements of where students should improve, feedback needs to attend to students' motivation. We want students to increase their effort and raise aspirations – and the messages required to achieve those goals can be different from student to student, depending on their past experiences and mindsets. Feedback needs to focus on looking forward, not back; whilst we are learning from mistakes and past performances, the goal is always to improve the next performance. Fairly obviously, there needs to be a next performance or else giving the feedback is a waste of time!

There is then the factor of dependency – SatNav syndrome. If we give too much feedback, students stop thinking for themselves. They need to do the work; they need to learn to self-correct, not simply learn to rely on having their mistakes corrected.

---

97. Wiliam, D. (2016) 'Looking at student work', *ASCD Educational Leadership*, 73(7) pp. 10-15.

Wiliam simplifies the complex issue of feedback quality down to this:

> The only thing that matters is what the student does with the feedback. If the feedback you're giving your students is producing more of what you want, it's probably good feedback. But if your feedback is getting you less of what you want, it probably needs to change.[98]

Authentic assessment

A key driver of the macro data tracking machinery is the perceived need to communicate the outcomes of assessment in a consistent form and to be able to make comparisons between subjects. There's an assumption that Leo's B in maths indicates better performance than his C in science. However, as reasonable as this might seem, at the granular, cellular level where learning happens, it's not much help at all.

The idea of authentic assessment is that, instead of being driven by the need to produce standardised outcomes, we are primarily focused on generating formative feedback in the form most useful for a particular discipline, whatever that looks like.

In maths and science, there are swathes of assessments where the answers are right or wrong. Most assessments will be straightforward problem-solving or questions requiring simple knowledge recall. This kind of 'difficulty model' assessment, as Christodoulou calls it, is common to lots of subjects. The difficulty of the questions determines the standards and raw scores of tests in discrete topic areas, referenced against a clear knowledge checklist, will tell you what you need to know. It gets a little more complex with multi-mark answers in science or geography, where mark schemes need to spell out a wider range of possible correct answers. The feedback outcomes from difficulty model assessments can be quite specific: the questions that were wrong need to be revisited and attempted again after further teaching and study.

In English and history where extended writing is the most common form of outcome from a learning sequence, comparative judgement might be more useful. These 'quality model' assessments require teachers to compare standards across numerous success criteria (grammar, spelling, depth of analysis, the flow of ideas, the level of originality or perceptiveness). The complexity demands that direct comparison is likely to be required between specific pieces of work and possibly some benchmarking exemplars. Whether or not marks or grades are awarded, these assessments are always based on teacher judgements even if

---

98. Wiliam, D. *ibid.*

tight rubrics and mark schemes are used; they are not purely objective scores as in maths or science.

Feedback is more complex here and teachers need to agree on the language of feedback that helps move students forward. Often this is where things go awry.

- *This paragraph lacks clarity.*

- *The conclusion doesn't address the question sufficiently well.*

- *The ending is too corny.*

This kind of feedback is too vague to move the learner forward; students would not know what to do differently – only that their work had fallen short. However, with good comments and specific examples – as we examine in **K11 Verbal feedback** and in the next section – feedback can tell learners much more than any form of grading.

- *Re-write this paragraph using the Point-Evidence-Explain pattern to make it clearer.*

- *In your conclusion, sum up both sides of the argument and then state which you think is the most persuasive.*

- *That 'it was all a dream' ending is over-used. Perhaps try a darker ending that leaves the reader wondering what happened.*

Of course, there is every reason to include simple knowledge recall tests in English and history as part of the diet of formative assessment: dates, characters, the sequence of events, background facts. Knowledge of these elements can be assessed in a raw marks form that is very useful before getting stuck into full-blown essays.

In languages, there are multiple modes of assessment that teachers need to employ to encompass the four skills of speaking, listening, reading comprehension and writing. No single grade can do justice to this range of learning elements and provide information that could be used as feedback. In other subjects such as art, music and drama, there will be some knowledge elements but, largely, the creative outcomes will be subject to teacher evaluation where the interpretation of success criteria will be the key aspect of the process. Are marks appropriate here? Or A-G grades? Or perhaps a simple Pass, Merit, Distinction might be more meaningful given the level of subjectivity. It is self-evident that a B in maths can't mean much in comparison to a B in art in terms of the actual learning so why try to line them up at all? We would do better to keep the information as raw and as close to the requirements for subject-specific forms of feedback as possible.

5.3 Feedback for excellence

BLOG: Lessons from Austin's Butterfly

One of my favourite educational references is the work of Ron Berger and his ideas about cultivating 'An ethic of excellence'[99]. A much-loved metaphor-rich video clip, readily available online[100], is Berger's story of Austin's Butterfly. I refer to this in nearly every training session I do. The video shows Berger telling the story of First Grader Austin and his attempts at 'looking like a scientist' (by which he means using the skill of scientific observation) to draw an accurate picture of a tiger swallowtail butterfly from a photograph. He shows that, by using positive and specific feedback solicited via teacher-led class discussion, through a series of redrafts Austin improves his work from a very basic first effort to a magnificent final drawing.

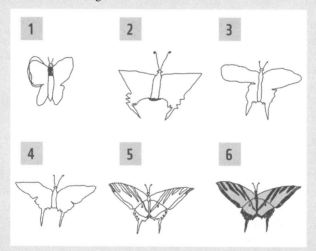

Beyond being an effective demonstration of the peer critique method, the story conveys several messages. Firstly, there is the idea that Austin was always capable of excellence – it's just that, to begin with, he didn't know what was expected or what he was capable of. But the wonderful final butterfly was in him all along. Linked to this is the idea that, too often, we accept work that is substandard; we associate certain students with

---

99. Berger, R. (2003)
100. Austin's Butterfly: Building Excellence in Student Work EL Education 2012 https://vimeo.com/38247060

their mediocre initial offerings without enabling them to push forward, insisting that they produce and experience excellence. Berger's philosophy is that every child should be given the opportunity to experience excellence:

'After students have had a taste of excellence, they're never quite satisfied with less; they're always hungry.'[101]

A second layer of thinking is that, in seeking to 'look like a scientist' at a photograph, the end product that would constitute excellence was there for all to see. Everyone involved could use this as a reference point to generate the specific feedback leading Austin towards the goal. From this, we can see that, in our various disciplines, a central task of successful formative assessment is to define our butterflies. Butterflies plural because there may be many ways to achieve excellence.

We need to spell out and exemplify what excellence might look like – including where there are multiple possibilities – and then devise iterative feedback processes that allow students to see the steps from where they are to where they could be in the detail of their learning goals. Austin and his teacher do not need a graded ladder or tracking system to help him improve; it's all about the detail of the work itself linked to a clear idea of what excellence might look like, modelled by an exemplar. Is his butterfly a D or an A? Who cares? It doesn't matter. The value is in the product itself.

Where students are set work that is too easy or where they have substandard work accepted, at the core of the issue is that teachers lose sight of expected standards. They don't define what the finished butterfly-equivalent should look like for each learner, taking account of their age and prior attainment. This is often because, in many cases, there is a sliding scale and it is difficult to know.

Take these questions:

- Why does your heart beat faster during exercise?
- What effect does dropping a ball from a greater height have?
- Was it right to kill Osama bin Laden?
- How is Harry Potter different from The Hobbit?
- Was King John a good king?

---

101. Berger, R. (2003)

It would be possible to have a good discussion about each of these questions with students aged 10, 13, 16 or 18. But what answers should be expected at each level? When should students start talking about haemoglobin and respiration? When should kinetic and potential energy start to feature? What distinguishes an A*/Grade 9 GCSE answer from a strong Year 7 answer about King John, Osama bin Laden or The Hobbit?

Around the world, there will be under-challenged children aged 14 making the same PowerPoint they were asked to make five years earlier; they will still be doing the same kind of percentages and fractions questions that they learned aged 10; they will be having the same discussion about food chains in a forest environment that they had aged 9; they will still be making some teachers happy saying King John was bad and bin Laden deserved to die instead of evaluating competing views in a coherent balanced manner.

At the same time, no teacher deliberately sets under-challenging work. What we need is to do a lot more work on establishing what standards mean, without using a proxy code; we should be doing it by looking at the actual work. Teachers should be discussing this extensively within schools and schools should be sharing this information extensively between them, defining the butterflies.

For any piece of work we should be setting out the most challenging success criteria we can conceive of for the task by referencing specific examples:In Year 8, an exceptional student should be able to produce work like THIS: (produce an actual example). It has the following features: (define the features).

- The minimum expectations we would have might look like THIS: (produce an example; define the features).

- In the 9th Grade, a six-mark answer to a question like 'How does an eye adjust to focus on near and distant objects?' should be structured like THIS with THIS level of scientific detail: (example given).

- Exceptional students in Year 7 might be expected to produce a poem analysis like THIS: (top end example on hand, with features identified).

- By the end of 7th Grade, the highest-performing students should be looking at solving simple simultaneous equations and Pythagoras' equation in problems like THIS; all students should be comfortable working out any percentage of any number and multiplying and dividing fractions such as THESE...

To me, this is the real scale. Turning all of this real assessment into numbers sucks the meaning out of it. Our obsession with grading is a distraction because knowing that the average for a class is B- doesn't mean much in terms of what they can actually do and what it looks like to achieve excellence. The key to real assessment of this kind, and the real standard-setting that it allows, is to have routine moderation processes. Schools could compile portfolios – writing, questions, work samples, book samples – from top, middle and bottom in each subject and gather in a room with schools nearby, every year.

Subject specialists should pore over each other's evidence of standards and see what everyone else is up to. This would have the effect of making everyone chase the best. Once you see what 13-year-olds can do down the road, you'd be defining your butterfly differently – it would be more and more sophisticated. But every teacher should know very clearly what excellence looks like, for every question they ask and every piece of work they set – not based on what they've always done, but based on sharp current information referenced against tangible exemplars.

How would you measure progress? Through the work. When I worked at the British School in Jakarta, a 3-18 school, every primary child had a 'First of the Month' book. On the first day of every month they would spend an hour writing on a fresh page in that book; the book would travel with them up the school. Over time, you could see their progress simply by turning the pages. It was wonderful – and powerful as an assessment tool for the teachers. If you turned all that into grades … I won't go there again.

Let's define standards by looking at the very best examples of work that students can produce – and let's share that information with our students and each other so that our sights are continually being set higher. Let's be very clear about the depth and rigour of the answers we expect students to give at each level in our curriculum so that we're not accepting work they could have produced years ago. It should be a routine part of departmental discourse to clarify expectations of standards, referring to the exemplar material on hand. Let each Austin make the best butterfly they can ... and not the one they could do already. It should be a matter of basic credibility for any teacher that they stretch the most able in their lessons – there is no excuse not to.

Making marking work as feedback

To conclude this chapter, a brief word about marking. A final part of this macro summative paradigm has been our approach to marking. For years now, marking has been largely a PR exercise where how the marking looks has been more important than what it achieves, with an appallingly low impact to workload ratio. Most marking is wasted. It doesn't lead to students knowing more, understanding things better or producing better quality work. This is in part due to the eternal marking paradox that those students who need the most help are the least able to interpret the real meaning of marking in order to adjust their thinking or performance. It is also partly to do with the time gap between the point when students did the work and the point when they get to improve it: it's often too long and everyone just wants to move to the next thing without making improvements on the last thing.

Despite these issues, school control cultures have demanded levels of marking – of red pen – that bear no relation to students' progress in their learning. As outlined in Part 2 **K13 Marking: Keeping it lean, K14 Whole-class feedback** and **K15 Close the gap**, there are alternative methods. Methods that are workload efficient whilst also moving students forward in their learning.

A new assessment paradigm?

If we put all the ideas in this chapter together, we have the ingredients for a more effective assessment paradigm to drive growth in our Learning Rainforest. Is it new? No. But it is certainly better than what dominates now. Instead of macro summative attainment tracking, we want to have a model made up of these elements:

- Maximum use of formative assessment: low-stakes, high-frequency testing owned exclusively by teachers and their students, focused on specific, clearly defined areas of knowledge and skill

- Judicious use of summative assessments that support the leanest possible tracking including the use of comparative judgement wherever subjective quality judgements are being made

- Responsive teaching, where feedback is informed by teacher-student relationships coupled to a range of 'minute-by-minute' interactions that elicit information about where students are in their learning

- Authentic assessment in subject disciplines, where the needs of each subject hold sway over the needs of the centralised data machinery

- Clear exemplars of excellence, where teachers have collectively defined their butterfly, working collaboratively in their subject teams using concrete examples of excellence to develop a shared understanding of standards

- Intelligent, lean marking approaches that acknowledge the limited effect marking has in relation to the demands it places on teachers

MANAGING THE LEARNING RAINFOREST

" EACH OF THE SPECIMENS IN THE LEARNING RAINFOREST IS REPRESENTED IN THE WONDERFUL ARRAY OF TREES WITH THEIR COMPLEX ROOTS, TRUNK AND BRANCH SYSTEMS THAT GIVE THEM STRENGTH AND STRUCTURE AND GLORIOUS CANOPIES WHERE THEIR CHARACTER FINDS EXPRESSION.

EXPLORING POSSIBILITIES

BUILDING KNOWLEDGE

ESTABLISHING CONDITIONS

" BUILDING THE KNOWLEDGE STRUCTURE:

- USING EFFECTIVE INSTRUCTION METHODS (K1- K10)
- USING EFFECTIVE FORMATIVE ASSESSMENT AND FEEDBACK METHODS (K11- K15)
- TEACHING FOR MEMORY (K16-K20)

" EXPLORING THE POSSIBILITIES:

- PROVIDING OPPORTUNITIES FOR HANDS-ON, AUTHENTIC LEARNING EXPERIENCES (P1-P10)
- USING ONLINE TOOLS AND OTHER RESOURCES TO SUPPORT STUDENTS AS INDEPENDENT LEARNERS (P11- P16)
- GIVING SPEECH ACTIVITIES A HIGH PROFILE AND CELEBRATING EXCELLENCE IN ALL ITS FORMS. (P17-P20)

" ESTABLISHING THE CONDITIONS:
- FOSTERING THE ATTITUDES AND HABITS NEEDED AS A BASIS FOR STUDENTS TO ACHIEVE EXCELLENCE: (C1-C5)
- ESTABLISHING EFFECTIVE BEHAVIOUR ROUTINES (C6-C12).
- DESIGNING A CURRICULUM (C13- C20)

6.1 The Learning Rainforest metaphor: Recapitulation

To conclude Part 1 of this book, I want to revisit the central metaphor, as this is the basis for organising the categorised strategies and ideas in Part 2.

The classroom is part of an exciting, complex rainforest made up of individuals with their own needs, individuality, prior knowledge, experience and ambitions, capable of expressing their learning in multiple forms. At the same time, within all of this apparent diversity and complexity, there are patterns and trends; there is a science common to all that guides many of the principles of growth and development.

All of this takes place within a curriculum environment where the three arts of the Trivium hold sway, where 'head, heart and hand' guide children as they engage in 'the great conversation': the philosopher kids and their teachers immersed in the accumulation of powerful knowledge as part of the journey towards becoming principled global citizens in the world of opportunities.

Each of the specimens is represented in the wonderful array of trees with their complex roots, trunk and branch systems that give them strength and structure and glorious canopies where their character finds expression.

The tree metaphor serves as a way of capturing the three sets of tasks that constitute great teaching:

Establishing the conditions (Chapter 7)

- Fostering the attitudes and habits needed as a basis for students to achieve excellence: having high expectations, teaching with rigour whilst also inspiring awe and making the whole process joyful (C1-C5)

- Establishing effective behaviour routines and developing relationships that support students' self-esteem, motivation and, crucially, their engagement with teacher feedback (C6-C12)

- Designing a curriculum where the knowledge and skills are structured in a way that supports long-term retention, builds confidence and allows connections to be made (C13-C20)

Building the knowledge structure (Chapter 8)

- Using effective instruction methods to build students' knowledge explicitly and deliberately: explaining, modelling, questioning in various ways and developing routines for practice (K1-K10)

- Using effective formative assessment and feedback methods that make teaching highly responsive and support students to improve continually (K11-K15)

- Teaching for memory in an explicit fashion, using a range of methods for learning by heart, making this a positive and joyful part of the learning process (K16-K20)

Exploring the possibilities (Chapter 9)

- Providing some opportunities within the overall curriculum for hands-on, authentic learning experiences, group activities and project work, with open-ended outcomes (P1-P10)

- Using online tools and other resources to support students as independent learners with occasional opportunities to lead learning based on their own knowledge (P11-P16)

- Giving speech activities a high profile as experiences in the enacted curriculum and finally celebrating excellence in all its forms (P17-P20)

It's important to see the interaction between the different elements as well as to understand each one. Each element supports the others. You can't hope to build a lush canopy of possibilities without building the knowledge structure to support it. Many of the ideas in P1-P20 could be horribly unproductive if students do not have sufficient knowledge to make them worthwhile. Any discourse that downplays the importance of knowledge, or pits knowledge as being in some way standing in the path of creativity is foolish; suggesting that we will somehow foster lots more creative wunderkinder without undertaking the knowledge-building process is misguided. That's the road to the scrubland of underachievement.

At the same time, unless the conditions for learning are sufficiently fertile, the extent to which a knowledge structure can be built will be limited. You ignore the basic conditions for growth at your peril. Teaching our subjects as specialists is very important from a knowledge curriculum perspective, but we are always teaching our subjects to specific people; individuals with whom we need to foster relationships if we are going to cohabit our learning spaces happily, give the right feedback and provide the right motivational cues.

Finally, it's important not to see the three elements of the tree as a simple linear sequence. When a tree grows, all three parts grow at the same time as they interact, each fuelling the growth of the others. The 'exploring possibilities' activities are not simply end products. They will generate learning that feeds back down to the process of building the knowledge structure (albeit less directly for many areas of the curriculum). Similarly, the business of learning itself, the experience of building knowledge through teacher-led instruction is enormously rewarding, and this feeds directly into reinforcing the conditions for future growth. The roots don't just support the tree; the tree feeds the roots. The links happen at every stage.

Mode A: Mode B. 80%: 20%?

If we get the sequencing right, and give each element of the Learning Tree the optimum proportion of our time and focus, then we will create a beautiful rainforest full of wonderfully awe-inspiring specimens. What might this look like in practice? I have found that, in giving some exploratory talks about the rainforest metaphor, some teachers have taken a look at 'exploring possibilities' and said, 'Great, I'll do lots of that'. But it's not a free-for-all.

As we explored in Chapter 4, even where there is ambiguity in research this does not mean that anything goes. It is clear that you need a big strong trunk of knowledge to make a fabulous canopy of creative, expressive, impressive learning outcomes. This is the hard part; this is what takes the time. But it's not all there is to a great education. To create a shorthand for this issue, I often talk about Mode A and Mode B teaching.

Mode A teaching is basically all the elements that make up Building knowledge (K1-20). This is the teacher-led instruction mode where you lead the learning from the front, deploying the full range of instruction and feedback techniques. Mode B teaching is doing anything else – including anything I've described in Exploring the possibilities (P1-20).

What's the optimum balance? This would be foolish to mandate given all the variables at play but, in my context, as a secondary teacher of maths and science, weighing up the opportunities and opportunity costs, I'm going for 80% Mode A, 20% Mode B. It's a guide. If pushed, I'd give more time to Mode A, not less, especially for maths. That's my orientation as a fairly traditional kind of teacher. In other subjects, this might be too much. My straw polls at various events suggest that this rings true for a lot of people. It's only an impressionistic split but I would argue that in any content-heavy subject, Mode B teaching needs to be kept to a level where it can always be meaningful, challenging and knowledge-rich.

6.2 The Managed Rainforest

With our three elements firmly in mind, let's now revisit the rainforest-plantation comparison. As discussed in Chapter 1, the rainforest is an environment where it is possible for things to go wrong. Not everything thrives automatically and that's problematic when we're talking about a child's education. A plantation has a lot to be said for it in terms of providing safety nets – even if it doesn't allow the freedoms and diversity we value. The compromise is to think of a managed rainforest; our attempt at securing the best of both worlds.

We might be satisfied that we've created a set of ideas that deliver for the majority but, if we're going to be truly great teachers, of particular importance is how well our model for teaching works for students at the extremes. In Part 2 I will look further into the idea of Teaching to the Top. This has always been a philosophy I've held dear. But we must also be sure that our most vulnerable students thrive.

Inclusion for Special Needs

In England there is a comprehensive government Code of Practice for Special Educational Needs and Disability (or SEND) covering children and young people aged 0 to 25. This Code[102] states that:

---

102. DFE SEND Code of Practice January 2015 via www.gov.uk

All children and young people are entitled to an appropriate education, one that is appropriate to their needs, promotes high standards and the fulfilment of potential. This should enable them to:

- achieve their best

- become confident individuals living fulfilling lives, and

- make a successful transition into adulthood, whether into employment, further or higher education or training

A great deal of the Code deals with the statutory duty of various agencies to provide the elements that make up a SEND student's education, health and care provision. It doesn't say much about what teachers should do, largely because there are so many variables. General advice covering SEND provision overall is only of limited use. It's important to get into the details of what any one child's needs are. The Code uses four helpful SEND categories:

- **Communication and interaction** which includes speech and language difficulties, ASD including Asperger's Syndrome and autism

- **Cognition and learning** including the subcategory of specific learning difficulties that encompasses a range of conditions such as dyslexia, dyscalculia and dyspraxia

- **Social, emotional and mental health difficulties.** Here the Code highlights the fact that students' behaviours may 'reflect underlying mental health difficulties such as anxiety or depression, self-harming, substance misuse, eating disorders or physical symptoms that are medically unexplained. Other children and young people may have disorders such as attention deficit disorder, attention deficit hyperactive disorder or attachment disorder.'

- **Sensory and/or physical needs** including visual, hearing, multi-sensory impairment

A quick glance at these tells you just how many specialist areas of SEND teachers might need to be familiar with over the course of their career – if not simultaneously. If you throw the particular needs of second language learners into the mix, it can feel rather overwhelming. From my experience, it can help to hold on to a few key principles:

Entitlements, not favours

If a student has certain entitlements, it's vital that you don't regard them as a burden or see the special work you do for them as doing them a favour. You need to give absolute priority to students who cannot access the curriculum without special support; meeting their needs is a bottom-line regardless of the other demands on your time. If you have a student that can't read the textbook or follow the standard instructions because of learning difficulties or physical impairment, you have to provide for them every time. You need to plan for their needs every lesson and always make sure they know what to do. Don't expect them to be any more grateful than any other student is for the support you give them.

Assistants assist; teachers teach

It is essential that you talk and teach directly to your SEND students to at least the same extent as you do for any other student even if they are supported by another adult. It's a classic error for teachers to assume that the assistant can do all the direct communication but they are meant to provide additional support, not replace you. For example, I've been told by several severely visually impaired students over the years how frustrating it is for teachers to talk about them, around them and not to them.

High expectations are the best form of inclusion

This means having the same high expectations for SEND children as for everyone else to the greatest extent possible. Obviously this depends on the details but in a mainstream context you want SEND students to behave within the school boundaries, access the same texts in English, complete all of their homework and take part in the same range of activities as everyone else, as far as is possible. In my experience, when SEND children underachieve at school it is often not because the expectations are too high for them to meet; it is usually because teachers' or the school's expectations are too low. This applies as much to standards of behaviour as it does to standards of work and levels of effort.

See the individual, not their SEND label

It can be useful to have a general understanding of the typical indicators and strategies that help support a range of identified special needs. However, in full-on rainforest style, SEND students tend not to conform neatly to the definitions. Often students have multiple overlapping needs or they fall somewhere along a spectrum of needs such that they require tailored support that is very particular to them. I've encountered lots of examples where a reverse Pygmalion effect has been in force; where students carrying a SEND label have been held back by institutional glass ceilings or teacher-driven low expectations.

Another dimension of this is more technical; labels are usually very broad, relative to a particular student's actual needs. Quite commonly the dyslexia label can be problematic because it doesn't tell you much on its own; it's more of an umbrella term covering a spectrum of specific learning difficulties. The risk of lowering expectations is serious where labelling isn't supported by specific information about actions to follow. There are also multiple label-free SEND students who might appear to have low cognitive function without an identified learning difficulty; they find school difficult and we need to gauge our expectations, pitched to enable them rather than limit, demoralise or inhibit them. This is always easier said than done.

Behaviour needs often have social origins but need educational solutions

In terms of SEND in the SEMH category, the social context or home learning environment is often a major factor. The Code says that we should aim to be neutral in respect of family context but my experience is that we ignore it at our peril. We need to be able to discuss parenting without it being taboo; this is not 'blaming the parents'. Quite often it's just that home and school are miles apart in terms of how we set and enforce everyday boundaries; with SEND students it's usually even more important to be consistent. Often low self-esteem through negative learning experiences is the root cause of a student's' behaviour issues but I would say that it is quite rare for this to happen in isolation from other social/family factors. Teachers have very little hope of transforming a child's home learning situation so the solutions have to be located in what we can control: what we teach, how we teach, our relationships and whatever additional provision we can offer to support learning beyond the classroom.

Inclusion for second language learners

In England, English as an Additional Language is the preferred term (EAL). This group of students also requires some additional consideration, some of this is around social and cultural inclusion where it helps to celebrate diversity and the value of multilingualism in general. However, one of the most important principles is to be very clear that, whilst language barriers may present some additional difficulties, EAL students do not have special needs remotely on a par with SEND students (except, of course, when they are also SEND students!). In general, some of the biggest issues to address are:

- Accessing the curriculum at the beginner stage: students of all levels need beginner-level language support just to access the resources and follow instructional input.

- Progressing beyond a plateau of functionality to fluency: it's common for students' EAL status to recede once they have grown in confidence. However, this can be premature, masking ongoing limitations in their comprehension and oral fluency. Teachers need to continue to model correct speech and encourage EAL students to continue to practise and improve.

- Maintaining high expectations for academic learning: EAL students are likely to have the same broad ability range as the other students in the class. Even at the beginner stage, we need to keep the level of academic rigour high. School structures need to support their language development as well as their academic learning; one should not displace the other.

Day-to-day differentiation: Gardening!

Looking ahead to the strategies in Part 2, I would like to stress that, at all times, I envisage that they apply to all learners. That is the reason why there is no separate strand of EAL or SEND strategies beyond what I've written above; they should be included in everything. However, sound as our intentions might be, the challenge of teaching students with a range of levels of prior attainment in one space can be daunting. How can we manage this aspect of our rainforest classroom in practice? I have three main messages:

1. Keep the curriculum goals and learning objectives the same; only differentiate the support needed to reach them

There's a classic Bart Simpson line where, having been put in a catch-up class, he says *'Let me get this straight. We're going to catch up with the rest of the class by going slower than they are?'* Bart raises a valid point. We don't want our SEND or EAL students to know less about history, art, science or literature. Every time you take a decision to allow the curriculum content to diverge for different groups of learners, you create gaps that are really hard to close later. Of course it depends on the precise needs of your students – as individuals and in the make-up of your teaching group – but as far as you possibly can, make your learning objectives the same for everyone even if that feels difficult.

2. Nurture the students at the extremes

This means that you go out of your way to forge relationships with all of your SEND students, making absolutely sure that bottom-line access is secure. You also do the same for the highest attainers. In all probability the strongest and weakest learners are likely to be the ones who you struggle with the most in terms of your planning and teaching. If you let them know very clearly that you are working for them, keeping an eye on them and giving them the special attention they need, they will have confidence that, when things aren't perfectly tailored to them, you haven't forgotten. Their parents will know this too and that helps a lot. If you are keeping these students supported and challenged and their parents happy, you'll be doing a great job overall.

3. Treat differentiation like gardening

You have a group of individual specimens with their own precise needs and qualities and your job is to get them to flourish to the greatest possible extent. But, as with gardening, you often need to focus on one specimen at a particular moment. You can't do it all at once.

You may feel that Mo is coasting a bit; he needs a push this lesson. It may be that Tamara has looked a bit bored of late. She might be finding things a bit easy; so let's really crank it up this lesson. The last time Ruby handed her book in it was a bit of a shocker; you'll need to sit with her this lesson and get a few things sorted out. Harun is always just below the top level. Why is that? Is this an Austin's Butterfly effect? Maybe he needs to do some re-drafting and you need to absolutely insist that he does it again and again until he's hitting the top level, truly delivering excellence.

That's real differentiation: keeping standards high for everyone, trusting that most learners learn in broadly similar ways, teaching them as a whole group and then pushing, prodding, nudging, stretching ... slow, subtle, nuanced, a step at a time, working around the class from lesson to lesson where needed to the greatest extent you can manage. It's not a performance you master each lesson; it's something you grind out over the long, long run.

As well as trying to be a teacher who champions the students with the greatest needs, the main thing is to keep differentiation at the forefront of your thinking, doing your best to keep everyone in each class moving forward without limiting them. It's never going to feel that you've got it absolutely nailed – and that is teaching!

That is life in the Learning Rainforest.

Individuality and commonality

My final thoughts on the managed rainforest metaphor are about the continual need to balance a desire to treat each of our students as individuals with their own needs and interests with the moral and practical imperatives that lean us towards providing all students with common educational experiences.

There is a joy in the diversity of the rainforest; we want our students to develop as individuals with opinions, ideas, tastes, preferences, personality – and a range of talents. The great strength of any community is the diverse range of individual skills, talents and personalities that come together to form the collective; the Learning Rainforest should be a celebration of individuality with a wide range of opportunities for children to express who they are. This is what Chapter 9 – Exploring the possibilities focuses on.

Some of our attention to individuals will encompass the preceding discussion about any special educational needs or disabilities, any additional language learning needs or any special attention needed for exceptionally able students, performing far beyond the level of their peer group. We also need to acknowledge that, at different points, students will have legitimate, genuine interests that are going to shape their attitudes and commitment to learning in different areas.

If we recognise that our students are going to diverge into multiple life paths as doctors, artists, dancers, mechanics, musicians, business people, film makers, bankers, charity workers, engineers, diplomats, retailers, teachers, lawyers, designers, programmers, politicians, journalists, soldiers, pilots and astronauts – then our rainforest has to cater for multiple eventualities. Ideally you want every one of your students – with their broad spectrum of personalities – to feel liberated by their education, set free to explore the world.

However, we are also faced with the important moral and social imperative to give every student in our care the maximum opportunity to enjoy educational success. This means providing them with the most broad and deep, knowledge-rich education we possibly can. This is our best bet when we don't yet know which path they will go down in the future or even what all the possibilities are. We need to make sure that no doors are closed prematurely. Many adolescent children would make short-term choices about their learning that are not in their long-term interests if we simply allowed their teenage desires to shape their curriculum. Of course we want to ensure that they enjoy the process of learning in the moment but, at the same time, we are preparing them for the future. It doesn't have to be a choice.

We also want our individual students to become engaged citizens of the local, national and global communities that they are all belong to. This means that, to a large degree, there should be a core body of knowledge from multiple domains that they all share. When coupled with the simple logistical practicalities of educating students in classes of 25-30 and the knowledge that students are more similar than different in the way they learn, teaching a common curriculum with the broadly similar learning goals for all is a reasonable basis on which to base most of our curriculum design work.

The Learning Tree metaphor can help to navigate the path between individuality and commonality. If we've invested sufficiently in creating fertile conditions for learning and then built a strong knowledge structure that might predominantly be common to all our students, we have the platform for exploring possibilities in much more individualistic ways. There is room for everyone to experience success and to develop a love of learning if we approach teaching with this spirit.

PART 2: THE LEARNING RAINFOREST IN PRACTICE

ESTABLISHING THE CONDITIONS

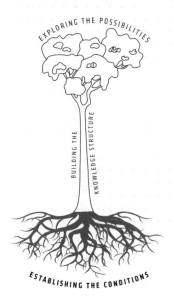

RELATIONSHIPS AND BEHAVIOUR

- **C 6** FOSTER RELATIONSHIIPS: POSITIVE, CARING AND DEFINED
- **C 7** ESTABLISH ROUTINES FOR EXCELLENCE
- **C 8** SIGNAL, PAUSE, INSIST
- **C 9** POSITIVE FRAMING
- **C 10** USE THE SYSTEM AS A LEVER, NOT A WEAPON
- **C 11** SILENCE IS GOLDEN
- **C 12** KEEP PERSPECTIVE

PLANNING THE CURRICULUM

- **C 13** BIG PICTURE, SMALL PICTURE
- **C 14** PLAN THE STEPS
- **C 15** SPECIFY THE KNOWLEDGE
- **C 16** OBJECTIVES v TASKS
- **C 17** SCAFFOLDS AND STABILISERS
- **C 18** SKILLS AND DRILLS
- **C 19** BUILD THE WORDS, PLAN THE READING
- **C 20** BUILD A TIMELINE

ATTITUDES HABITS FOR EXCELLENCE

- **C 1** JOY, AWE AND WONDER
- **C 2** TEACH TO THE TOP
- **C 3** RIGOUR
- **C 4** PITCH IT UP
- **C 5** PYGMALION

Attitudes and habits for excellence

C1 Joy, awe and wonder

Arguably one of the most important habits needed to create fertile conditions for learning is to communicate a sense of joy in what you and your students are learning and doing. Starting a lesson with a grim apology – 'Sorry, guys, this stuff is hard and boring but we just need to get through it' – is hardly going to fan the flames of inspiration. Life is short; there is probably enough drudgery in the world to drown us all if we let it; so let's not add to it with our teaching. We are not talking about lessons being a bit of a party, all fun and games, or teachers as entertainers putting on a show; not at all. We are talking about making the process of learning joyful, even when, at times, it can be tough going. How do we do that? Here are some ideas:

Share your passion

You always have permission (that you can give yourself) to teach the things that get you excited about your subject. Read that special poem that gets you fired up, show that fascinating maths puzzle with the neat solution, enthuse about the extraordinary story, or talk about that cool exploding watermelon video (a great backdrop for discussing energy and momentum conservation in a wonderfully joyous way). My daughter's English teacher made a superb video guide to ten books he recommended to his classes. He is incredibly passionate about the books and he transmitted that passion to his students. At my son's school, various teachers earn the title 'legend'; the ultimate badge of respect. These are teachers who are usually a bit 'old school', quite formal and unashamedly traditional in their methods, but who are absolutely, infectiously passionate about their subjects.

Adopt strategies that couple rigour with intrinsic motivation

Here is an example. English Paired Dialogue: Using a method called Paired Dialogue, Y12 students read sections of *The Remains of the Day* that are allocated to them in pairs. The room is full of the sound of students reading to each other. They subsequently annotate their texts, using the reading experience to inform their analysis of the use of language before a report-back which includes more reading aloud and probing questioning in a dialogic style. The students love it; joyousness abounds.

I could write a long list spanning all subjects and lessons of all kinds: a buzzy run-through of quick mental maths questions, a joyful exercise in German using vocabulary related to battling knights to recount invented gruesome tales, students giving an exposition of differentiation from first principles in calculus, students writing programmes in computer science to make a simple counter – simply thrilled by their achievement, students mastering a routine in gymnastics, students in full flow engrossed in their personal art projects.

There is joy to be found in every corner of the curriculum and in every classroom.

Build joyful relationships

I'd suggest that sharing in the joy of learning is characteristic of great teacher-student relationships. The teacher and students laugh together, share in the fascination of the subject together and generally bond through their exchanges, their questions and their journeys off-piste. If those relationships are edgy, negative, disdainful, based on autocratic teacher tendencies, there is usually a dreary joylessness and the learning feels stifled. If there is occasional laughter, mutual respect, room to express interests and passions and veer off into new corners of the subject from time to time…if there are joyful relationships, then great teaching and learning are far more likely.

Celebrate achievement as its own reward...

For many of us, the greatest joy is from seeing a student achieve; to be there when the penny drops; to see the smile on a student's face and feel the smile on your own when you can say, 'Wow – that is a great question; that is a superb piece of work … you're starting to write beautifully now … you've really nailed it … what a superb idea…'. Wow. Never mind the stickers and the stamps, the grades, the levels, or exam success – or even the future employment prospects or university places – in the here and now, the simple but utterly magnificent joy of achieving, of making those steps toward the big audacious goals, that is reward enough. That is the joy of learning.

Inspire awe and wonder

Take time from the groove of instruction and practice to contemplate the subject in hand, instilling a sense of awe. This is how the seeds of a deep-rooted love of learning are sown. We're not just learning this stuff because we have to; or because it is useful. We are learning it because it is just so fabulously, fascinatingly awe-inspiring. There is no greater motivation to learn than this. In a five-period day, with exams to prepare for and a pile of marking to look forward to, you may feel your inclination to inspire awe may be on the low side. But who else is going to do this if you don't? In fact, we should aim to make it our default mode, our natural disposition, to seize every possible opportunity to fire our students' imaginations and to stoke their passions. This is as important to a school's contribution to social, moral, spiritual and cultural education as any number of assemblies. Is it unrealistic to think of inspiring awe as a habit of great teachers? It's not all *Dead Poet's Society* table jumping; it can be quite subtle. And look how much material we've got!

As part of his Latin workshops at my school, my step-dad, Larry, (a retired professor of Medieval Latin) introduced students to a poem that he described as 'the most beautiful poem ever written in any language'. An audacious claim. But did it grab attention? You bet! They listened intently to his rendition of the 13th-century *Carmina Burana* manuscript. The theme of anticipation of post-coital sleep also seemed to capture their imagination!

In maths, the fundamental truths inherent in the patterns, theorems and axioms are all worthy of being marvelled at as well as studied and learned, from simple patterns linking the Fibonacci sequence to natural forms to wonderful unifying ideas at a more advanced level such as $e^{i\pi} = -1$.

As a physicist, I naturally feel that most of my subject is awe-inspiring. Playing with a pair of magnets is a wonderful thing, just sensing that invisible mysterious force. Seeing a simple current carrying wire moving in-between a pair of magnets, well that is extraordinary. Imagine Faraday's surprise and delight. Making a simple motor ... well, we're becoming ecstatic now!

In literature, or art or music, we can get stuck into a groove of doing the formal analysis or making technical comparisons. But we must also be sure to capture the spirit of a piece of art, to bask in its glory, for its own sake before we start dissecting. Great English teachers will focus as much on how the words make them feel as they are spoken and experienced – as much as on their technical function and wider meaning. In history, as well as learning the chronology and the causes and effects, we need also to consider the human courage displayed or the sheer enormity of certain events.

For me, and I hope for you too, this isn't just a bit of icing on the cake. Inspiring awe is a core function for teachers. We need to take every opportunity we can to communicate our own feeling that life is full of wondrous things that are there to be studied, discovered and enjoyed.

As well as transmitting our enthusiasm to students and modelling the importance of seeing awe and wonder in the physical and cultural world that surrounds us, we also have an opportunity to shine a light on our students' work. Encouragement and praise that keep students motivated, engaged and on track, can sometimes be taken up a notch or two into all-out awe.

C2 Teach to the top

'A rising tide lifts all ships.'

Joseph Renzulli[103]

Every class is a 'mixed-ability class'. There is always a range. Do you plan to teach to the middle and then try to push the very top end with some extras? No. I've always found that it is a win-win to cater explicitly for the highest attaining students in any group; to 'teach to the top', pitching every lesson and the general thrust of every unit of work to stretch them. In doing so, everyone benefits. The curriculum content is always at its most challenging so everyone is exposed to it; top-end students enjoy their learning, feel valued and feel normal. (Their parents love you for this.) The learning environment in each lesson is characterised by high expectations. This raises aspirations and, through appropriate scaffolded support, all students are pulled along in the wake.

Importantly, this isn't something you do from time to time; teaching to the top is a total philosophy. Some of the elements of this approach include the following:

- Plan learning objectives, resources and questions with the highest attainers in mind. Don't allow your concern that this might be too much for some students to deter you. Always have in mind that you must not put a lid on your expectations for any student and resolve never to dumb things down. *Take the lid off and see what happens.*

- Find out what your students can do before you launch in with a topic via some form of preliminary formative assessment. Simple questioning can do the trick. There's nothing worse than being 'taught' stuff you already know or that is far too easy. You can't stretch students to their limits if you don't know where the limits are. I would suggest that where teaching is at its weakest, it is often where a teacher has underestimated what their students are capable of, failing to build on what they can already do, on what they already know.

- Celebrate intellectual curiosity and make it normal to do things that are difficult and academic in nature. Turn all those hideous pejoratives – nerd, geek, dork – into badges of honour. Champion students with a general all-round passion for knowledge and understanding and never let anyone diminish them for it.

---

103. Renzulli, J. http://gifted.uconn.edu/schoolwide-enrichment-model/rising_tide/

- Don't talk down your own knowledge or make a virtue out of ignorance. If you struggled at school then find a story to tell about how you overcame struggles through hard work and determination; don't inadvertently become a role model for acceptable low academic aspirations or the idea that success at school doesn't matter too much. (Too many people do this about maths, for example.)

- Embrace the ideas of **Rigour (C3)** and **Pitch It Up (C4)**.

C3 Rigour

I would suggest that it is always true that great lessons are characterised by a high level of rigour. Rigour is part of a great teacher's attitude. You don't settle for low-level disruption, sloppy thinking, mediocrity, laziness, half-hearted writing or incomplete answers. You can't do a bit of rigour every now and then; it is part and parcel of every lesson, relentless and automatic.

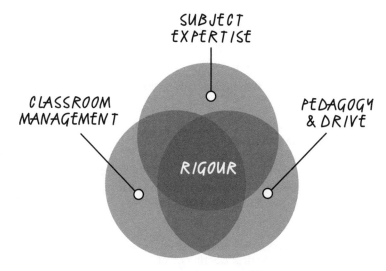

The precise form of rigour is usually highly subject specific but there are some common characteristics.

- The teacher pitches the material very high; there is no doubt that the highest attainers in the room are challenged and engaged.

- The teacher presents a strong command of the subject and uses that to select appropriately probing questions and tasks. This is different to passion which, on its own, can actually mask a lack of rigour if we're not careful.

- The teacher can respond intelligently to questions and can back-fill or widen discussion with examples, counter-examples and tangential ideas.

- Students are required to give precise answers and extended answers.

- The use of accurate subject-specific terminology is expected and reinforced.

- The teacher is prepared to challenge and accept challenge back; it matters that things are right – or that they are examined for truth and the general tone of the lesson is one of searching ever deeper.

- There is usually a general sense of high expectations in a range of areas: concentration span; extended writing; independence and self-help; maturity and sophistication *etc*. All these things reinforce a rigorous approach to learning in the classroom.

- The focus is on intrinsic reward and motivation through the learning; rigour is rarely associated with 'having a bit of fun'; but actually, in great lessons, students get engrossed in rigorous tasks and enjoy the feeling of making progress. Serious endeavour, rigour and enjoyment are intertwined.

How does rigour come across in different subjects? Here are examples from lessons I've seen:

Y7 Geography: Students plotting graphs, being drilled in the precision required, points in the right place; aligning multiple variables in the appropriate columns; starting the line in the exact spot required and getting the decimal places correct. This early training allows them to tackle complex synoptic tasks later on at GCSE and A Level where accurate data analysis is an assumed prerequisite for a range of problem-solving challenges.

Y12 Maths: Students asked to identify a general formula to cover all possibilities to define the factor theorem, comparing the method with long-division of polynomials where the vertical alignment of each power of x was critical. The ability to identify different equally valid methods was key, whilst also challenging students to select the most effective.

Y11 Physics: Students needing to produce a five-mark answer to describe and explain the function of a transformer using electromagnetism and the concept of induction. The scope for waffle is huge so the teacher has to filter out misconceptions, challenge any sloppy use of terms (current, potential difference and magnetic field) and ensure all students can relate the theory to the practice.

Y12 History: Students reading and discussing the latest examiner's report for the American Civil War sources paper, to see how subtle the requirements are in terms of using prior knowledge in conjunction with interpretations of sources to answer a question, then applying this to a sample question.

Y9 Art: Students set a challenging multimedia project with a high degree of freedom but also a tight brief in terms of the progression of ideas from a particular stimulus. The rigour comes through the pace expected, the depth of thinking behind the composition and the level of detail in the application of various painting techniques.

Y13 Economics: Students in pairs identifying the key consequences for global businesses of reducing interest rates; sharing the answers and defending their positions under questioning. The rigour comes from expecting students to weigh up the relative effects of competing trends and come to a conclusion, again, using appropriate terminology and citing relevant examples.

Y9 German: students given a translation task, using various resources to identify the grammatical features of a sentence and the required word endings. A strong understanding of cases is developed from Y7 to allow students to experiment and explore new and unknown phrases.

Y7 English: students discussing structure and imagery in 'The Lady of Shallot', following a student presenting an extended exposition of the key elements of one section. The rigour comes mainly through probing questioning and challenging soft answers that don't go far enough or are too sweeping.

In each case, the level of the work is pitched right up to the top; the expectations of students in terms of work ethic are also very high and the focus on detail, accuracy and precision is strong. Rigour in this context goes hand-in-hand with creativity, open-endedness and experimentation; in fact, the more rigorous the general approach is, the more confident both teachers and students are to then go 'off-piste'; conversely, if the rigour is lacking, everyone feels insecure in the whole process and no-one ventures anywhere near the edge.

C4 Pitch it up

This is a component of **C2 Teach to the top**. To pitch it up means to ensure that the enacted curriculum is characterised by conspicuous challenge for all where every opportunity is taken to explore a subject in depth. This can have numerous dimensions:

Acceleration through depth before speed. Don't make it a race to finish early. Although some high attainers can benefit from learning at a fast pace, there is a risk of skimming through at the expense of the breadth and depth of learning. Take time to explore interesting questions, more extended problems, wider reading, more artists, poets and composers, more practical examples instead of moving on to the next topic.

Selecting high impact questions. For example, here is my son's first homework from his secondary school:

It began with an explanation of the ideas of Greek philosopher Democritus who observed that water behaved in similar ways to sand – it could be stirred, poured and mixed. His hypothesis was that water might, therefore, be made up of small particles akin to grains of sand but smaller than the eye can see. He called these particles *'atoma'*. The questions that followed were:

- What is the difference between science and philosophy?

- What observations did Democritus make?

- What was his hypothesis?

- What properties of liquids could be explained by Democritus' hypothesis?

- Does his hypothesis explain the behaviour of solids and gases?

How about that for an introduction to secondary science? It's not just the material itself – it's the message of embedded high expectations and the notion that young students will not be patronised.

Choosing challenging texts

For example, at KEGS, new students used to start their learning in German with a unit called 'Fun with *Faust*' and in French with 'Kids can do *Candide*'. The teachers introduced students to authentic texts in literature and showed them that they could engage with the rich vocabulary. Similarly in English, the selection of texts can be crucial in determining the pitch. You could read *Hamlet* or *Blood Brothers*. Both have value but if you want to pitch it up, you'll choose *Hamlet*. You would choose *Of Mice and Men* over *Holes* or *The Diary of Adrian Mole*. This isn't elitism. In fact, the elitism lies in the assumption that some children cannot access these texts whilst others can.

A challenge I make to teachers sometimes is to ask: imagine you believed your next class was a year older – in the next grade up. You teach them with those age-related expectations notched up a year. When do you or they notice? Or does it go just fine? If so, who is holding them back – them or you? The message is to keep the pitch of the material we teach as high as possible; let's set audacious goals and strive to meet them.

C5 Pygmalion

The idea here is to try to recreate the Pygmalion effect with students that we know. If we set higher expectations for every member of our class and truly expect more from them, can we make the same kind of impact as found in Rosenthal's study (referenced and discussed previously in Chapter 4)? It's hard to fake a placebo effect but we can learn the lessons. These are captured in four areas:

a. The climate effect: To be kinder and more encouraging

b. The input effect: To teach the more demanding material on the basis you expect it to be learned. As soon as you decide not to teach something to students on the basis that it's too hard, you've closed a door to them. That decision might be needed but, as in **Pitch it up**, you need to be careful not to do this prematurely.

c. Response opportunity: To ask more questions and give more time to respond; *ie* to believe this is worthwhile for all students, not just those you already believe will give good answers

d. Feedback: Giving more differentiated feedback, leading a student to higher quality responses

If you mentally scan through your class list, are there students in there that you are already writing off just a little? Are there students who you will accept lower quality answers and writing from? Imagine them all as Austin with beautiful butterflies in them, waiting to get out – if you can just show them the standards that are possible and not put a lid on your expectations (see also **P19 Third time for excellence**).

Relationships and Behaviour

C6 Foster relationships: positive, caring and defined

It is a mistake to try to mandate a particular form of teacher-student relationships. Even in schools with hyper-strict behaviour-management systems, individual teachers need to establish their own relationships and be themselves within the parameters of agreed expectations. There's a huge range of approaches but if I survey the many hundreds of teachers I've seen and worked with, there are some general patterns.

Great teachers foster relationships with their students based on genuine mutual respect, where there is no argument about expected standards of behaviour.

They achieve this in different ways – sometimes through the gravitas of maturity and experience; sometimes through amazing warm, interpersonal interactions with every child – but they create an environment where learning always thrives and there is a sense of the teacher and their students enjoying each other's company. Their rapport with students is palpably positive and caring. The relationships are also clearly defined.

Positive: Interactions are warm and friendly; human. Everyone assumes the best intentions; they forgive mistakes and give the benefit of the doubt. The language is positive and respectful (see **C9 Positive framing**) even if there's an edge of intensity in the drive for success and especially when behaviour needs to be challenged.

Caring: Teachers recognise the power they have in the relationships and are not autocratic; their default mode is to be kind and trusting; interactions take account of natural emotional responses to challenge and insecurity. Mistakes are acknowledged. Students feel known and that they are in the hands of someone who cares. It is perfectly possible to be strict and caring – as any parent knows – but there are lines which can be crossed in either direction where this no longer holds; when a teacher is not strict enough or not caring enough to create the right conditions for learning.

Defined: Students know where they stand. Teachers are responsible for their students; they have a position of authority – along with a host of professional obligations – and this does not go both ways. It's problematic to blur the lines. Along the full spectrum from what might appear to be warm and fuzzy to what seems more formal and distant, great teachers establish excellent relationships. Whatever their style, the boundaries are clearly defined; there is room for everyone in this space.

In any school, there will be discussion about the issue of authority. It forms a key element in the whole school ethos as we discussed in Chapter 2 as part of the traditional-progressive debate. My personal perspective is that the concept of a 'democratic' classroom is misplaced, especially where students are children. Even when teachers are uncomfortable with the language of authority and compliance, the fact is that they underpin excellent behaviour in any school where there are rules of any kind. They're part of establishing the conditions for excellence in learning. Compliance doesn't need to equate to suppression – and all those factory-school memes; it's a part of life. Just as with bus-lane tickets (good for public transport) or speeding fines (good for public safety), the whole community benefits from enforcing the rules so it has to be done.

This never means that children don't have rights or that they have to become inherently compliant. In fact, it could be argued that it is the right of the majority of students to learn in an atmosphere where learning thrives that needs to be safeguarded; expecting compliance to some rules is part of helping teachers to do just that.

C7 Establish routines for excellence

One of my educational heroes is Bill Rogers. His guidance helped me enormously to find an assertive presence in a classroom that was not also autocratic with a tendency towards shouting. Probably my favourite Bill Rogers phrase is 'you establish what you establish'.

This refers to the establishment phase with a new class and your subsequent maintenance of expectations. Right from the start, anything you allow becomes established as allowed; and anything you challenge is established as unacceptable. A typical issue is noise level and off-task talking. If you do not challenge students who talk while others talk, you establish that this is OK; it is no good getting bothered about it later. Similarly with noise level, if you ask for 'silence' and then accept a general hubbub – then your message is 'silence means general hubbub'. If you want silence – you have to insist on it.

Bill Rogers is great on the whole area of planning for behaviour; investing time in setting up routines – a signal for attention, how you come in and out of the classroom, the noise level, asking and answering questions. Routines for excellence can include how work is presented and any subject-specific requirements such as using appropriate units in physics, protocols for safety and so on. The pattern to follow is:

- State what you expect explicitly, modelling what your expectations are as well as writing them down.

- Rehearse all the routines multiple times so that students learn how to do what you are asking them to do.

- Reinforce these precise expectations continually. As soon as you drop your guard, the message can be that you no longer care – and then the standards can start to slip.

The start of a new term is a good time but at any point, if you are not happy with the behaviour in your lessons, you have to address it explicitly. Otherwise, the message is that you accept it.

C8 Signal, Pause, Insist

This is one of my favourite 'silver arrow' strategies – a term I use on my blog for a simple idea that cuts through your ingrained practice and makes a big impact. Effective classroom management is multi-faceted but if you can do this, you can do anything. When a class is full of students talking, after an activity or discussion or simply because that has happened spontaneously, you need to regain full control with everyone listening, silent and giving attention:

- Signal: You give the agreed signal for attention that you have rehearsed multiple times. Typically this is '3, 2, 1, and Listening' – or something similarly punchy. Or it's a raised hand – a silent signal.

- Pause: You wait, adopting an assertive stance and position in the room, scanning for eye contact with everyone – it's absolutely normal that some students take longer to break from their conversation (adults are exactly the same).

- Insist: You insist on full attention. Liam ... Suki ... *I need you looking this way and listening* ... Thanks. You do not do anything until you have full attention.

You now give the instruction or direction you want to give. To gain attention, you ask for it, you expect it, you insist upon it, so it happens. Signal. Pause. Insist.

C9 Positive framing

This is very simple but packs a punch. It's an idea promoted by Bill Rogers and Doug Lemov (see *Teach Like a Champion* Technique 58 which has the same title[104]) and others. To me, positive framing suggests that, instead of using negative language of correction, you focus on stating your positive expectations.

- Instead of 'Will you stop talking' you say 'I'd like everyone listening, please'.

- Instead of 'John, stop turning around and distracting Mike' you say 'John, I'd like you facing this way and getting on with your work... thanks'.

- Instead of 'Alice, this work is really poor' you say 'Alice, I know you can do much much better than this'.

- Instead of 'Daisy, what's wrong with you, why are you always late' you say 'Daisy, you are capable of arriving on time every lesson and that's what I expect from you'.

---

104. Lemov, D. (2015), p. 426

- Rather than get into a 'whodunnit' saga with unknown or ambiguous miscreants you say 'Most people are doing a great job focusing on this task' – or on packing away their apparatus/paints/tools – 'Let's get everyone meeting the same standard. Thank you'.

After watching Bill Rogers, I found myself saying 'thanks' all the time … and it makes a difference. Of course, this isn't an absolute rule. It's not some kind of mind game or neurolinguistic voodoo, and it's not to say that, from time to time, you don't need to zap someone with your absolute line-in-the-sand disapproval (Controlled severity is another of Bill Rogers' great concepts).

Positive framing is about minimising conflict, maintaining positive relationships and keeping the atmosphere of a classroom upbeat and positive so that there is maximum focus on learning.

C10 Use the system as a lever, not a weapon

The context of your school, the demographic it serves and the philosophy and values of leaders and governors will have a major bearing on the type of behaviour system you are working with. Most schools will have the equivalent of a 'choices and consequences' system whereby students know the rules and the possible sanctions[105]. The theory is that they understand the rules and therefore make a choice to follow them or accept the consequences. Ideally this will be consistent and predictable. Some schools have 'no excuses' approaches where there are no warnings before a sanction is given. In others, there are one or two warning stages before sanctions are imposed. The consequences might be logged de-merits, detentions or immediate removal from the lesson, leading all the way to potential exclusion from school depending on the situation.

The goal and challenge for teachers is to use the system as a lever for excellent behaviour – not simply as a weapon to punish poor behaviour. There is a significant difference. Even in highly defined systems, in most schools there will be a range of teacher approaches. Some teachers will use the system punitively – giving out sanctions, following the letter of the rules but not appearing consistent or fair. There can be an unsatisfactory 'scattergun effect' when students can get through the warnings on multiple infringements within a few minutes of arriving into the class. Bang, bang, bang – Out. That's not our goal.

If we use the system as a lever, we're securing excellent behaviour by using the sanctions judiciously: we're firm, consistent, strict. But we are also

---

105. Schools will have rewards systems too. In my view these should be used exclusively for rewarding achievement, not for simply following the basic rules.

conspicuously fair, positive and kind. This isn't remotely about being soft; it's about getting the spirit right, building relationships as well as maintaining high expectations (see **C12 Keep perspective**).

Language of choice

One of the keys to getting the balance right is to be consistent in using the language of choice as you reinforce your expectations ... *'Keisha, you can hand that fidget toy over to me and get on with your work, or we can talk about it after school with your parents'*. The 'establish what you establish' principle can be harder to maintain than you might want. If standards are below the level you want, with multiple or persistent infringements, you need to have the patience to return to rehearsal mode rather than try to sanction multiple students back into compliance. Try to reinforce the habits of excellent behaviour rather than leaving it to students to decide whether they fall on the right side of the choice-consequence line.

Narration

Whenever you give sanctions, you walk through the rationale with the student and the class as a whole; you narrate your decisions. *'Clara, you were talking out of turn again, after you had had a warning with your name on the board; that means that you now have a detention as I warned. Now I want you to show me you are listening and engaging in the class discussion'*. This helps to avoid any sense of arbitrariness and reduces students' tendency to say 'I got a detention for no reason!'.

A key area for school ethos and policy is to deal with defiance and rudeness at the point of sanctions being given. In my experience, some students genuinely struggle with accepting their sanctions graciously; at first. Emotional behaviours are part of the matrix of special needs as we explored in Chapter 6. Some students are going to be frustrated – either with you or with themselves – and verbalise their feelings. It pays to allow some space for certain students to reach a point of acceptance but, as soon as you can, engage them again in positive dialogue to re-establish the relationship you need for learning to continue. Narration of sanctions for SEND students in particular is vital. This doesn't mean you accept rudeness or defiance – but it can pay to take an educative position rather than a punitive one. It's a subtle area that is highly context dependent.

Be the adult

It is important to always be the mature adult in the relationship and to model this conspicuously. With the most challenging students sometimes you need to step off the ladder of sanctions and create space and time to talk to them as people, away from peer influences, helping them to get a better perspective on the way their behaviour affects others, saving them from self-destruction. This is especially important if you need to repair any damage done in any previous exchanges.

Focus on the purpose

Finally, always try to focus on the primary purpose for any behaviour management rules and routines and reinforce this in your own mind and in your interactions with students: you are trying to set them free to grow through their learning, not tie them to the floor in a straitjacket. Excellent behaviour is for learning; it's fertiliser for the rainforest.

C11 Silence is golden

There's a particular kind of learning atmosphere that I love to create every so often to inject some real purposefulness and focus: silence. Not just 'quiet': absolute, total, complete, you-could-hear-a-pin-drop silence.

If a silent atmosphere is created in the right way, with the right spirit, it means this: 'OK; we've done all the talking, we've thrown up all our ideas ... now it's over to you to bring it all together, to get really stuck in and produce something that shows what you've learned, by yourself'. It's intense; intensely productive and intensely concentrated. And then, after an appropriate time has passed, 'Right then, let's see what you've got' ... the silence breaks and the output is revealed.

The reason I include this obvious-sounding strategy is because I feel *Silence* is often misused:

- The teacher calls for 'silence' when they think a class is too noisy. 'OK... let's have silence! I want you to work silently.' The noise level drops but the teacher then accepts a general murmur; they didn't want silence at all – just a little less noise. Here, the students come to understand that 'silence' means ... 'carry on talking, but just a bit less loudly'. Nothing has really changed.

- The teacher is FED UP and demands 'SILENCE!' They enforce it – absolutely. Nobody breathes...the electric fence is fizzing in anticipation of a transgressor to FRY!! Here silence is properly oppressive. Scary. It signifies heavy discipline and constraint ... not the freedom to express ideas without interruption. It's not a great atmosphere to work in; it's just a dark cloud that won't shift. It's miserable.

- The teacher wants to talk so asks the class to be silent. 'I'm talking so you should be silent' ... but the silence never arrives because the teacher is talking! Wanting silence to fill with your own voice is a contradiction. What they want is for the class to *listen*. But being silent and listening are not the same thing. Silence is for everyone. It's all or nothing.

When I say, 'Alright class, let's spend ten minutes working in silence', I'm talking about a special atmosphere that students know means something specific. And it's very powerful:

- For a start, it gives them time to think properly. A classroom full of noise is often bewildering ... silence can set you free to really think.

- Silence creates focus; students know it won't last for too long – so they have a limited time to get into action and that often yields a great burst of productivity. Finally, pen is put to paper and the writing starts or the paint flows or the measurements come thick and fast.

- The social pressure in any group is strong ... the need to engage in the endless stream of commentary is oppressive – even if an average teenager will never admit it. Silence is liberating on many levels – if it's done in the right spirit.

- Finally, silence puts everyone on the spot; the 'ask a friend' option has gone and students have to rely on their own resources. This is a 'no conferring' situation. This tells you more about how much they've learned than many other activities; what they produce in that time is down to them alone; the passengers need to get up front and drive!

The silence I'm after is always absolute. There is no talking at all. None. Not even from me. It's heads down and no nonsense. If someone needs help, it's a whispered whisper. It's time limited, notified in advance. Silence becomes oppressive if you don't know how long it's going to last or if someone else is controlling the end point.

It's positive – never punitive. I want my students to embrace the silence, not fear it or resent it. I keep it back for particular occasions and don't overuse it; I want to preserve it for when we really need a burst of positive action, free from the noise.

It's not a sanction; it's a haven. The beautiful sound of silence.

C12 Keep perspective

Teachers want to teach; they don't really want to be rule enforcers. It's just part of the job; you can't do one without the other. Fortunately for some, this can all be very light touch and you do feel that you can just teach. However, sometimes, in some contexts, the level of enforcement required can seem overwhelming and this is disheartening for teachers and students alike. In difficult situations we need to keep perspective:

1. First things first

This really depends on your school context – the default standards of behaviour and the way behaviour is managed across the school – but it often pays to build up layers of expectations a step at a time rather than trying to enforce multiple rules simultaneously. The first-things-first approach concentrates on all the behaviours and routines that directly infringe on learning. In your classroom you need students to be safe, ready to learn with all the equipment they need, listening and being respectful to you and each other. That's already a lot to manage. If those things are not happening, it really isn't worth getting into any other issues. Some changes in behaviour will require whole-school initiatives that you can't engineer alone – so stick to the things that you can control and keep rehearsing the routines. As an early-career teacher, finding that assertive voice and persona is the bedrock of nearly everything else and rehearsing routines is a good way to build it up.

2. Remember the positives

This means that it pays to balance the corrective language of enforcement with your positive affirmation for all the students doing the right thing. Bill Rogers calls this 'the black dot in the white square'. We need to remember to acknowledge the square of clear space (the positive behaviour that dominates) even if all we're seeing is the dot that spoils it. In practice this means that you publicly acknowledge all the students who are on time, who have all their equipment, who met the homework deadline, who fell silent bang on the signal for attention – before you admonish the minority who did not. Sometimes it's enough simply to do the positive affirmation instead of any correction; the message is clear.

Once you start doing this as a matter of routine with a class, I have found that it is transforming. What can feel like a battle – of attrition, of relentless negativity, creating an atmosphere that everyone dreads – is switched around. You find yourself saying, 'Well done, brilliant, thank you, that's fantastic' all the time and students who have earned that acknowledgement appreciate it – even if they are just doing what they are meant to.

3. Reset at any time

It's important for your mental health and the wellbeing of your students to be prepared to start afresh any time you need to. If you ever feel that behaviour with particular students is getting you down, preventing learning or causing stress, step off the track and take time to regroup. Go back to basics and re-establish all your expectations and routines once again.

4. Work as a team

The final thing to say about relationships and behaviour is to stress that, however isolated you might feel in the classroom from time to time, you're part of a team. As with any team, you need to play your part but it is the job of the team as a whole to support behaviour in a school. It's important to draw strength from that, accepting support when you need it and giving support back in return, doing your bit to maintain agreed protocols so that the behaviour system can take the strain, not each individual teacher.

Planning the curriculum

There is a good debate to be had about the value in discussing generic teaching strategies or whether these are really just details of the enacted subject-specific curriculum (see Chapter 3). Is there such a thing as pedagogy – how you teach – that can be separated meaningfully from the curriculum – what you teach? For example, we can talk about 'questioning techniques' but, ultimately, good questions are subject-specific in nature. If the answer is that we can't separate them, then we need to remind ourselves continually that everything we read about general approaches to teaching – in this book and countless others – needs to be contextualised in the content of subjects if it is going to have any impact in a lesson some time in the future.

The curriculum content is clearly something you cannot do in any detail in a book about teaching in general. However, there are planning processes that are common across subjects and, as we have explored in Chapters 2 and 3, there are plenty of decisions to be made, however prescriptive you may feel your curriculum framework is. The next set of ideas and strategies are about aspects of the curriculum that you can plan for in advance as opposed to things you act out once you get into the classroom. That is why they are included in 'creating the conditions'.

In our overarching metaphor, if the conditions set by our planned curriculum are not sufficiently rich in nutrients for developing knowledge, then our learner-specimens in the rainforest will not thrive. The content of the curriculum is a limiting factor in the ultimate quality of education a school provides, however well you deliver it. With that in mind, in general I feel that teachers should spend a lot more time talking about the details of their curriculum – at the enacted level as well as the planned level – relative to the time they spend talking about behaviour, assessment and generic teaching strategies. For the purposes of this book, I have tried to give examples from multiple curriculum areas just to give the generic planning idea some real curriculum flavour.

C13 Big picture, small picture

As we know from cognitive science, new knowledge sticks to knowledge we already have in our long-term memories where we construct schemas for sets of ideas, making ever more complicated networks of connections. However, it can only build up in small chunks, processing through our working memories a few ideas at a time. In order to support learning new material, we should, therefore, be conscious of the need to organise our ideas so that the individual components have some kind of structure when assembled.

When students encounter a new idea or fact, how does it link to what they already know? Where does it fit into the big scheme of things? As a student I always wanted to know the course structure and the scale of each module so I could gauge the depth needed for each component of learning and allocate study time in the right proportions. When I get a new book I check how many pages it has so that I always know where I am in the scale of the narrative. I think this is fairly common. It's a well-established idea that a contents page and chapter structure is helpful to guide readers through a textbook. The big picture is necessary in order to make sense of the details.

A good everyday example is how we conceptualise locations in terms of geographical areas of ever decreasing size: UK. England. Greater Manchester. Chorlton. Keppel Road. Number 66. Upstairs. Another example is chronological as explored in **C20 Build a timeline** – we like to know how far along we are in any process; knowing where we are in time and space matters if we're going to make sense of the world. We need to be able to zoom out and take a wide view and also zoom right in to see the detail.

In practice, students benefit from seeing an overview of everything they're going to learn so that they can see where they're going. This might include a topic structure overview like these excerpts from a geography course:

Geography:

- Physical
    - Water and Rivers
        - Flooding
            - River management
                - Hard engineering solutions: Dams and river diversions
- Human
    - Development Processes
        - Urban and Rural Environments
            - Urban environment in LEDCs
                - Favelas

You can see that, once the topic structure emerges, connections between areas can be made. Here, there will be case studies of flooding in less economically developed countries that tie in particular inter-related aspects of human and physical geography. This applies across all subjects, in the detail.

Another helpful big picture reference is to map out a rough timeframe for the course structure where that is appropriate, showing students when assessments are scheduled and where each topic fits in the sequence.

Every examination specification and textbook has a form of organisation of the subject content. The task for teachers is to provide the overview for the curriculum students will actually experience. As described in **P15 Co-construction: Sidekicks**, I have had success in engaging students in producing these things themselves because they were so closely involved in planning their own learning alongside me. However, that might not work in every context.

The point of this is not merely to have the documents sitting in the background. It is to use them as a roadmap for the learning. The roadmap is as much a conceptual tool as a simple time-management tool. You need to make it an explicit part of the learning process to regularly take your bearings, linking the specific area of focus in any series of lessons to the bigger picture.

Thinking Points: What do the content outline and timeline look like in your subject context? Do your students have access to the information they need and in a format they can readily access? Could you involve them in constructing it as part of the learning process? (see **P15: Sidekicks)**

C14 Plan the steps

One of the key tasks for curriculum planning is to map out the incremental conceptual or practical steps in any learning process. How do students progress from novice to expert in the particular domain of your subject discipline? It's important that, within each discipline, the curriculum has coherence so that as you move through a sequence of topics or units, you are revisiting key concepts, creating a spiralling effect; continually building on prior learning whilst also expanding the range of ideas that are in play.

In art, for example, how do students move from small-scale life-drawing activities, prescribed by the teacher for developing specific skills, towards more complex, larger-scale pieces with different media and a high degree of student input and freedom of expression?

In sport how does a player improve and become more successful? What are the most important skills to master at the beginning, what should come later, at what point is it about strength and fitness over technique? Where do match-play and tactics play a part? If students are only going to work on a few things at a time, there is a sequence that needs to be understood and planned.

In English literature, how can we move up the scale from simple, supported responses to reading a poem or play to 'convincing, critical analysis and exploration; a fine-grained and insightful analysis of language and form and structure supported by judicious use of subject terminology'[106]?

In science, how do we build students' conceptual models so that, when watching magnesium burn with a bright flame in their Bunsen burner, they can get behind the tangible things they see and relate this to the process of metal combustion in oxygen at a particle level, the release of energy through ionic bond formation and the related transfer of electrons in an atomic model.

In maths, how do we progress from confidence with arithmetic and an understanding of the fundamental properties of shapes towards algebraic problems involving trigonometric functions and Pythagoras' equation? At a more basic level, moving from arithmetic with integers and place value in Units,

---

106. English GCSE Marking criteria AQA via http://filestore.aqa.org.uk/resources/english/AQA-87022-SMS.PDF

Tens and Hundreds to fractions and decimals is quite a big leap and the path to follow needs some expert concept sequencing.

In history, do you teach broad-brush scene-setting epochs and general themes before engaging in some deep-dives to explore specific events? OR do you do it the other way around – teach about Romans, Tudors and Nazi Germany as separate topics before, later, linking them up with general historical concepts? It might well be a combination but you have to start somewhere; you have to know what the master plan is.

In French, do we want students to be able to say *'L'année dernière je suis allé à Paris. C'est une ville extraordinaire. Je suis impatient d'y revenir encore une fois'* with confidence, knowing what it means but before they fully understand all the grammatical components? Or are we going to build up phrase-level understanding by working up through the tenses – present, past, future – and only expect recall of phrases when students have a sound grammatical underpinning? (See the discussion on knowledge organisers in **C15 Specify the knowledge.**)

These are huge fundamental questions that ought to occupy a great deal of teacher discourse in subject teams. Or, at least, they should play a major role in the thinking of the person entrusted to write the scheme of learning that everyone will follow. The mistake is not to have the discussion and to assume that everybody knows these things intuitively. The sequence of concepts will have a major bearing on how successful your curriculum plan is in securing deep understanding and high levels of performance from your students.

In my previous book, *Teach Now Science*[107], I highlighted three core concepts for science teachers to consider: particles, energy and scale. At various points in the study of science, these key concepts are absolute prerequisites for moving forward to a deeper understanding. You can't explain chemical or physical change in any detail unless you have a model of materials being made up of atoms, ions or molecules and some sense of the scale at which this operates. This is the key to understanding how we breathe, what happens to our food and what plants need in order to grow successfully. The role energy changes play in nearly every process in science is also a vital element: what form does energy take; where is it stored; how is it carried? The large scale of the Earth, solar system and beyond is also important in order to fully understand the phenomena we observe every day.

Thinking Points: Do you have a clear rationale for your topic sequencing? What

---

107. Sherrington, T. (2014)

are the main conceptual or practical stages that students will need to move through in your subject discipline? What is the optimum sequence? Is this planned into a spiralling curriculum so that students can revisit ideas as well as build on prior learning as they move along the novice-to-expert path?

C15 Specify the knowledge

In the geography unit mentioned in C13 above, we can see that students will study favelas. But what exactly are they meant to know about favelas? In order to be certain that your students are learning what they need to know and what you want them to know, it is very powerful to spell this out in some detail. For example, it could be the following:

Geography: Favelas

- **Favelas**[108] are **shanty towns** in **Brazil**. The main example is in **Rio de Janeiro**. They are made of basic materials such as **tarpaulin, corrugated sheets, broken bricks** on land which they **neither own nor rent**.

- Houses have no basic amenities such as **running water** or **toilets** so diseases like **cholera** and **dysentery** are common.

- **Unemployment rates are high**. Most people who do have a job work in the **informal sector** so their **income is not guaranteed**. There are **high rates of organised crime**.

- Rio is **hemmed in by mountains**, so **during tropical storms landslides are common**. Makeshift houses in favelas offer little protection to people and **houses are easily washed away** by the **heavy rain and mud**.

With a little more formatting, this would become a learning checklist or knowledge organiser for this topic. Students could self-assess their knowledge of these key points, checking their recall of the specific details.

- What are the basic materials? *Tarpaulin, corrugated sheets, broken bricks.*

- Which diseases stem from poor basic amenities? *Cholera and dysentery.*

- Which phenomenon is common during tropical storms? *Landslides.*

It is possible to construct helpful knowledge organisers in every subject. In order to support retrieval practice, it is important for abstract ideas and concrete examples to be presented side by side.

---

108. Source: BBC Bitesize http://www.bbc.co.uk/education/guides/zk32pv4/revision/11

Science: Reactions of metals

- Metal + Acid → Salt + Hydrogen

  - *eg* Zinc + Hydrochloric Acid → Zinc Chloride + Hydrogen: Symbol Equation $Zn + 2HCl → ZnCl_2 + H_2$

- Metal + Oxygen → Metal Oxide:

  - *eg* Magnesium + Oxygen → Magnesium Oxide: Symbol Equation $2Mg + O_2 → 2MgO$

- Oxidation is the loss of electrons or an increase in oxidation state by a molecule, atom, or ion.

- Reduction is the gain of electrons or a decrease in oxidation state by a molecule, atom, or ion.

Lots of other science topics can be well supported with diagrams: the key organs of the body, parts of a plant cell, features of the kinetic theory particle models for solids, liquids and gases.

English: *Animal Farm* by George Orwell

- 'Four legs good, two legs bad.' Snowball's speech, Chapter III

- 'All animals are equal, but some animals are more equal than others' From the Seven Commandments, Chapter X

- Snowball represents Trotsky; he is a supporter of Animalism (Communism) who is expelled by Napoleon (Stalin).

- Napoleon: Expels Snowball and executes animals. Establishes himself as dictator. Controls with fear. Becomes Jones at the end.

- Snowball: Devoted to Animalism and the education of lesser animals. Hero at the Battle of the Cowshed.

History: Civil Rights Movement key dates

- 1955 Montgomery Bus Boycott challenges segregation on buses

- 1960 Freedom summer begins with lunch counter protests

- 1963 March on Washington: Martin Luther King's *I have a dream* speech

- 1964 Civil Rights Act: outlaws discrimination based on race, colour, religion, sex, or national origin1965 Rise of Black Power. Malcolm X assassinated

- 1968 Martin Luther King assassinated

Maths: Key facts to be learned by heart:

- Powers of 2: 1, 2, 4, 8, 16, 32, 64, 128, 256, 512, 1024; *eg* $2^9 = 512$

- Cubed Numbers: 1, 8, 27, 64, 125, 216, 343, 512, 729, 1000; *eg* $7^3 = 343$

- Area of a Trapezium = ½ (a + b) h

- Volume of a cylinder = $\pi r^2 h$

French: Specific phrases to be learned:

- I love going /to the movies /with my friends. *J'aime bien aller /au cinéma /avec mes amis.*

- I do not like /to go shopping /on weekends/ because there are /too many people. *Je n'aime pas /faire les courses /le week-end/ parce qu'il y a /trop de monde.*

- Last year, /I went to Paris. /It is an extraordinary city. /I look forward to visiting again /another time. *L'année dernière, /je suis allé à Paris. /C'est une ville extraordinaire. /Je suis impatient d'y revenir / encore une fois.*

- When I got home, /I realised /that I had lost /my keys. *Quand je suis rentré chez moi, /je me suis rendu compte /que j'avais perdu /mes clés.*

The idea of knowledge organisers has been developed extensively by the pioneering staff at Michaela School in Brent, London, as described in their book, *Battle Hymn of the Tiger Teachers*[109]. Crucially, the power of the documents lies in the way they are used systematically to support self-quizzing and daily knowledge retrieval practice. It is not about giving out crib sheets to stick in books for general reference.

At Michaela, in French, for example, the level of recall is supported relentlessly through various call-and-response activities as well as written knowledge tests. Using the example above (although this is one I made myself), a teacher would say the English and students would respond with the French translation. It's fun and engaging but, at the same time, expectations of recall are very high. Even beginners quickly develop confidence as they learn to say whole phrases like '*J'adore aller /au cinéma /avec mes amis*', in stages and then all at once, knowing exactly what it means. It's a superb basis for subsequent grammar work. The same level of rigour around the recall of specified knowledge can extend across the curriculum.

---

109. Birbalsingh, K. (ed.) (2016)

It's important to keep in mind that a knowledge organiser is always only a framework for key factual knowledge that students benefit from being able to recall readily. It is not meant as a definitive, reductive version of all relevant knowledge pertaining to the subject in hand. That would be absurd. You can't capture all there is to know or the spirit of *Hamlet* or *Frankenstein* on a side of A4. The document is a springboard but, importantly, it is one that is common to all learners – not just those that already find it easy to organise their ideas and remember things.

It is also worth considering that you don't have to pre-make the organisers. I have seen excellent examples where teachers have issued a formatted page onto which students write the key learning points as they emerged in a lesson – essentially a form of structured note-taking. Here the students were then going to use these documents as the basis for subsequent retrieval practice and the teachers made sure that their students all had recorded the knowledge requirements very precisely.

C16 Objectives vs tasks

Very often, in the busy flow of everyday school life, although teachers might have an overarching idea of the broad learning goals, they plan the individual lessons in terms of tasks. They think about what students will do. For example, in an electricity topic, students might make some circuits with different components, measure voltage and current readings, plot graphs, discuss their findings, answer some follow-up questions…and so on. Some students will get more done than others and that's the crudest form of differentiation there is. At the end of all of this activity, there's an assumption that they will have learned various relevant aspects of the science topic in hand.

Although task-planning is a common, practical way to think about lessons for the week, it is far from ideal; it's just hit and hope. Teaching in this way can lead to a lot of dissipated energy, wasted time and unfocused learning. My experience is that my lessons and those I observe are much better when the learning objectives are very clear; when teachers are conspicuously clear about the purpose of all the tasks and have a reasonably tight goal in mind for that specific lesson as part of a sequence.

The learning objective for the electricity example above might be:

For students to recognise:

- that voltage and current vary in direct proportion for a fixed resistor

- that the curve for a light bulb shows that its resistance changes as it heats up

- that the resistance increases as shown by the gradient of the curve

This sounds obvious enough but it makes quite a difference. It makes you ask yourself, 'Why are they doing what they are doing?', which can then lead to a more efficient use of time, cutting out activities that don't support the learning objectives directly. It helps sharpen your questions and provide more focused assessment feedback.

In science, if you want students to develop practical skills, to become familiar with apparatus and gain an understanding of the complexities of measurement, then a hands-on experiment is an essential task for that objective. But if you want them to make a connection between an abstract idea and its manifestation in a real setting, then a teacher-led demonstration is likely to be far more effective.

The same applies in other subjects. For example, in history GCSE, it's useful to make a distinction between a learning objective about the historical content – for example understanding the significance of the Tet Offensive in Vietnam – versus an objective to understand the structure of a written answer that meets the assessment requirements of a ten-mark answer on a source paper. These things may overlap in the source analysis task, but what is the main learning you are after?

In English, it makes a difference if you are focusing on knowing and understanding Falstaff's character development in Act II in broad narrative terms rather than the more technical ideas about Shakespeare's use of structure and language in the text. Each of these can be developed more sharply if your objective is clear during the task of 'reading and analysing Act II'. Of course these things interact but students get a firmer grasp if the focus in any given lesson is precise. The terms 'narrative', 'structure' and 'language' need to be learned clearly before students can use them – obviously enough – but that requires some sharp sequencing of learning objectives.

In maths, if you want students to know how to learn how to solve simultaneous equations by substitution, then it makes sense to show them how, model several examples and get them to practise their own before checking how they're getting on. A group problem-solving task or extended lecture that minimises their practice opportunities wouldn't be as effective. The specific learning objective helps to identify the most efficient and effective strategy.

If you want students to practise their ability to use language spontaneously in French, a role play or group task is going to help deliver that learning objective because they need interaction in that form. You can't learn to be spontaneous if you are not given the opportunity to use your knowledge in that way.

I have seen plenty of learning objectives in classrooms that are really just a list of tasks. Is that helpful? It might be…but it's not the same thing at all. The most important thing is that you, the teacher, know what the learning objectives are; get that very clear in your mind. You really don't need the students to write them down slavishly in their books. I don't understand why schools make teachers do that.

Finally, the value of thinking in terms of learning objectives is that they often span over a whole series of lessons whereas tasks are often one-offs. If you are being truly responsive in your teaching, you will be planning to reach certain learning goals over a certain period of time, planning at the level of weeks. Each lesson's plan will then depend on where your students got to last time. The main thinking has to happen at the medium-term scale not at the lesson-by-lesson scale.

C17 Scaffolds and stabilisers

One of the challenges we face as teachers is knowing how much help to give. There are many examples of structured support across a range of learning experiences: arm-bands in swimming, stabilisers on a bicycle, the vocabulary crib-sheet in language learning. They are all designed to provide support in the early phases of learning, with the explicit goal of removing them later on. The question is, when? If we leave the support structure in place for too long, students develop a dependency; an over-reliance on the support and a mutually reinforcing fear of failure, satnav style. If we remove the support too early, they can fail badly and develop the fixed mindset fear that could inhibit their future learning.

I remember teaching my daughter to ride her bike. It was a classic parenting moment. With stabilisers, it was easy. But, once they were off, she didn't find it easy. One day I was running along behind her, pushing her along to give her momentum. After a while she said 'you can let go now'. The beautiful thing was – I already had! She was away; I was so proud of her in that moment I actually cried.

So much of teaching is the art of building confidence and minimising the consequences of failure, showing the way so students can go it alone. A crucial element is the explicit determination to take the supports away in the end and it helps for students to be fully aware of that. In lessons it is often very easy for students and teachers to create the illusion of learning when the supports are all around. Over the years I've seen a lot of lessons where students are immersed in 'learning' based on supportive resources; they've been saturated with facts and ideas but, all along, they've been wearing impermeable skins that leave nothing behind. The 'in the moment' learning hasn't left a deep enough impression. All of us need to guard against that.

For example, if you look at your German vocabulary sheet you might read directly from it: *'Ich muss Hausaufgaben machen';* *'Am Vormittag habe ich ferngesehen'.* Easy: 'I have to do homework'; 'In the morning I watched television'.

Students can practise these things repeatedly in the class, giving the impression that they're getting the hang of the structures. BUT – take away the vocab sheet and what do you have? That's the question.

What they need to do, explicitly, is learn the vocabulary sufficiently so that they can put the elements together without help. That requires a shift in emphasis: if the goal in the lesson is for students to aim at doing this unaided from the start, they will process the information differently compared to a situation where all they need to do is produce the goods from the sheet. They need to develop the techniques for retaining key phrases, building up their internal resource-bank. That requires lessons with opportunities to wing it a bit, speaking unaided using what they know without the worry that getting it wrong might matter too much.

There is a similar situation in English. Writing frames are great: lists of interesting or effective openers, closers and connectives can be found everywhere. Students can use them really well to produce well-structured pieces of writing. I remember my daughter beaming after a test because, as she put it, 'I got in my "crimson" and my "consequently"' (words she never normally used). My son used to like setting the scenes for his stories with the same description: 'There was a grey monotonous sky'. This was him using scaffolds to build his writing around. But what is left after the supports are removed?

The trick is to make it more routine for students to move from guided practice to independent practice: to 'do one with help and then do it on your own'. That approach should be built-in. I once visited a primary school in a very deprived area in England where the valiant Year 1 teacher had been working on adjectives: the wall was covered in rich vocabulary to describe a villain in the story they were reading: scary, crabby, wicked, unkind, terrible, grumpy, selfish. They'd used these words in their writing – with the word-wall for reference. But when the children were asked to describe the villain in the class discussion with books closed, they reverted to the basics 'he's bad, he's old and mean' and simple things like that. It was an uphill struggle. They didn't own these words; they needed to go much further to absorb them, internalise them and make them their own.

So – what to do? Give them more help? More scaffolding? I don't think so. Firstly I think we need to work with students to improve the link from the surface learning to the underlying models; deeper models will lead to deeper recall. Secondly, we need to do more testing for the recall itself alongside contextualised deployment of new ideas.

One way or another, the stabilisers have got to come off in the end – and you need to be prepared to take the risk that they will fall or else they will never ride off on their own.

C18 Skills and drills

Although there is ongoing debate about the specifics, education research supports our everyday experience that we get better at things we can practise. Whatever you might read about the mystical 10,000 hours, there is no neat correlation between the amount of practice and the level of expertise you will reach: you might take to the piano relatively easily but struggle in perpetuity to play a decent round of golf or swim fast. Life's a bit more complicated.

With that caveat aside, it is clear that we can't get better at things unless we practise. This applies to performing new maths skills, to writing, to learning a language and to anything physical from painting to playing a sport. It even applies to teaching itself. A great pianist will continue to practise their scales over and over again; a great tennis player will hit hundreds of serves and hundreds of backhands, over and over, looking to strengthen specific skills so that they are absolutely embedded. This is so that, during the performance or the match, these things flow instinctively, on demand at the time they are needed.

As discussed earlier in the book, the task for teachers – and coaches in sport or music – is to break down complex tasks into component skills that can be practised repeatedly through drills. A football coach will create a set of skill drills that the players can improve on outside the arena of a match. They will also give some match practice to see how the skills come together. Finally, they will assess players' performance in each match. In combination – skill-drills, practice match and real match with feedback at every point – you have the recipe for improvement.

Sometimes the drills are essential just to get going. One of my (fairly trivial) challenges in life is playing FIFA football on a games console. Basically I can't do it. I realise that this is because I'm always overwhelmed by the number of controls. My son has done all the drills; he knows that Y means a through-ball and how to sprint and slide tackle. He's internalised that and does these things reflexively. I have to think about every movement and it just doesn't work. The last time we played, to give me a chance, I was Barcelona, he was Gillingham; I was 3-0 down at half-time and gave up. I'm not ready for the match situation because my basic skills aren't good enough. If I were to persevere I would need the whole thing broken down and to commit more time to practice.

The challenge, then, is to create curriculum elements that serve as effective drills. What might these be?

In maths, nearly all basic arithmetic operations can be drilled: multiplication tables and related divisions, number bonds to 100 or 1000, substitution into equations, squares and cubes, multiplying and dividing by powers of 10, putting fractions and decimals in sequence, operations with fractions, finding the next terms in a sequence...an endless list. Basic multiplication and number bond practice takes students a long long way; the more secure they are the better.

In geography and science, students get better at drawing graphs and presenting data, the more often they do it – provided, of course, that they are getting appropriate feedback in-between each attempt. In art and technology, each technique will improve in the level of fluency and precision as students engage in more practice. The challenge is to identify skills that can be repeated in isolation – and not always in the context of larger-scale pieces. There will be certain painting techniques or joints with resistant materials that could be practised on small samples repeatedly before students embark on longer projects where these small-scale skills can be deployed.

In areas such as history and English, it seems to me that teachers have an almighty task to rein-in the expansive complexity and scope of the subject matter so that students can write coherently – and secure appropriate credit under exam conditions. These subjects are unconfined in many respects and essay-writing is massively open-ended; there are so many ideas and possibilities to grapple with. The task is to isolate elements, to find order within that expansiveness so that students have scope for defined practice – like the FIFA analogy. These can be around the progression from sentences in different styles to paragraphs that serve particular functions to paragraph sequences and essay-planning, putting ideas together in a linear order. It links to the ideas in **C14 Plan the steps.**

Thinking Point: What are the elements of your curriculum that you can use as drills to enable students to practise repeatedly and thereby see gains in their performance?

C19 Build the words, plan the reading

A key component in successful learning is reading. The more fluent students are with reading the more independent they become and the depth to which they can explore the content of the curriculum increases. A part of this process is the development of vocabulary – either incidental words that are used to convey ideas in general or the technical subject-specific terminology that is used to explore domain-specific concepts.

In the spirit of establishing the conditions for learning, here are two things that teachers can do in this crucial area:

1. Deliberately build word knowledge and confidence

This involves being specific about the words that students should know and use, not simply leaving it to chance and hoping they will pick things up. This is absolutely essential for many SEND and EAL students but it benefits everyone, including students who are 'word poor'.

You might identify common non-technical words that students struggle with alongside the technical words in any given subject and include them in your knowledge organiser. You might use a vocabulary book or simple back-of-book glossary that students compile with words as they emerge spontaneously.

However, two things are vital if any word lists are going to make a difference:

- You have to be definite about the words that students should know and record them – not simply toss them out into the ephemeral ether of a lesson to be forgotten about by the next lesson.

- You need to engage students in active processes that require them to recall the words: how to say them, spell them and use them. It's amazing how often you can find students who are not confident saying a word out loud even when it is one they encounter frequently at school – words like remarkable, spontaneous, extraordinary, photosynthesis, decomposition, denominator, transformation, confrontation, specific, accommodation, commendation, appropriate, reflection. A mixture of technical and non-technical terms. Call-and-response practice, spelling tests, 'use the word in a sentence' tests and so on help to consolidate word use. Multiple-choice questions that require students to select the correct use of a word are also very helpful. Whatever you do, it's not enough just to hope that words 'sink in' through familiarity.

2. Plan the reading

A key part of the resource planning for many curriculum areas should be the reading material that teachers and students will use. The text selection should honour the spirit suggested in **C4 Pitch it up** – *ie* not over simplified or dumbed down. Students can't learn to read sophisticated texts if they are not given the opportunity to. Ideally texts should be selected that help to explain the concepts in hand or provide interesting perspectives and contexts.

It is an obvious but powerful strategy to select a section in a textbook – say in history, geography or science – and to read it through as a class. Sometimes you want to read through for fluency, making sure the overall meaning is clear. At other times you need to stop at specific words and take time to explain them and record them for future reference and practice. In doing this you are using a good source to impart information but you are also modelling the process of independent study: you are showing your students how to read a textbook; when to skim and scan; when to read for deeper comprehension; when to read in order to follow a specific set of instructions.

I would suggest that students' reading diets in schools are generally too low and are usually confined to too few subjects: mainly English and history. However, if we are going to give students the best possible curriculum experience, they need to read a lot every day and most teachers will have a role to play. You can't leave this to chance – especially if you believe that students' enacted curriculum experience should not be too dependent on which teacher in a team they happen to have that year. Reading requires planning; a key task in devising a great scheme of learning is, therefore, to plan the reading and to source the sources!

Thinking Points: What resources do you have that will support this goal? Are the reading materials available for everyone? Are they of the appropriate quality? What routines do you need to establish if you are going to build words in a systematic manner?[110]

C20 Build a timeline

In my experience, the power of chronology in providing a framework for our curriculum is hugely powerful, yet underutilised. In this section I want to give a big push to the importance of understanding the scale and sequence of historical eras; a framework for locating every event and every historical figure relative to every other. This is the big picture; the story of everything we've ever known and ever done. It's a schema that everyone develops to a degree

---

110. A favourite book for further reading about reading is Barton, G. (2012) *Don't Call it Literacy*, Routledge

but, very often, students have trouble getting the scales right and all kinds of misconceptions can take root; they need help.

As a science teacher, I find that a strong historical framework is essential in developing the concepts and making connections between them. One of my all-time favourite books is Bill Bryson's *A Short History of Nearly Everything*[111]. Bryson pulls together various strands of science so that you get a sense of the significance of certain discoveries and theories. For example, the audacious revelations of Darwin's *On the Origin of Species* are all the more remarkable given that the prevailing wisdom regarding Earth's age in the mid-19th Century didn't allow sufficient time for evolution to have progressed as far as it has. Geological science later developed to yield an Earth-age entirely compatible with evolutionary time-scales; the discovery of plate tectonics provided further supporting proof and our current knowledge of genetics absolutely seals it.

There is a wonderful story to tell about human understanding of our existence on a planet orbiting a star within a spiral galaxy and our composition from elements – some of which formed during a supernova explosion. From Ptolemy to Copernicus, Galileo, Newton, Einstein and Hawking, the story of how ideas have changed can help us to understand the ideas themselves.

The interaction between the history of science and the history of human development is obvious enough. As we learn about social development, settlement and urbanisation, the technology of communication and transport, the development of medicine and healthcare and the quest for sources of energy that meet demand, we are gradually building up a complex multi-strand timeline of interacting themes. These themes sit alongside, and interact with the parallel timelines relating to politics, revolutions, monarchies, empires, wars and individual acts of courage or foolishness. In turn, all of these themes interact with the development of culture – music, literature, language and philosophy. In some ways, the whole of the curriculum is one giant timeline.

A key question for curriculum designers, not least those responsible for the history curriculum, is deciding what to include. Where to start? A typical English history student will encounter some standard topics: Ancient Greece, The Romans, 1066 and all that, The Middle Ages, The Tudors, The Stuarts, The Victorians and then WWI and/or WWII. They may also explore some unifying themes: science and technology, church and state, monarchs and elected governments, revolutions and wars, food and clothing, women, children, poverty and so on. The hope is that this matrix of themes and specific areas

---

111. Bryson, B. (2003) *A Short History of Nearly Everything.* Random House.

of study will lead to a rounded view of history in the end. However, one of the difficulties is that these studies are spread over so many school years that it is difficult for students to knit them all together – especially if they only remember what an eight-year-old might remember about the Roman Empire.

The central dilemma for planning a history curriculum is to achieve the optimum balance of coverage and depth – as referenced in **C14 Plan the steps**. Twenty years ago I completed a Master's in Development Studies. My final dissertation focused on UN Intervention in Somalia from 1991 to 1993. It was a very focused study of one particular conflict but it required knowledge and understanding of a wide range of other aspects of history. A key resource was the fabulous *World Politics since 1945* by Peter Calvocoressi[112]. Understanding Somalia and the UN in 1991 required an understanding of African history, colonialism, post-war American hegemony and the development of the notion of humanitarian intervention. It also required some understanding of neo-Marxist and neo-liberal theories of economic development and their origins. I had a lot to catch up on. Gunmen hijacking food convoys or shooting down US attack helicopters in Mogadishu were the details in a much bigger picture.

So, how do we build this balance into the curriculum? There is only so much we can teach in the time we've got. One approach is to focus on a selection of key reference points; the key events. Before diving into any individual events or stories of individuals, it is instructive to get a sense of what else was going on. To help recall and retain some of this in an ever-improving historical schema, perhaps it would be worth ensuring that students learn the key dates, embedding them in their knowledge organisers.

Do we simply allow the chronology to develop organically over the course of students' education or should we make it much more explicit as an overarching or underpinning aspect of the curriculum? Should we be asking colleagues in history, science, English, music and elsewhere to be contributing to timeline education in a more concrete, explicit manner? This is the discussion to have in your school.

Here is rough idea of what it might start to look like:

---

112. Calvocoressi, P. (2008) *World Politics since 1945.* Routledge.

	1500	1600	1700	1800	1900
Literature	Shakespeare			Shelley Austen Dickens	Great Gatsby Animal Farm Sylvia Plath Harper Lee
Science	Galileo	Newton	Watt: Steam Jenner: Vaccine	Faraday Pasteur Darwin	Einstein Watson, Crick and Franklin
History	Henry VIII Elizabeth I	Mayflower Nth America Civil War England	Industrial Revolution USA Independence	Victorians Abolition of Slavery UK Civil War USA	WW1 Suffragettes WW2 Civil Rights
Music		Handel Bach	Mozart	Beethoven Tchaikovsky	Gershwin Elvis Beatles

This selection, as with any other, is highly selective. Too many dead white men? Too Anglo/Euro-centric? Almost certainly. But the key to challenging that is to specify the alternative stories and historical figures that must feature – not just raise the issue in general. Harder still is to decide what to take out given that curriculum time is finite.

We're not asking students to prepare for a pub quiz, swotting up some dates to impress their mates. We're preparing them to create a much more ambitious and complete historical schema of everything that could ever fit on a timeline. The idea is that every time a student meets a new book or poem, new scientific theory, a new composer or a new historical figure or event, they are encouraged to open up their (metaphorical or physical) master timeline to link it to what they know already, looking at the picture first, then drilling down to the specifics. It seems to me that this should constitute a required element for a truly excellent school curriculum.

BUILDING THE KNOWLEDGE STRUCTURE

CHAPTER 8

K 6 THINK, PAIR, SHARE

K 7 WHOLE-CLASS RESPONSE

K 8 MULTIPLE CHOICE HINGES

K 9 GUIDED PRACTICE

K 10 SAY IT BETTER

FEEDBACK AND REVIEW

K 11 VERBAL FEEDBACK

K 12 RESPONSIVE TEACHING

K 13 MARKING: KEEP IT LEAN

K 14 WHOLE-CLASS FEEDBACK

K 15 CLOSE THE GAP

K 16 TEACH FOR MEMORY

K 17 DAILY, WEEKLY, MONTHLY REVIEW

K 18 FACE IT

K 19 LEARNING BY HEART

K 20 HOMEWORK = GUIDED STUDY

EXPLAIN, MODEL, PRACTISE, QUESTION, FEEDBACK, ASSESS

K 1 EXPLAINING

K 2 MODELLING AND METACOGNITION

K 3 CHECK FOR UNDERSTANDING

K 4 PROBING

K 5 GO DIALOGIC

Mode A teaching: 80%?

In our metaphor, building the knowledge structure is at the core of the whole process of creating the rainforest. I have suggested that, in practice, the strategies involved here might dominate daily school life – especially at secondary schools in typical academic disciplines. A short-hand I like to use is 'Mode A' teaching – because this is what you do most of the time. I've suggested that 80% is a rough proportion – but that is just to give a perspective on the balance as discussed in Chapter 6. It's not scientific by any means and you'll have your own view depending partly on which subject you teach.

The core elements of Mode A teaching are about effective teacher instruction: explaining concepts and procedures, imparting information and telling stories; modelling what is expected in terms of standards and thought processes; giving time to guided and independent practice; effective questioning to check for understanding across a whole class; immediate feedback that is responsive and moves students forward; assessment that is largely formative, focusing on specific areas of content.

Explain, Model, Practise, Question, Feedback, Assess

K1 Explaining

Explaining is a great art. I recall watching a skilled chemistry teacher at BIS Jakarta explaining a range of phenomena observable from a demonstration of the simple process of boiling water in a beaker using a Bunsen burner. With students gathered around, he drew attention to the initial formation of a layer of condensation on the outside of the beaker and posed a key question – where did it come from? This hooked students in and he then explained how this had originated in the combustion of the Bunsen's gas – not the water inside the beaker. It was crystal clear and spellbinding. A firm favourite lesson I saw at KEGS was an English teacher giving an extended exposition of how Darwinian ideas have been expressed in literature including Tennyson's 'red in tooth and claw' as referenced in the poetic writing of Richard Dawkins in *The Selfish Gene*. The blend of literature with the science was superb. A colleague at Highbury Grove shared his brilliant method for introducing algebra using a jar of sweets to represent an unknown variable that can be taken from, added to and multiplied without us knowing its actual value. I took it on board and found it immensely useful.

At the core of a great teacher's skill-set is the ability to explain the concepts, theories and techniques that make up their subject. On the reputational scale, there is no doubt that teachers who explain things well, making the complex simple, score highly as Great Teachers. I've observed countless lessons where the teacher exposition accelerated the learning process for everyone through the clarity of the explanation. It can be a joy to listen and learn as an expert teacher tells the story that lifts the fog and makes it possible to see clearly.

A quote often attributed to Einstein is, 'If you can't explain it simply you don't understand it well enough'. Even if he didn't say these exact words, it makes good sense! For me there are two implications:

- Getting students to explain ideas to the teacher and to each other is a great way to determine the depth of their understanding. In asking questions, we are often asking students to explain things to us. In fact it is a bread-and-butter element of great lessons that they are rich with explanatory dialogue.

- As teachers, for high quality explanations to be habitual, we need to know our subjects, taking time to develop our own capacity to explain the key concepts simply. I think departmental professional learning time would be well spent with colleagues rehearsing the ways they explain the more difficult material. Too often we assume we can do this but, over the years, I've found this is a key area for improvement and experimentation, for me personally and for others.

Explaining doesn't have to suggest didactic one-way traffic, but equally it might well be that an extended teacher exposition is exactly what is needed to cut through some key ideas so that students can engage with them quickly and put them to use with more advanced material.

In talking about explaining, we are obviously talking about doing this in conjunction with probing questioning (K4). We're also talking about gaining attention and engagement in the process; not merely explaining into a void oblivious to our students' capacity to receive. We also need to consider multiple lines of attack: if we're being responsive in our teaching, it's often no use simply repeating an explanation again – it's about finding another way in for those students who need it. We need to have at our disposal a repertoire of explanatory tools that we can use habitually and instinctively as we seek to bring the barriers down.

A quick guide to explaining

Most of this may seem obvious but I think it is worth spelling out: we can always explain better. Alongside **K2 Modelling and metacognition**, here are five ways to support explaining well:

1. Tell a story

It's hard to beat the power of a good narrative. Most explanations require you tell a story, breaking down a set of ideas or situations into a sequence, building from what students already know, leading through some logical steps and finally breaking through to the new understanding – the light bulb moment – as the climax, the punchline. The great art of explaining is to know the steps and to tell these stories with confidence and clarity. Some of the best teachers I've seen were great because they were good story-tellers; you would hang on every word, wanting to know what happens next.

An important feature of a good explanatory story is to make connections from abstract ideas to everyday life. A superb example of this (easy to find online) is Professor Brian Cox using a disintegrating sand castle as a model of entropy. It works brilliantly, seeing how order turns into disorder over time in a context that feels real. There are countless examples in every subject from pizza-slice fractions to differential calculus, examples of every art form, every scientific phenomenon, every feature of language, every geographical process. Getting your stories straight is a good place to start in planning a lesson or a scheme of learning.

2. Use models

You can't teach science properly without models but this also applies to other subjects. In developing deep scientific understanding, it is important to develop models of atoms and molecules and to relate them to macro everyday materials – this takes time. For example in understanding the chemistry of burning magnesium, an atom-level model is necessary to explain observations and link them to the formula form equation.

A great science teacher will automatically explain observations by building models, here linking the observation that the 'shiny metal stuff' turns into white powder to an abstract model that explains the chemistry, showing that new substances are formed. Enabling students to construct ever more sophisticated mental models is the key to all good science teaching. I used to love stretching out a big sheet across my lab as we tried make space-time to explain gravitational fields … it worked well. These aren't merely tricks up your sleeve; they are ideas that should form your core knowledge and are embedded in your default mode teaching habits.

3. Use pictures

The idea of being a 'visual learner' has now rightly been chucked in the pseudoscience dustbin but 'dual coding' is strongly supported by cognitive science[113]. I'm not alone in loving a diagram. There are multiple situations where a verbal description fails to register on its own but when given alongside a visual sketch of the same information it makes sense in a well-designed combination. One of the least well understood phenomena (I find) is the origin of the changing phases of the moon (do not say it's the Earth's shadow…!!). However a simple diagram showing the relative positions of Sun, Earth and Moon make it all come clear.

Possibly the most important diagram for all early learners is the number line. The key to good numeracy is a strong mental model of numbers in sequence and scale. This then builds up to rectangles of rows and columns to make equivalent multiples and then images of fractions in different shapes. In any subject, flow diagrams of concepts, sequences of procedures or timelines or events are all hugely helpful.

4. Develop useful analogies

Another vital weapon in the arsenal is using an analogy to make sense of an abstract idea. Possibly one of the most difficult concepts to convey in science, from my experience, is the relationship between voltage and current. When I was at school – and I still remember this vividly – our teacher Mr Taylor (remember him with the Starsky and Hutch stripe on his car mentioned in Chapter 1) told us to think of throwing oranges through a tennis net. Really! The harder you throw (more volts) the more oranges would get through each minute (current) and the size of the holes would link the two (resistance). It worked for me…and I still use it. There are also analogies using the flow of water with a pump for a cell, traffic flow or the movement of people down corridors…all kinds. The key is to evaluate how good each analogy is – they all have limits – and to make that part of the learning.

5. Take the learner's perspective

It can often be true that a certain teacher can explain something much more effectively than someone with supposedly greater subject expertise. This is because they do a better job of seeing the learning goals from the perspective of the actual novice learners in front of them. It's an important teacher skill to gauge the depth of explanation required, building on students' prior knowledge and then pushing them on from there – not going in too deeply too soon or assuming a generic explanation will succeed. A Headteacher once told me one

---

113. *eg* Kirschner, P. A. and Neelen, M. (2017) 3starlearningexperiences.wordpress.com/2017/05/30/ double-barrelled-learning-for-young-old/

of his school's maths teachers was particularly successful at securing grades 4/5 from lower-end students but this same teacher was not confident to teach at 8/9 level, never mind Advanced Level. His success came from anticipating the common misconceptions and knowing how to build confidence with the core topics for students who often struggled.

A key consideration ahead of any teaching sequence is whether you can explain the concepts. This sometimes requires practice and discussion with colleagues and probably should be a central area to focus on in department meetings.

K2 Modelling and metacognition

Another powerful tool in your instructional repertoire is to model everything you want your students to do yourself. Often teachers set students tasks that they do not do themselves, especially when any extended writing is required. I am suggesting that it is powerful to show students how you approach tasks yourself; you show them how it is done. There's no point talking in theoretical abstract terms when you can just provide an example and walk it through. Instead of talking about iambic pentameter, sonnet form, a piece of computer code, an artistic technique or a physical skill in PE, show them in action – lots of times. Multiple examples are important for students to identify what constitutes the general rule, what is specific to a particular case where specific examples require special treatment.

This extends to lots of situations:

- Write out a full answer to a science question.

- Show fully worked solutions to the maths problems.

- Write out your own introductory paragraph and conclusion to the essay.

- Produce an example of the art assignment you've set in real time – not simply 'Here's one I prepared earlier', which makes it all seem to happen by magic.

Linked to direct modelling of this kind is metacognition. As discussed in Chapter 4, metacognition scores very highly in several research surveys. The idea is to make your thought processes explicit to your students to demystify them: creative thinking, writing tasks, mathematical problem-solving – anything. As you go through the modelling process, you should verbalise your thinking:

The question has four marks; I want to list the four key points: these are A, B, C, D. I then need to sequence them. It makes sense to start with C, which leads to B, so I'll write my paragraph as four key ideas C, B, A, D. Then, I read it through afterwards to check for spellings and punctuation and fluency.

The question asks for the shaded area of the circle inside the square. We are not told the radius but I know the equation for the area of the circle is πr^2. So if I label the diagram showing the radius r, I can see quickly that, for the square, the length is 2 x r. So I know I know the area of the square is $(2r)^2$. Now I just need to divide them....

I want to create an effect that creates an illusion of depth so I will use the vanishing point method, but I want it to be slightly off-centre so that the composition is more interesting; I also want to create a texture with a random stippling effect to make it feel natural, using the white space to suggest light so that the contours I can see with my eye are reproduced in the painting.

A further extension of modelling and metacognition is to do this together with the class in the form of live writing. Here you work with the class to discuss each decision about the words to use, where to start, what to write next and what the overall structure of the writing will be. It works brilliantly for creative writing, making the creative decision-making process less mysterious.

If I use a burst of short sentences with short words, it creates drama: 'The door opened. He stood still. Nothing moved. It was dark and silent.'

Finally, it's important to model the dialectic and creative elements in whatever it is you are doing. If there are competing views or ideas or multiple possible correct solutions or responses, include this in the way you model your own response. Where there is no one right answer, you may need to model multiple responses yourself to get that point across.

K3 Check for understanding

Very simply, you need to make sure that your students have learned what you want them to learn. To do this, you need to check by asking them to demonstrate this to you, not by merely asking, 'Are you ok with this? Is everyone happy to go?'. Doug Lemov calls this 'reject self report' in *Teach Like A Champion*[114]. It is so obvious, but something I have seen repeatedly is where teachers ask a whole class something like, 'Ok? Everyone understood?". This invariably is met with a mix of nods, shrugs and muttered acknowledgements. It doesn't tell you anything. Even if a student says clearly that, yes, they have understood, you don't know for sure unless you check. Similarly, 'Any questions?' is a poor strategy when directed at a large group. The awkward silence does not indicate that nobody has any questions.

---

114. Lemov, D. (2015)

The strategy here is to ask routine questions that require students to demonstrate their understanding or the level of fluency with a particular skill you want them to develop. At the basic level of instructions for a task it pays to check. *'OK, before we start, John, please run through the instructions for the task'.* John now has to give his version of what he thinks you've asked him to do. Other students can chip in with corrections if he makes mistakes.

This applies to the content too. You can do a verbal check: *'Daisy, before we move on, recap the key argument about the causes of failure of the tsunami warning system'.* This could be directed towards a number of students so that, by sampling the class, you get a sense of where they are – as one part of your overall formative assessment repertoire. Alternatively, you might use some pre-prepared hinge questions alongside a whole-class response method like mini whiteboards as explored in K7 and K8.

K4 Probing

This was the first blog post I wrote in a ten-post series called Great Lessons: Probing Questions.

On my recent learning walks and in recent formal observations, I've been struck by a simple thought: when you walk into a lesson where the teacher is talking and you immediately think, 'Yes, this is a great lesson', what is happening? It is this: the teacher is asking probing questions. There is an intensity to it: solid classroom management is securing complete attention from everyone...eyes front, listening intently ... and the teacher is probing. This is what they could be saying:

- That's interesting, what makes you say that?

- That's true, but why do you think that is?

- Is there a different way to say the same thing?

- Can you give an example of where that happens?

- Can you explain how you worked that out?

- So what happens if we made it bigger or smaller?

- Really? Are you sure? Is there another explanation?

- Which of those things makes the biggest impact?

- What is the theme that links all those ideas together?

- What is the evidence that supports that suggestion?

- Does anyone agree with that? Why?

- Does anyone disagree? What would you say instead? Why is that different?

- How does this answer compare to that answer?

- But what's the reason for that? And how is that connected to the first part?

- How did you know that? What made you think of that? Where did that idea come from?

- Is that always true or just in this example?

- What would be the opposite of that?

- Is it true for everyone or just some people?

- Is that a direct cause of the effect or is it just a coincidence, a correlation?

- Not sure if that's quite right ... have another go ... is that what you meant?

- That's the gist of it ... but is could you say that more fluently?

It seems to me, on reflection, that the natural tendency to hold exchanges like this with individuals or a whole class is a key feature of excellent teaching. At a whole-class level, the dialogue is conducted with some energy and passion, moving from student to student, bringing the students from the back and the corners into the fray. There is discipline; everyone listens to everyone else as the probing continues. Each respondent gets at least one teacher bounce-back but often repeated exchanges, dialogues, develop as deeper and deeper answers are sought.

Spontaneously, as an interlocking element, the whole-class exchange is re-directed regularly so students discuss in pairs or groups, giving everyone an opportunity to engage. Here, the students adopt the modelled approach *and begin to probe themselves; they ask each other questions in a probing style*:

Is it is A or B ... does it get bigger or smaller? Why does it get smaller? And how does that work? Do we have enough for a four-mark answer? Have we explained it enough?...

Then, the probing continues as the teacher circulates or when the class is brought back.

I started the blog series with this because I like to think that an excellent teacher would be excellent in a field or on a desert island with no kit, no resources and nothing to write on. It is just you and them…and a really good key question. A less confident teacher will not probe enough, will accept surface responses or will not create the intense atmosphere of active listening required from the class. Sustaining probing dialogue with any number of students that engages them all is the hallmark of a great teacher; it's where we should begin. It's the number one habit. Probe, probe, probe…

K5 Go dialogic

It's a natural, sensible tendency for teachers to want to spread questions around a class, involving as many students as possible, keeping them all interested, listening to each other and thinking about the question in hand. However, from time to time it is worth exploring what happens when you focus more intensively on just one student to probe more deeply into a set of ideas.

The idea of dialogic teaching was popular amongst colleagues at KEGS who had been inspired by the work of Robin Alexander[115]. It is well worth reading their account in the KEGS research journal *Learning Lessons* (Volume 2, Issue 3)[116]. In this issue they report on their work with extended teacher-student dialogues in English A level classes, where, typically, the following types of open prompts and questions were used:

'Talk to us about…'

'Why…?'

'What do you think…?'

'Help us to evaluate…'

'How is this shown…?'

'Can you explain…?'

'What questions do you now have…?'

They concluded that successful dialogues had the following features: they had

115. Alexander, R. (2006) *Towards Dialogic Teaching: Rethinking Classroom Talk*. Dialogos UK Ltd.

116. KEGS Learning Lessons via http://www.kegs.org.uk/force_download.cfm?id=941

to involve reasoning, hypothesising and 'thinking aloud'; needed to last for long enough to make a difference; had to include more 'wait time' (for both students and teachers); were perhaps best done with 3-5 students overall in the middle of a longer lesson, *eg* following pair or group discussions; presentations; prior to writing; prior to a whole-class 'plenary'.

I have explored this method in my own teaching. Normally, when a class has been set a question to discuss in pairs, I tip-off one pair that I'll be asking them to share their response with the class. This gives them time to be ready; they're not surprised to be asked. Then, I bring the class to attention and focus on one student in this pair asking for ever-greater clarity in their response. Here's an example from a Year 10 chemistry lesson:

Looking at rates of reaction curves, what do the graphs tell you about the reactions in each case?

- What were you saying in your pair? *The reaction finished at the same point in each one, but they just did it at a different speed.*

Typically enough ... they stop there without volunteering an extended verbal answer. But then the dialogue starts:

- OK, that's right. Is it the acid or the limestone that determines that the reaction is finished? *The acid is used up.*

- And how did you control that to make it the same? *We measured out the same volume each time.*

- So what feature of the graph tells you that the reactions have finished? *They become a straight line because no more gas is being produced.*

- Why is it a curve and not a straight line? *It goes up quickly to start with because there is more acid to react with and more reactions take place and then it slows right down ... it gets less steep.*

- Good ... and what's a more sophisticated term for 'goes up quickly'? *The gradient is greater.*

- Excellent ... so how is the gradient different for the three different experiments at the start? *The gradient was the greatest for the small chips.*

- Very good ... and what is the feature of small chips that makes the gradient greater? *They have a greater surface area so there are more reactions on the surface.*

- Which does what? *Which makes the reaction happen more quickly ... at a greater rate.*

- Ok. Now try to put that all together in a full answer all at one go with all the correct terminology saying what happened and why.

Ta-dah! The final response was superb, linking these ideas together.

This approach clarifies the understanding of that student and makes them link ideas together. However, because everyone else is listening with in a highly focused manner, they all get to put their thoughts together. I think it works well because it models the thought process of one person…it's not a case of pulling together different people's ideas. There's an intensity to it; a hot-seat aspect that makes that one student really think hard about terminology, sequence of cause and effect and so on. It makes you, as the teacher, listen to their answers closely and, by not moving on to a new student, you create a dialogue that deepens rather than widens the thinking. That's often a powerful effect. In some lessons where question spreading is the norm, students often throw in new ideas rather than deepening the idea that's already in hand.

I think it is important to finish with a re-constructed answer of the kind you want – a full, extended answer. Students can then write down their versions of the same thing having seen this modelled. You can't do this all the time, but every so often, it is very worthwhile to Go Dialogic.

K6 Think, Pair, Share

Here is another popular post from teacherhead.com – **The 'washing hands' of learning.**

Whilst some ideas from my professional learning have helped me to frame an overarching philosophy for teaching or have augmented my armoury of teaching tools, there is one simple strategy that has transformed the way I teach every lesson, every day: **Think, Pair, Share**

I used to be a 'hands up' merchant just like a lot of people. Then, at a training session in the early 2000s delivered by a superb trainer, the seed was sown that 'hands up' might not be such a great idea. It is so obvious when you think about it. In fact it is rather alarming that such a poor and even harmful strategy is still so deeply ingrained in pedagogical practice. For years I'd fought my way through the forest of hands – 'Oo, oo, oo, me, me, me!!!' – OR faced the tumbleweed of deathly silence; those 'blood out of stone' moments when you scan the room desperately looking for someone willing to give you an answer and everyone is staring at the floor. And of course there would often have been kids at the back wishing, 'Please, please, don't ask me, I haven't got a clue'.

But the solution came: every time you ask a question, get the students to think first, then discuss it in pairs before they answer. Lightning bolt. This simple strategy has transformed how I teach – and helped develop an entirely new way of thinking about teaching. I've since often referred to this as the 'washing hands' of teaching. This is the commonly cited hospital analogy where the single simplest act with the greatest impact is to ensure every hospital worker washes their hands after each patient contact, *ie* changing something that you do all the time every day has an enormous impact.

I think it is worth revisiting just why 'hands up' is such a poor strategy:

- Only one person gets to answer at a time so you have no idea what most people are thinking.

- The answer can be offered before others have had a chance to work it out for themselves.

- Students can opt out of answering or thinking altogether if they choose to. They can hide.

- It is difficult to express confusion or simply to say that you don't know the answer.

- In the 'forest of hands' scenario, the competitiveness inhibits less confident students (and there are gender-specific behaviours here that can't be ignored).

- In the 'blood out of a stone' scenario, you can't tell if students are really stuck or just too unsure of themselves to offer a public answer.

- Very often 'hands up' goes together with closed questions with very short 'think time'. We are not comfortable with silence – and expect responses within seconds of asking a question.

- Ingrained patterns of behaviour develop: students who always put a hand up and students who never do.

So, what changes when you ask routinely, 'In your pairs, discuss…'?

Crucially, in doing this you are creating a small bubble of security around each pair; a safe space where they can think for a while and say whatever they like. 'I think X', 'No, I think Y' … 'I haven't got a clue', 'I wasn't really listening', 'It is more complicated than that … maybe it is X except when it is Y?'

- In this bubble it is safe to admit you don't understand and the pair can pluck up the courage together to report this back. It's much easier to say 'We don't get it' rather than 'I don't get it'.

- Every single student can engage in answering the question; they are all generating answers simultaneously – and there is less chance of hiding. Shy students will speak to their partner; the blood comes out of the stone! It has an immediate effect.

- Two heads are better than one. If the question is a good one, pairs can debate their answer. They can then rehearse it and feedback to each other ...'Yes, that sounds good but maybe also say this...'

- When the teacher brings the class together to hear answers, the students are repeating something they have rehearsed. It is easy to report back 'We thought that maybe it is XYZ' when you have already thought this through compared to being put on the spot with a cold question. It is crucial in the report-back phase to ask selected pairs directly to share their discussion. This ensures that everyone is prepared to report back in case they are asked. Using a building process is also key here: ask if students have anything to add, to challenge, any better or different answers? And so on. It is not always time-efficient to get each pair to share their answer.

I could go on ... it is just such a powerful change. Still now, it is by far the most common piece of feedback I give after lesson observations: 'If you had asked them to discuss in pairs at those key points, the learning would have been better'. The question is, why do teachers still ask for hands up or accept it when students take them down the hands-up cul-de-sac? What are the barriers to adopting 'in your pairs' as the default mode of questioning?

- For some it is about behaviour management. To repeatedly stop and start a classful of kids talking is more difficult than keeping a lid on them and taking one answer at a time. Good stop-start strategies need to be developed and rehearsed.

- It can be overwhelming dealing with all the answers that are generated. After 15 paired discussions – what do you do then? The key is to encourage active listening and the process of building on previous answers as you sample the responses. Sampling is valid –

and much much better than only taking a couple of cold hands-up responses.

- Students default to hands-up themselves and have to be trained out of it – which can be a drag. Yes, it can, but it soon works if you ignore students with hands up and get the pair discussion going. If you reward 'hands up', that is what you'll get.

- It can feel like a sledgehammer to crack a nut if you only want to know 'What is the capital of Spain?' or 'What is 3 x 4?'. Well it is. But is that a good question in the first place?

This is the crux; think-pair-share forces us to ask better questions. There is room for a few sharp closed recall questions in a lesson but if we are looking for evidence of deeper thinking, answers that model literacy skills as well as content and, generally, are probing to a deeper level of understanding, then 'hands up' with closed questioning is never going to be enough. If you want to see if students know their facts, a quick quiz for everyone is more effective in any case.

Once you are into the groove of routine 'in your pairs' questioning, you find yourself asking better questions – it all flows.

K7 Whole-class response

It is impossible to engage with the thinking and understanding of every student in a class simultaneously unless you employ some form of technology or, much more simply, the magic of dry-wipe mini-whiteboards – the modern-day slate. I think every classroom should have them. Why are they so great?

I usually introduce this at training events by giving all the participants a pen and board and asking them questions of various kinds. This example from an old 11+ exam always works well – because it generates a good range of responses.

I ask people to work out what the ??s should be. They should show me their answers or write a big question mark or draw an unhappy face to indicate if they're not sure. Then, on a countdown, all at once, I ask them to show me their boards. This is an important part of the strategy: 1, 2, 3, Show Me!

Across the room people hold up their boards showing me their answers. There are some correct answers[117], some wild guesses and quite a few 'don't knows'. It's a great demonstration. Without the boards, how else would I know every student's response at once? There is no more efficient way to know a) who knows and b) who doesn't have a clue.

However, the crux of this is that I can give immediate feedback – and ask follow-up questions. To those who got it right, the least important thing to know is the actual answer; the question is, 'How did you work it out?'. Then to those who were slightly wrong I'll ask, 'What made you think of that?'. It is such a rich source of two-way feedback; it's immediately compelling – and the reason so many teachers use them a lot.

Mini-whiteboards have lots of other uses as these examples show:

- What are the main reasons for rural to urban migration? (4 marks). Use the whiteboards to jot down your four key points. At a quick glance you can see a range of responses; it is possible to draw out common answers, the off-piste but not entirely wrong answers and all manner of variants before agreeing on the best ones.

- Write a sentence in French (or any language) saying what you will be doing to tomorrow. The ephemeral nature of the writing often gives students courage to take some risks, worrying less about accuracy and more about stretching their vocabulary and use of grammar.

- Write a haiku; write down the five key dates; write out the key equations; solve this equation in four steps; sketch out the sequence of the life-cycle of a star; jot down the main events in Act IV Scene II. These are all the type of quick checks that can fit on a whiteboard so that you can see multiple responses simultaneously.

- Draw a diagram to show... (model of convection, pattern of erosion, water cycle, graph of $y = 3x - 4$ and so on).

In each case, there is the same sequence of events: Every student is attempting to answer every question. This can be as individuals or can be used to generate pair/group discussion. The teacher is able to see every single response which almost always yields the following:

- correct answers – including the variety within that idea of 'correctness' leading to the 'How did you work it out?/What was your thought process?' question

---

117. The correct answer is T (triangle in front); S (black square).

- common errors or misconceptions that can be challenged or corrected

- unexpected answers or approaches that add depth/interest/flavour to the proceedings

- students admitting that they are unsure or don't know (and how else would you know?)

The pitfalls with whiteboards are the following:

- Making them too difficult to get out; it is a disaster if you have to book them; they should be accessible spontaneously. Best of all, get them out all the time. (I'm not a fan of 'back of planner' whiteboard inserts because they are too small and teachers tend not to use them.)

- Failing to take account of all the responses in shaping a lesson. I have seen teachers ask for responses on whiteboards, only to say, 'How interesting', and move on regardless. The point is to use the students' responses to inform what happens next; to explore the responses actively.

- Using them too little (leading to tedious novelty item behaviours) or too often (the students become jaded and the impact wears off). They are great for new ideas and for revision/consolidation.

In my view, the various smartphone apps that can be used for engaging with online quizzes have potential – but none of them are as good or as immediate as a set of whiteboards simply because of the amount of information you can capture. Where online tools are better is in storing responses, averaging up scores or counting up the range of answers to a multiple choice question or providing a quick visualisation of the results.

K8 Multiple choice hinges

This is a powerful strategy for gaining an idea of how well your class has understood some key concepts before you decide to move on. It's a time-efficient stock take. The format of hinge questions[118] requires that everybody answers them using multiple-choice responses that allow you to gather information from every student very efficiently. This would be a good use of mini-whiteboards, voting apps or lettered voting cards.

The challenge is to design the questions so that they give you as much information as possible about the success of your teaching. The design process takes time so, in doing this, you should focus on key areas of the curriculum

---

118. See Matt Bromley in Sec Ed, January 2017. http://www.sec-ed.co.uk/best-practice/teaching-practice-hinge-questions/

where the questions are going to be useful for lots of different classes, well into the future. Here are some examples:

Grammar

Look at this sentence: Alice ran quickly down the dusty track.

$$A \qquad B \quad C \qquad\qquad D$$

- Which word is a preposition?
- Which word is an adverb?
- What is the subject in the sentence?

Each bullet point is a separate question and the A-D choices could be mixed up for each one – but the idea is that students should be able to identify the grammar terms in a real sentence if they can be said to have understood them.

Maths

Which of these identities is incorrect?

A. $(a + b)^2 = a^2 + 2ab + b^2$

B. $(a + b)^2 = (-a - b)^2$

C. $(a + b)(a - b) = a^2 - b^2$

D. $(a - b)^2 = a^2 - 2ab - b^2$

This set of choices is aimed at students for whom the mechanics of multiplying brackets is straightforward. At this level they should know the concept of an identity, recognise agreements with plus/minus signs and some standard identities. The time limit of a couple of minutes would govern the level of fluency expected in recognising the errors. Here, more than one could be correct so students have to check them all.

History

In Roman history[119], what were the auxiliaries?

A. non-'Italian' Roman citizens

B. barbarians settled outside Roman borders, selling goods to state merchants

C. barbarians settled within Roman lands, required to provide military service

---

119. Taken from Sparknotes http://www.sparknotes.com/history/european/rome3/quiz.html

D. from beyond Roman borders, co-opted into service under legionary commanders and tribal lords

Good hinge questions combine concepts in them so they go beyond simple recall; they show some more subtle understanding. Detractors should be plausible but part of the learning is to know why they are wrong as well as spotting which answer is correct.

Science

The ozone layer in the atmosphere is important because:

A. It provides protection against ultraviolet radiation

B. It helps scatter blue light

C. It provides condensation nuclei for cloud formation

D. It creates the greenhouse effect

As with the history example, the detractors are plausible and are correct for other components of the atmosphere. The common misconception of ozone being linked to the greenhouse effect is included deliberately to see if students are successful in avoiding the obvious pitfall.

The key purpose of the strategy is to use the hinge questions at the right point, part way through a learning sequence. It's a moment of diagnosis: do we move on or should we have more input and more practice? If you are getting 80% success rate or more, you could probably afford to move on, taking note of students who have yet to master the concepts. Any less than that, you would probably be leaving too many students behind.

K9 Guided practice

The importance of guided practice is highlighted in the research overview in Chapter 4. The practice phase of any lesson is often the core activity. Planning the nature of students' practice time is one of the main tasks in lesson planning and resourcing. However, the focus here is on the need for guided practice.

The example I usually offer to illustrate this is the case of typical staff training on a new IT system. The trainer will come in and demonstrate the new database or homework logging system. It's quite complex but they explain it well and always make it look easier than it is. Everyone is encouraged to use the system to practise but, because the computers are in offices, everyone returns from the training room to their workspace. When, finally, you choose to practise your new skills, the trainer is not present and you flounder, forgetting the most basic things. You've gone straight from an instructional phase to an independent practice phase and it is often a disaster. The key to success is to bridge from instruction to independent practice with guided practice.

Here the teacher is present as students first embark on their own practice based on the content that has been modelled and explained previously. The teacher's skill in deciding how much help to give is crucial; you only need to give just enough to keep the learning on track; not too much to build dependency and not too little so that students give up. A key role in the guided practice phase is to ensure students are pitching to the right standard, using the models of excellence you've already shared as a guide. It is also important to pick up on any early misconceptions. If lots of people are getting stuck it might indicate that you need to explain things better, gathering everyone together for further instruction before any independent practice is attempted.

K10 Say it better

This is a quick win – a silver arrow – that can make a massive difference if you use it routinely. To keep life simple, imagine that the whole-school literacy strategy could be reduced to this: every time students give a verbal answer and before they are asked to write anything, ask them to re-form their initial responses into well-constructed sentences using the key words and phrases you've discussed. Do it relentlessly, every time.

What does the graph tell us?

- First attempt: *It goes up.*

- Second attempt: *The speed on impact increases as the mass of the trolley increases.*

What happens to Lady Macbeth?

- First attempt: *She kind of goes mad; she feels bad.*

- Second attempt: *She starts sleep-walking, because she feels guilty about her role in King Duncan's murder.*

There are several things going on here. You are reinforcing high expectations – that you won't accept weak answers. You are giving students time to rehearse, to think and then deliver an improved response immediately. You are also making it normal for students to express ideas verbally in an extended fashion. Over time, a 'say it better' approach leads to students offering more extended answers first time around. This organic form of rhetoric is vital even if you have lots of structured speaking activities going on elsewhere (see **P17 Structured speech events**).

Feedback and Review

K11 Verbal feedback

The purpose of feedback is to help students move forward with their learning – not simply to describe how well they've progressed so far. This means that feedback needs to be conveyed whilst a learning process is underway to allow for the information about how to improve to be acted on. Ideally, any feedback should be given promptly so that the improvement can be immediate, misconceptions can be corrected quickly and subsequent practice can be more effective. Verbal feedback, given in the moment during a lesson is by far the most effective way of doing this. The evidence of giving verbal feedback should be that students' work improves; there should be no need to generate artificial evidence of verbal feedback with stamps and stickers!

Didau and Rose summarise the features of effective feedback very succinctly in their *Psychology* book[120]. Feedback should be:

- Specific and clear

- Focused on the task, not the student, targeted to increase task commitment

- Explanatory, focused on improvement

- Designed to attribute outcomes to factors student can control

- Designed to link outcomes and effort

This all applies to the verbal feedback given in class. A useful example of verbal feedback in practice is with coaching an athlete such as a javelin thrower. The outcome is clearly measurable – the distance thrown – and so the improvement task is also clear – to throw further. Certain forms of feedback are going to be limited in their use:

Good job. That was awesome. Just try again and you can do it: Praise feels good; it can be motivating. The 'You can do it' mantra might also provide some growth mindset stimulation. However, unless the athlete does something different, it won't help them.

You are too slow and your release timing is off. This might be accurate but neither of these comments helps the athlete to run faster or improve their timing. The 'You are slow' comment risks reinforcing a fixed attribute mindset. It might feel that the timing issues are random – and not within their control.

---

120. Didau, D. and Rose, N. (2016), p86

More effective feedback might include some reference to what the athlete is doing well and then provide some more specific, explanatory guidance. The latter part might go something like this:

Try to release the javelin just at this point here as your arm hits this position here; that's going to give you the best trajectory. Practise just doing that.

You are capable of running faster; push harder and trust yourself to hit the release point at a greater speed.

In general, your feedback needs to focus on how to put things right – how to make things better in some detail – rather than on describing what is wrong or making generic, wishful statements. As discussed in Chapter 4, growth mindset orientated urgings have limited impact unless they are directed at a specific strategy to work on. Keep that in mind when giving any feedback.

Importantly, as we discuss in **K15 Close the gap**, you must also ensure that the students do what you've asked, that the feedback is acted upon. Giving good feedback is only part of the battle; the hard bit is making sure that there's a positive response. This is where strongly positive relationships kick in – creating an effective interface between your feedback and your students' capacity and motivation to turn it into improved performance.

K12 Responsive teaching

As discussed in Chapter 5, according to Dylan Wiliam, formative assessment or 'assessment for learning' are perhaps better thought of as 'responsive teaching.' I think this is as much a teacher mindset as a set of strategies. If you adopt responsive teaching as a disposition, it means that you go into every lesson with a rough plan of what your learning goals are (see **C16 Objectives vs tasks**) but you also take along a stash of contingency plans for ways to adjust the course of the lesson depending on how well your students respond. Instead of being fixed in how you see your lessons panning out, you are agile, flexible, adaptable, anticipating changes in direction, ready to respond and redirect in response to what is happening. For some teachers this is quite a shift.

To do this well, in addition to the mindset, you need to have some tools:

- Methods of identifying how well students are doing – formative assessment tools that you use to take bearings throughout the lesson.

- Methods of adjusting your teaching or students' practice in order to keep on track towards your goals. If necessary you may even need to change the goals – to go further or to retrace your steps depending on the progress your students make.

Here's a small selection of what you might want to include in your responsive teaching repertoire.

Questioning strategies: Whole-class response with whiteboards, probing and dialogic questions, quick quizzes, hinge questions, cold-call questioning, randomised questioning. The full gamut of modes of questioning is there at your disposal; in each mode, student answers need to be met with an appropriate response. You need to use the feedback you are gaining as a teacher from your students' answers to decide what happens next. More examples? Further explanatory exposition? More practice? Or, jumping forward to the next thing. This applies to the class as whole and individuals within it.

Success criteria: Clarity about the learning goals is vital: defining our butterflies; spelling out what excellence might look like. This can involve producing pre-determined success criteria alongside some exemplar work or it can be a process of generating an agreed set of criteria through class discussion, making that part of the learning. What will it look like if you have produced excellent work on this task? The strategy is then to continually reference students' work against the agreed criteria. Are you there yet? What's missing? What do you need to do next? Ask them – or just tell them – but always keep the specific learning goals in mind.

Self-assessment: Teachers don't have time to do all the assessment themselves. It's essential that students learn how to self-assess. This might be through simply checking their work against the correct answers, self-quizzing and testing their knowledge of a section of a knowledge organiser or self-assessing against the success criteria. This last strategy can be difficult and needs to be taught and modelled explicitly. Students can develop the skill of using mark schemes and success criteria quite accurately after practice.

Students as resources: There are lots of ways students can be used as resources for each other: the class critique method is superb for eliciting feedback from a group; peer assessment – where students use success criteria or answer sheets to give feedback to each other; peer instruction and student-led demonstrations – where students lead the learning (see P12 and P15). You can also ask students to echo the metacognition strategies you have shown them, asking them to walk through their thinking. This tells you a lot about the depth of their understanding.

Wiliam's book *Embedded Formative Assessment*[121] is packed with more practical strategies to deliver on his five categories for delivering responsive teaching. It is worth remembering his suggestion that, unless you have adjusted your teaching

---

121. Wiliam, D. (2011)

in response to students' learning, you have probably not used formative assessment – or used it well.

K13 Marking: Keep it lean

Let's make an assumption: there are only two purposes of marking:

1. for teachers to engage with the detail of students' work so they know how well they are doing, where they need to improve and how this might have a bearing on subsequent teaching

2. to provide students with information about where they should improve and how to do it

Given that marking has massive workload implications it is important than any marking you do is delivering on these two fronts. My strong recommendation is that marking has the following features:

- Be selective: only mark at the frequency and depth that students have the capacity to respond to – you do not have to mark everything and there is only so much that a student can work on at any point.

- Only mark work that you will return to for students to improve or correct. Don't mark work that is old and will never be returned to simply for presentational purposes. It's literally a waste of time.

- Be formative: restrict written comments to those that inform students how to improve or give instructions for actions they should take; otherwise use codes.

- Think of all marking as an instruction for what students will do; make sure it leads to them doing more work than you are!

- Every time you mark books, give students time to respond to the comments and feedback immediately.

- Use presentation as a proxy for wider standards. If students are required to maintain high standards of presentation, the rigour involved can translate to other aspects of the work – it suggests that their work matters. If you accept poorly presented work, it gives the opposite message.

Further advice about marking lean is included in the table below – a piece of work shared with me by staff at Saffron Walden County High School[122] as featured in the Closing the Gap blog post mentioned in K15.

---

122. Table created by Nathan Cole, now Head at Wilson's School, and Jo Sansome, now at Colfe's School.

Reduce workload and increase impact:

Instead of...	The teacher...	The student...
Writing annotations in the body of a piece of work and giving an overall comment	Only writes annotations in the body of the work	Writes an overall review highlighting two strengths and one area for improvement
Writing annotations in the body of a piece of work and giving an overall comment	Only writes an overall comment	Annotates areas of the work where the areas of strength are apparent and where improvements need to be made
Writing extensive comments	Only gives one strength and one possible improvement	Works to 'close the gap' on the one issue identified
Writing 'Well done you have…' next to good aspects of work	Puts a double tick next to the best parts of the students work	Adds the reasons for the double tick
Marking every question in detail	Only marks the highlighted questions in detail	Marks or peer marks the work before it is submitted
Writing out a full solution when a student gets a question wrong	Writes a hint or the next step	Completes the correction
Correcting work when a student makes a mistake	Writes WWWT? (What's wrong with this?) or RTQ! (Read the question!)	The student makes their own correction
Marking only extended pieces of work	Reviews in class students' initial plans for this work prior to marking the extended piece of work	Does not hand in rubbish!
Giving back work and moving straight on...	Gives students specific skills or corrections to work on and time in lessons to 'close the gap'	Students read and start to engage with marking before working on the 'close the gap' task the teacher has identified

K14 Whole-class feedback

This is a very powerful idea that constitutes quite a surprisingly radical change in established teacher culture. I first encountered this idea via a superb blog by English teacher Jo Facer[123] from Michaela school in London where she outlines the approach used in her lessons. I have since seen this developed in various

---

123. Facer, J. (2016) Giving Feedback the Michaela Way https://readingallthebooks.com/2016/03/19/giving-feedback-the-michaela-way/

schools and teachers are always very positive about the impact it has on their teaching and their workload.

The method is simple:

- Take all your students' books in and read through the work that you want to give feedback on.

- Instead of making any marks in students' books, make notes on a sheet or in your planner as you go through the books. This will form the basis of your whole-class feedback. You might want to include the following:

    - Common technical errors and misconceptions

    - Common areas for improvement either in the substance of the work or in the presentation

    - Common spelling and grammatical errors

    - Particular books that demonstrate excellence to share with the whole class

    - Particular students whose books are below par and will need special attention

- Ideally the following lesson, give the books back out and run through your comments. Give students redrafting tasks to address the common issues, check their spellings, search for the common errors and make immediate improvements in their books, possibly in a new colour of pen so you can all see where the improvements are being made.

- Show the examples of excellence and talk individually to the students who need special attention.

Compare that process – which is very quick to do – with the laborious process of writing individual comments in each student's book in the hope that they will then read your comments, interpret them correctly and then successfully act on them. It seems like a no-brainer to me. Whole-class feedback is more efficient by far and, because of the time saved, students will receive the feedback more promptly which means it is likely to have more impact.

Some schools have devised standard marking sheets so that teachers are prompted to look for specific things and so that the findings from each marking process can be shared with colleagues in a common format. Managers are now no longer looking to see that teachers have covered the books in red pen; they are looking to see a flow of improvements in student work.

K15 Close the gap

One of my most-read blog posts[124] (astonishingly with over 80,000 views) is based on a visit to Saffron Walden County High School. Here they have developed a simple but powerful shared language around feedback and improvement. 'Close the gap' was the phrase used across the school to signify the process of acting on feedback to secure improvement. Each department was free to interpret this in their own way so the details are very subject-specific but the language was always the same. The gap is the difference between the standard of work a student has produced so far and the standard they would reach if they acted on the feedback.

With this method, whenever feedback is given, in whichever format, the teachers always then give the instruction to close the gap. I heard this all around the school at SWCHS. Students understand this as the cue to engage with the feedback and make improvements to their work during lessons as part of what is often called Directed Improvement and Reflection Time (DIRT). This happens every time so that there is no longer the disheartening experience of producing copious amounts of marking comments only for students to ignore them. Once teachers see their marking as having a direct impact with the confidence that their comments will be responded to, they trust the process and become more precise in what they write; they start 'marking lean' as I describe in K13 above.

At SWCHS, I saw this work in many different subjects:

- In art, students were closing the gap acting on the feedback written on post-its, both peer-marked and teacher-marked. A grid system was used for recording teacher feedback and student actions.

- In English, students were re-drafting sections of their work, closing the gap by trying to build in the grammatical and stylistic content from their feedback.

- In science, A4 feedback sheets were stuck in books with a large box where students had to record their gap-closing work.

- In maths books, students were making attempts to identify and correct errors in response to teacher feedback.

- Humanities books showed where 6- or 8-mark answers had had to be re-drafted taking account of teacher feedback on previous attempts.

- In technology, *closing the gap* on ongoing projects meant that feedback

124. Sherrington, T. (2012) teacherhead.com/2012/11/10/mak-feedback-count-close-the-gap/

and self-assessment were recorded and dated, logging progress as the project proceeded through stages.

In every case, closing the gap appeared to be making an impact and the teachers all seemed to feel that it had helped them re-focus their marking so that comments were actionable and the overall volume realistic.

K16 Teach for memory

There is teaching for understanding in the here and now and there is teaching for remembering later. Obviously they are linked: the better students understand now, the more they're likely to remember later – but it's not the simplest of links. For sure, you can't claim that your students have learned anything unless, at some point later, they can still demonstrate the knowledge and skills you taught originally.

I'm often dismayed by the things students can't remember from six months ago and, in line with research explored in Chapter 4, I've found that it pays to make the business of recall very explicit. Building knowledge in long-term memory obviously helps students to pass exams but it also helps them to understand subsequent work and makes them better educated in the long-run. It's worth doing for its own sake.

Take this example of a piece of information:

The nearest star to our sun is Proxima Centauri (part of the Alpha Centauri system. Pronounced 'Sen-TOR-eye'). The distance to Proxima Centauri is 270,000 AU to 2 significant figures where 1 AU = the Earth-Sun distance.

It's quite easy to imagine the gap-fill worksheet in a typical classroom:

1. The nearest star is called ....

2. The distance to this star is..AU.

Students who complete this worksheet during the lesson minutes after being taught about the information will happily fill in their sheet, answer a few questions, stick the sheet in their books and skip off to break. They may never encounter this information ever again. Even if they were asked to pronounce Proxima Centauri in class, they may never say the words again. They may never be asked to recall the distance, ever again. What have they learned? ... What will they remember in an hour, a week, a month, a year?

I'd say that this type of super-short-term 'learning' is all too common. The teaching has been wasted. There is not remotely enough emphasis on the process of securing the information in long-term memory. The topic has been 'covered'. But what does that mean exactly? Students will later say – 'Yeah, we did that thing about the nearest star'. They'll be familiar with it – but will they have learned it? Of course, some lucky ones will and some won't. But it's not merely a case of knowing some bits of google-able pub quiz info; in this example it's about them having a really secure understanding of the universe in which they live.

Let's work on the basis that we actually want all our students to remember the things we teach them. Teaching students so that they can actually remember things is our job; that IS teaching. And this is not *instead* of teaching them to understand or be creative; it's simply part of the whole process – building a knowledge structure strong enough to last.

As a physics teacher I often found that the less confident students were operating on shaky ground too much of the time in terms of their basic recall. Their basic physics vocabulary wasn't secure enough; they mixed things up and morphed ideas together. For example, they might start talking about Force and Energy as if they are the same thing; they might write $R = I/V$ and not realise it is wrong. They might even think that Joules, Watts and Newtons are more or less the same thing – or have a guess. This gets more confused as the ideas become more sophisticated. Gravitational Potential (V, units: J/kg) and Gravitational Potential Energy (U, units: J) become intertwined with each other. Some students are virtually tossing a coin to decide whether to measure the gradient or work out the area under a curve to find a change in potential. Asked to find the mass of a planet, they might calculate this to be 8×10^7 kg and not flinch because they don't automatically reference this to the mass of Earth = 6×10^{24} kg, thereby realising they might be a few powers of 10 out in the calculations.

It could be that students are becoming too reliant on their ability to look things up on the internet or that, for too long, most of the equations and constants they needed were given in a formula book during the exams. Knowing things off by heart has not been part of the deal for many years (recent English exam reforms are changing that). My feeling is that it is actually the weaker students who suffer the most because of this, not the strongest who have other resources to draw on. I concluded that my students would benefit from more explicit emphasis on memorising elements of the material I was teaching. I became a driller-killer for units, equations, quantities, definitions and graphical methods and this paid dividends.

It is obviously important to know where the equations come from and to be able to apply them to different situations but if you know them by heart, 'S = ut + ½at' or 'v² = u – 2as' are obviously wrong and you are less likely to make mistakes. For some students it was too optimistic to expect understanding to precede the recall; often they could learn the equations by heart and the deeper understanding could follow later.

How do you teach for memory?

If we're teaching something with the explicit goal that the students must remember it later – at various spaced points in time – then it informs how we give the information and what we expect students to do with it. It's just no good exposing students to information hoping it sinks in somehow after a few immediate recall exercises. To begin with it helps to tell the class that any given information isn't just *some* information. It is *the* information. It matters. We could present it as a neat knowledge organiser (as outlined in C15) so that students can see exactly what they need to know. As we teach it, they could be engaging with the information knowing that, in 20 minutes and then again next week, they'll have a test on it.

Try it. If I tell you the Indonesian phrase '*Kamu sangat cantik*' (you are beautiful) or the number sequence 343 454 565 676 and ask you to learn them so you know them next week – you will automatically start to process that information so you can recall it. You break it down, perform some mental drills and try to generate a connection to things you already know that will trigger the recall later. It's entirely different from just seeing the information at a glance and moving on with no expectation of future recall.

There are lots of elaborate memory methods – such as forming memory palaces or using the power of narrative. There are two main methods I find particularly useful. One is to set quick-check tests using mini-whiteboards for immediate feedback or short quizzes in exercise books with a delay after the material was last covered. I also often tell a class that they all need to learn some specific knowledge from memory and be prepared to go through it with the class next week – chosen at random.

The other method is drilling. This is when something is highly repeatable and students can be set several questions that are more or less the same to go over and over. Ten Density questions; Ten $PV = nRT$ questions; Ten '6-mark answers' ... and so on. Eventually, the method sinks in and becomes routine.

In some cases, choral chanting can help; you guide students as they practise saying things out loud, using the Learning by heart method explored in K19. Your job is to make sure, by checking, that every student can do it properly. All of the things below could be taught for understanding and taught for memory; one reinforcing the other.

- Neutralisation: Acid + Base = Salt + Water (nitric acid → nitrates; hydrochloric acid → chlorides)

- Momentum change = Area under Force-time graph, called 'impulse', units Ns, a vector

- Just War Theory: War must be a last resort when all other means of solving dispute have failed / war must be for good, and against a serious threat of evil / goal must be to restore peace, law and order / there must be some chance of success / weapons must not be used excessively / decision must be made by a lawful authority

- *Of Mice and Men* George Quote: 'Whatever we ain't got, that's what you want. God a'mighty, if I was alone I could live so easy.'

- Characteristics of Living Things: MRS GREN (movement, respiration, sensitivity, growth, reproduction, excretion, nutrition)

- Vietnam War Dates: 1968 Jan, Tet Offensive, then March My Lai, then Nov Nixon elected, then Jan '69 Vietnamisation Policy (Martin Luther King assassinated April '68)

- RE Christian basis for being anti-prejudice: Galatians 3:28 'There is neither Jew nor Gentile, neither slave nor free, nor is there male and female, for you are all one in Christ Jesus'

- French grammar: I am going to hit him: *Je vais le frapper* (Direct object pronoun); I realised: *Je me suis rendu compte* (useful, interesting, structure)

If we make it important enough and build in the routines, students can memorise anything.

K17 Daily, weekly, monthly review

As outlined in Chapters 4 and 5, regular low-stakes testing is a highly effective formative assessment process as well as providing an effective process for developing long-term memory. Regular review or retrieval practice, as it is known, strengthens our capacity to remember what we have learned; the more we practise recalling information, the easier it becomes and the more secure our long-term memory for that information becomes.

As discussed above in K16, teaching for memory needs to be explicit. Given the volume of knowledge we want our students to have, it pays to make recall activities a routine part of any sequence of lessons. It takes practice to establish this as a snappy, time-efficient, low-stakes routine, conducted in a disciplined fashion, at a frequency that really helps your students to retain the knowledge you've taught them.

For this to work well you need to establish a pattern that you can stick to:

- Identify the specific knowledge elements that lend themselves to snappy tests and make sure all your students have a clear record via some form of checklist or knowledge organiser broken into sections that students can focus on.

- Introduce a quizzing method that students are familiar with and can organise readily. Are you going to read out the questions, prepare a test sheet or use a PowerPoint slide? How many questions will you set? Not too many because of the time to go over them – but enough to make an impact.

- Develop a quick method for self- or peer-checking of the answers – *eg* with answers on a visualiser or PowerPoint slide.

- Establish a routine that returns to the same knowledge elements repeatedly so that the recall is strengthened. It's absolutely amazing the things students can remember if you quiz them on the same things often enough – sections of poetry, equations, vocabulary from any subject, sets of dates and facts of all kinds.

- Testing needs not take up too much time in any given lesson and should happen often enough to become low stakes and habitual. Use daily, weekly and monthly reviews for retrieval practice of a range of material that you have taught before. Vary this between focusing on specific topics and testing on a range of topics – interleaving the concepts and spacing the practice on any given topic so that important knowledge elements are returned to frequently.

Any stress and pressure that comes from this kind of testing will come from you. You can make it the healthy pressure that comes with a bit of drive and urgency for success, not the stressy kind that is inhibiting and worrying. If you create the right spirit, regular testing can be low key, no-nonsense and even fun and motivating. As students see that, through the regular testing, they are finding the recall more and more fluent, they view the whole process very positively. Importantly, none of this should be overburdened by data collection; it's a learning process – not a piece of record keeping. Save the data collection and tracking for other tests and assessments; they should feel very different.

K18 FACE it

How do you teach students to revise for exams? It's something lots of students struggle with. Based on her experience of taking students through GCSE exams, the FACE It idea was devised by my wife, Deb O'Connor – a Deputy Head and former Head of Science in various London schools. It is a simple and powerful formula to convey the essence of good learning and revision. Neatly, it also forms an acronym with another layer of meaning: **FACE it!** Daunted by revision for exams? FACE it! Think you know it already? FACE it!

Facts: Identify the key facts that need to be known and learn them. Memorise them. Test yourself. You can't explain something if you can't remember the key facts. This is the place to start.

Apply in context: Use recall of facts to solve problems in new contexts; it's not enough to learn isolated facts. Test your knowledge in different scenarios using questions in books and past papers.

Connect to other ideas: Increasingly you need to make links between topics – *eg* Energy and forces in science from different areas (*eg* mechanics and magnetism); comparing the use of techniques between different literature texts; pulling different maths concepts together in one problem; seeing common patterns in historical events or geographical processes.

Exam practice: Use past exam questions to rehearse the process of responding under time pressure, demonstrating your knowledge and understanding, taking account of the marks available.

This simple formula gives students a structure for the process of revision that can otherwise seem nebulous and overwhelming: learn the facts; apply them in context; connect to other ideas; practise exam questions. It may seem obvious – but for a lot students it really isn't.

Very often it is poor attention to the first two elements that cause weaker students difficulty. They graze over the content of their revision materials endlessly but ineffectively; they don't truly learn the key facts to a level that allows them to recall them later. Even then, they might only learn their facts in isolation – for example a quote from *Animal Farm* – without learning how this could be applied in context – *ie* knowing to use that quote as evidence to support an argument in an essay. It is the combination of doing both the learning for memory and the practice of applying this knowledge that makes the difference.

With lots of practice with the FACE it model, students can build up their confidence. For example, in biology:

- Facts: learn the equation for photosynthesis; the role of chlorophyll; the starch test; the concept of limiting conditions; the concept of gas concentration.

- Apply in Context: learn how a graph of crop yields vs CO_2 concentration relates to the equation; learn how results of covered leaf or variegated leaf experiments can be explained.

- Connect to other ideas: link work on crop yields to nitrogen cycle, nitrogen-fixing bacteria and use of nitrate-providing fertilisers.

- Exam practice: complete exam questions: *eg* a CO_2 graph needs to be analysed for 4 marks; some leaf starch test results need to be explained for 3 marks.

'FACE it' works for the revision process in lots of content-heavy subjects. It also works as a description of learning at a more general level. In fact it reads as an expression of the Trivium (with a different E):

- Facts: grammar; knowledge

- Apply and Connect ideas: dialectic; discussion, exploration, problem-solving

- Express the learning: rhetoric, extended verbal answers, written responses, models, productsTaking this a bit further, you could tell your students to 'FACE the Fear', the very real fear of exams and revision.

K19 Learning by heart

Learning by rote has become a much-derided process – part of the anti-traditional rogue's gallery of memes that characterise schools as 'Gradgrindian'. This is totally misguided in my view; a real tragedy because learning by heart is not only very useful – it can also be a source of great joy. Let's take a look at an example from poetry. Here is the opening stanza of one of my favourite poems:

'The Love Song of J. Alfred Prufrock' – T S Eliot

Let us go then, you and I,
When the evening is spread out against the sky
Like a patient etherized upon a table;
Let us go, through certain half-deserted streets,
The muttering retreats
Of restless nights in one-night cheap hotels
And sawdust restaurants with oyster-shells:
Streets that follow like a tedious argument

Of insidious intent
To lead you to an overwhelming question…
Oh, do not ask, 'What is it?'
Let us go and make our visit.

Read those wonderful words. There is something magical about the way the rhythms and rhymes and the use of language work together to create images, atmospheres, feelings… Wouldn't it be great if you could say those words any time you wanted to because you knew them by heart? Shouldn't it be at least some small part of every child's educational experience that they learn some poetry by heart? I would say so.

Having decided that learning this stanza by heart is our goal, how do we go about it? Very simply it is by breaking it down into small sections – perhaps a line at a time – and repeating the lines in your head or out loud, reading them to begin with and then attempting to say the lines without referring to the text. Each time you master a line you add another and keeping going over it from the beginning. The best way to get students to engage in this process is to do it together through choral chanting. That helps with the emphasis of key words and phrases. You have to return to it repeatedly, engaging in various forms of recall: group performances, call and response, tagging around the class with students saying a line and then handing over to one of their peers. Over the course of a few lessons, you can get any student to learn any poem – if you commit to it.

Of course this is how actors learn their lines and singers learn the words to their songs. It's an ancient art. The aim is to make it a joyful and rewarding experience. The end result is that, once learned, a poem, speech or song can stay with you forever – and the more often you retrieve them the stronger that process will be.

When I worked at KEGS, there was a superb cross-curricular project where students learned poetry in English, Latin and French by heart. The philosophy was very much that many written poems should be enjoyed as language that is spoken aloud and that, in learning them by heart, the experience was deeper. The results were inspiring. One of my fondest recollections from working at Highbury Grove was, in one of my last assemblies, hearing a Year 9 student recite 'If' by Rudyard Kipling from memory.

Where else can this method pay dividends? As part of the same oracy initiative that led to the 'If' recital, teachers in French asked students to give presentations about themselves from memory in French. I saw a lower-ability Year 9 class where students each gave their presentations to the class – something neither they nor their teacher believed they were capable of until they had tried. In fact the teacher told me that her own scepticism that her students could learn extended passages of French by heart had held her back. Only once she saw that they could do it did she really commit to the process and began to push students to extend the range of what they could say.

At Michaela School, the learning by heart method is an embedded process in the French curriculum with magnificent results. They also have their students reciting Shakespeare soliloquies ensemble before they sit down for lunch; on my visit in 2017[125], the *Othello* speech I heard was spoken with real energy and joy. There was nothing austere or Gradgrindian about it.

This method also applies to content-heavy subjects where there is a high volume of material to learn in sequence. As well as regular retrieval practice via short quizzes, the poetry-style learning by heart method can apply to things like dates and events in history, where the sequence matters, strings of information like the order of the planets, quotations in English, sequences of chemical reactions, sets of equations such as the 'suvat' equations of motion in maths or physics and lots of sequences of vocabulary in any language.

K20 Homework = Guided study

'You are not doing it for me; you are doing it for yourself'

That is one of my all-time favourite teacher-clichés. There are lots of modes of learning that students might engage in for homework including some extended writing tasks, challenging extension questions and open-ended project work. However, as I explored in Chapter 4 via the John Hattie blog post, a lot of homework tasks of this kind are problematic, especially for less confident or younger students. If students cannot get help when they are stuck and the homework is likely to create conditions where students struggle and flounder, it risks having a negative impact.

The most secure forms of homework to complement Mode A teaching are likely to be when they are essentially a form of guided study; where you are giving students the tools to learn to study independently based on work they have already done. As well as making homework very much doable, thus serving as a means to build confidence, it also helps to create the culture where they are doing this for themselves and not for you: their homework is just a structure to support their own private study.

---

125. teacherhead.com/2017/02/26/the-michaela-way/

That shift in emphasis helps to put all kinds of things into perspective: the nature of the tasks; the resources you provide and expectations in relation to marking. The staple diet might consist of self-quizzing in preparation for recall tests – using knowledge organisers as prompts, for example – and routine sets of questions for practice and consolidation on what they have already learned. Both of these forms of homework can be self-assessed in class, thus giving students immediate feedback.

You might add in some activities such as pre-learning or pre-reading specified bits of material (see **P13 Flipped learning**). It might also be appropriate to set the task of making notes or doing some research following a set template. If you provide the structure in advance, these can all be valid, helpful homework tasks.

The key thing is to make sure students have the tools they need once they leave your classroom: the resources, the guidance, the sources of information. If you are going to throw your students in the deep end, do it during a lesson when you are there to support them – not when they are at home with the possibility that nobody can give them the help they need. Your main goal is to build confidence; to help them build their knowledge through processes they can do at home without too much support.

EXPLORING THE POSSIBILITIES

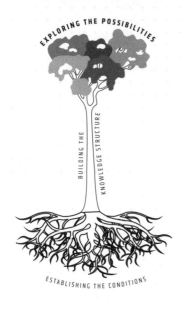

CHAPTER 9

EXPLORING THE POSSIBILITIES

BUILDING THE KNOWLEDGE STRUCTURE

ESTABLISHING THE CONDITIONS

Mode B teaching: 20%?

Having made the case for giving a central role to Mode A teaching (building the knowledge structure), the ideas and strategies presented in this chapter are examples of different aspects of teaching that also make a major contribution to the enacted curriculum overall. There is always a danger in presenting ideas separately in a series like this that they might be regarded as disengaged from the Mode A strategies for building knowledge. However, as with Peter Hyman's 'head, hand and heart' or the grammar, dialectic and rhetoric of the Trivium, each element interacts with the others continually to create the whole. In the Learning Rainforest, Mode B teaching strategies will happen alongside and interwoven with the more direct instructional Mode A teaching. Although they might occupy less time, they are still vital.

The title 'exploring the possibilities' signifies that we're building on knowledge to see what might be possible; we're creating conditions where learning and knowledge can be expressed in different ways and can go down a range of paths. At the same time, it's important to stress that all of these activities are also ways of building knowledge in various forms and of reinforcing the positive learning mindsets and classroom climate that create conditions necessary for further learning.

In deciding which strategies to use, we need to be clear about the purpose. Some modes of teaching will certainly be more effective than others in certain circumstances as we've discussed at length in Chapter 4. However, beyond considering the issue of what is effective at any given moment, there is also the question of designing a whole curriculum experience over the course of a student's education. We want this to be as rich, challenging, motivating and multi-faceted as possible so that we have the best chance of truly developing 'the whole child' with the maximum level of knowledge and cultural capital. As I said at the end of Chapter 4, sometimes we don't do something because it is necessarily the most effective – because 'it works'; we do it because we give it value for its own sake – we think it should form part of a student's learning experience. Many of the Mode B strategies fall into that category.

Projects and hands-on learning

P1 Hands on

There are lots of subjects that are inherently 'hands on' because they are about making things: art, technology, food tech, computing, media studies all warrant space in the curriculum – that's a macro curriculum design issue. Here, I am more concerned with situations where there is a decision to be made about whether to deal with a topic in a purely theoretical manner or whether there are practical, physical experiences that need to be designed in. This is a constant question for science teachers to consider but it also applies in other areas.

Given how much time students spend sitting still in rows of desks – for perfectly good reasons – I would suggest that we should take every legitimate opportunity possible to mix up the pen and paper and questioning with hands-on experiences. Sometimes this is important for the learning itself; at other times it's simply for the experience. Where possible you might include authentic experiences such as those in **P7 Keep it real**. However, very often you have to engineer hands-on experiences in and around the school.

Here are some examples I've seen or used in different areas:

In the elementary stages of learning maths, the use of what are called 'concrete resources' is very powerful. This goes beyond being experiential; it's a core process in constructing secure mental models. These include counting blocks for forming tens and units or rectangles representing multiplication patterns. It's fascinating how the development of firm mental models and experience of physical manipulation interact. There's still a pervasive, false notion that this belongs in primary school – but plenty of secondary-age students still need the physical model-building to support their mental models.

Later on, maths teachers have chances for students to do hands-on things like ripping the corners off a paper triangle to see that the three angles combine to form 180° along a straight line. This works with any triangle at all and it's powerful to see this for yourself. Of course there are hundreds of hands-on maths activities when studying construction in geometry. Schools are full of areas to measure, scale drawings to make based on real measurements and there are lots of opportunities to collect real data when learning statistics. You can do all of these things entirely in abstract out of a textbook or you can make them more hands-on.

I could make a massive list of hands-on experiences for science. Students can perform hundreds of hands-on experiments for different reasons: to develop measurement and observation skills; to support their conceptual understanding. They can also be used simply to gain experience of different phenomena such as magnetism or chemical reactions. Students can make their own electro-magnets, they can explore ways to make an effective parachute to safely land a dropped egg, they can make their own pH indicators from foods.

None of these things is a requirement; they are hands-on experiences that make the subject real.

When studying plants, students should handle real plants. (Sounds obvious but all too often this can be 100% book based.) Students can be given the chance to grow geraniums, pondweed or beans in various experimental conditions or simply to nurture some plants of their own in the classroom or out in the school grounds. Then, instead of studying the theory of photosynthesis and plant nutrition for some hypothetical abstract plants, you can talk about the actual real plants that students are familiar with. A lovely thing to do in studying ecosystems and populations is to collect insects with pooters (pots with a straw) in some long grass from the school grounds or to get students lying face down on the school field (or nearby park) to see how many different plant varieties are there and how alive grass is with invertebrates. Grass is teeming with life!

In conducting demonstrations in a science lesson, you can often get students to handle all of the apparatus while you do the talking. Students can light the splints, release the airtrack riders, press the switch, add the chemicals, take the readings, drop the collapsing can into the water. If it's fun to do, let some students be the ones having the fun, not you, putting in place whatever safety measures you need.

In geography, a hands-on experience might involve making maps or using real maps, building contour models, handling rocks and fossils, using various computer-based simulations (flooding, tsunamis, weather patterns, population and migration patterns) and engaging with any number of artefacts that represent different countries and cultures.

History lessons are very often brought to life with some real artefacts that students can touch. I remember a school trip to the Tower of London where students passed around pewter spoons and various other artefacts from the Tudor period. They loved it. The mocked-up plates made of stale bread that the nobles had used to mop up the juices from meat caused a real stir: when they were discarded, peasants would seize on the chance to get hold of the scraps. Having contact with these items hugely enriched the subsequent lessons. The same applies to studying religious education. We used to have access to a superb collection of Sikh artefacts that students could examine as part of that unit of work.

Finally, in common with **P8 Get creative**, excellent hands-on experiences can include making multimedia products to communicate their knowledge and understanding. Filming and editing an information video is a great experience if approached in a rigorous manner and I've seen students produce superb examples across the curriculum. As with anything, this can be done poorly; the content can be low level and students can make it into a jokey mess-around. It's up to teachers to set standards, to demand rigour and to ensure that the process supports knowledge-building as well as providing opportunities for wider learning.

P2 Ambiguity and uncertainty

As discussed in Chapters 2 and 3, there are multiple goals for teaching. One of them is for students to learn the knowledge that we determine should form their core curriculum. This will include a lot of factual knowledge that we, as the curriculum designers, will present as true and certain. Rightly and necessarily so. However, another goal is for students to develop the capacity to question and challenge, to engage in the dialectic of the Trivium; to contribute to the debate; the conversation. There are plenty of areas of the curriculum where there is ambiguity and uncertainty; where knowledge claims demand to be put under scrutiny.

In my experience it is problematic to leave these elements of learning to chance; it is better to plan them in so that you can be sure that every student has the same opportunities and you manage the boundaries of the debate – for good reason, as we shall see. A good strategy is to plan activities that deliberately introduce ambiguity, conflict, uncertainty or competing ideas at the right point in the curriculum.

In creative subjects and in English literature, the very nature of subjective creativity lends itself very well to this. What is art? What makes a good composition in music or drama? What makes a good design? What is great literature? It's helpful to explore these questions by presenting students with contrasting examples. It is often through comparison that students can see where different artistic elements have relative strengths. Is it that anything has artistic value or cultural significance if we assert that it does or are there some thresholds?

The point is not necessarily to reach a consensus – to reach the 'right' answer; it is to teach students to explore the issues and to make a reasoned case, to go beyond mere assertion of their preferences. They will need to use all the appropriate technical language in the process. One typical example I saw was an excellent graphics lesson where students were evaluating the merits of different classic logos. Whilst they could express a preference quite readily, they were challenged by the need to justify their choices using the design language of graphics.

History is another subject laced with competing theories. There is a level at which students simply need to know the key historical facts and perhaps the accepted consensus around the narrative of events, their causes and consequences. However, this is fertile territory for introducing dialectic. The challenge is to give students enough knowledge so that they can engage with the different perspectives in a meaningful manner. For example, in studying WWI, there are fundamentally different interpretations of various elements. One common WWI meme is the characterisation of the 'top brass' as blundering or wilfully negligent commanders wasting thousands of lives in pointless attacks including the battle of the Somme, the epitome of military futility. The counter view is that, whilst errors were made, generals were fighting a just war against German imperialism and ultimately made good decisions that led to victory. This is a rich seam of dialectic possibilities to explore.

However, it is vital that the exploration is conducted in a controlled manner so that students don't regard the process as one of picking a side based on some hunches or shallow allegiances; we want them to engage with evidence, source material and contemporary expert analysis. The process of engaging with the history of WWI presented through competing claims will be a far richer experience than if they were to be given one simple narrative presented as the truth.

In science, there is also plenty of scope for embracing uncertainty. However, again, caution and control are needed so that students learn when it is appropriate to have opinions, where it is not and where theories or practical situations contain ambiguities and uncertainties. Examples include developing a good understanding of variation within a population and to appreciate the difficulty of determining precise growth conditions; populations of plants will grow to different heights and we need to learn to talk in terms of probabilistic concepts about trends and variation from the mean.

Numerous science experiments are far more complex than the neat theoretical models we present with heat losses of all kinds tending to spoil the simplicity of our calculations where everything adds up. If you are looking to deliberately introduce uncertainty, as well as growing plants, experiments like burning foods can be interesting. Students can see that the energy from burning crisps, nuts and pretzels can be used to heat up water in a boiling tube. We can control the volume of water and measure the temperature rise. But the question is what this tells us about the foods. You get some impressive flames and good temperature rises but so much of the energy is lost to the surrounding air that the measurements can't accurately reflect the energy content of the food. Comparing official data for food energy content from the packets against our measurements presents some interesting material to allow us to consider various aspects of experimental procedures, fair testing and the limits of validity and so on.

There are numerous debates that swirl around in science and it's important to embrace them whilst being aware of the scope for legitimate debate. Here are some examples:

- Nuclear Power vs Wind Farms. This is a technical debate where both sources of electricity have positive and negative features. It is possible to make an argument on either side in any given context. The important thing is for students to understand the issues first. All too often this kind of debate is put in the curriculum before students really know how nuclear power works. The spooky 'magic moon beams' of radiation can be excessively demonised or the idea that wind turbines are 'too ugly' gets overplayed. An informed debate is possible but only at the right point.

- Evolution vs Intelligent Design. This is a non-debate so don't make it one. Evolution is as secure a scientific theory as gravity or electricity. It's not OK to allow students to decide that 'they don't agree with it' as if this is simply a matter of choice. Obviously creationists of various faiths might feature in some of your classes but you shouldn't allow yourself to bend the facts of science to avoid the awkwardness of the challenge this issue will present them with.

- Abortion: Right or Wrong? Here there are certainties to teach around legal rights and technical procedures. However it is a legitimate area for debate, steeped in ethical dilemmas, philosophical questions and social and emotional considerations. It's absolutely essential to allow this debate to happen, guided within parameters that keep things factual where they need to be.

There are parallels in other subjects too. Debate is important; but not everything is up for debate.

P3 Play detective

Whilst it is undeniably more effective to use direct instruction methods for the majority of knowledge-based teaching situations, where students have the appropriate prior knowledge it can be a very powerful method to use an investigative approach. This applies to any situation where students have the capacity to spot and make sense of patterns. Here is one excellent example from language teaching at KEGS:

Grammar Detectives

Students are asked to look at sentence such as *The little boy builds a complicated model aeroplane*. Their challenge is to translate this and work out the rules. Using their knowledge of German, their dictionaries, the classroom wall displays and peer instruction, they work out how the sentence is structured; the tenses, cases and word endings. Here is the response from one group after ten minutes or so: *die kleinen Jungen baut eine komplizierte Modellflugzeug*. Is this correct?

This type of approach was quite common at KEGS. The teachers broke up their normal instructional delivery with opportunities for students to work things out for themselves. Languages teacher Alex Steele wrote this piece[126] to explain an activity they called the James Bond mission:

> Building on the code-breaking stuff we'd done before, I did the James Bond mission lesson with Y7 and it seemed to work very well; they produced some excellent responses to a collaborative translation challenge which evidenced good understanding.
>
> The context of the lesson stems from a story we tell beginner learners about how German verbs work – essentially, that when Germany was unified in 1871 all the verbs came together for a big conference, where they had to decide on a set of rules. The 'weak' verbs – not wishing to rock the boat – accepted the rules and just got on with it. The strong verbs (some stronger than others) decided that they would 'rebel' in various ways against the rules.
>
> So, having already introduced weak verbs, the premise of this lesson was to discover exactly how certain verbs rebel in the present tense. Groupwork (pre-set by ability to optimise or remove support structures as required) with a dictionary (including verb list in the centre), they had to conjugate the 16 verbs and discover that there is a vowel / phonic change in the 'du and er/ sie/es/man' forms of the verb. The next stage – after I had claimed that these 16 verbs had divulged (after intense interrogation) that there were 8 even stronger verbs to find – was to use the lists again to hunt out the 8 extra-strong verbs and realise that 'sein' (to be) is the strongest and most rebellious of all verbs. Quite dry and dusty stuff in real terms but the James Bond mission slant made it more fun! I did a similar thing with *Mission Impossible* for my Y9 beginner French group last year to discover the perfect tense.

---

126. teacherhead.com/2014/04/23/pedagogy-postcard-18-problem-solving-playing-detective/

This is a great example of where a strongly motivating approach is blended with absolute rigour. Once students are guided through an investigative approach to one aspect of grammar, they realise they can apply this to other unknown grammar situations and they become even more confident language learners. Clearly there is a baseline of prior knowledge required for any given level of discovery – here that baseline was certainly present at a high level – but that's something to consider.

I've seen similar approaches work well in history, maths, geography, science, and English where learners use their prior knowledge to investigate new learning, to identify patterns and propose rules and connections. Done well, this can be an excellent way to build confidence and true independence with learning. This is never a replacement for mainstream Mode A teaching. In my view, it only ever really works well, with the right level of rigour, where the approach is just one part of the overall scheme.

P4 Deep end

As a teacher I have always found that, to stretch students, you need to teach them to embrace the struggle of wrestling with new concepts. A favourite mantra of mine is *'if you're not struggling, you're not learning'*. Obviously that needs further unpacking but it's a good way into the discussion. It's akin to the fairly tired cliché about stepping out of your comfort zone. Some students panic when things move beyond their sense of being in control. The solution to this can't be that you always pander to their sense of unease; you've got to get them through it – to help them develop some resilience in the face of intellectual challenge.

Deep End is a strategy for making this experience something you plan rather than something that takes students by surprise. The panic normally arises because people are not expecting to suddenly feel out of their depth. However, just as with a literal deep-end dive, it's entirely different if you know you're about to do it. The experience of a controlled deep-end dive then provides you with something to draw on when it is less planned.

You need to design a challenge that is going to be genuinely demanding; something way beyond what students might normally do unaided, or it might be a multiple-step task that requires sustained focus and independent thinking. It can help to explicitly label the task as a Deep End Challenge – so that students become familiar with the process. Before they start, you should run through some strategies for managing in the situation.

Before they say, *I don't know, I can't do it* and give up, they should do some practical things: read the task carefully; note down the concepts or facts in the task that they know; jot down some related information that they've learned recently – such as some contender equations in maths or science or some possible concepts from history or English that might be relevant; make a plan for any extended writing before they embark on the task, listing the key ideas in bullet points. They then need to explore the task, making any connections they can, draw on their knowledge and problem-solving experience and make an attempt to deliver on the task. If students have a set of preparatory tasks to perform that are functional, they are buying thinking time through which the solutions start to emerge.

Examples of this I have seen are with the application of knowledge in new scenarios in geography and science that require good explanations perhaps using calculations; unseen poetry analysis in English, perhaps with a new genre; photographic landscape analysis work in geography to identify and explain settlement patterns; source analysis work in history; large scale painting in art; extended devising and performance work in drama linking multiple elements and performed to a high standard; peer coaching activities in PE such as giving the half-time team talk; computer programming trouble-shooting activities. There's an endless list.

Importantly, once students have experienced the struggle, they need to have some resolution through exploring correct solutions or examples of excellent responses. This is rich territory for exploring metacognitive strategies and examining how we know what we know and how we approach problem-solving. During the task, teachers need to decide whether students are struggling too much or for too long, gauging when and how to bail students out – a few clues and prompts are often needed for some students, whilst others can get there on their own.

I have found that, sometimes, it is the teacher who breaks first – they don't like to see students struggle and they intervene prematurely, giving the game away. Learning to develop a tolerance for deep-end struggle is part of a teacher's development too.

P5 Groups: Goals and roles

One of the elements of the traditional-progressive debate concerns the value of collaborative learning or working in groups. In my view, instead of making this an either-or, black-white issue, the question we should be asking is this: what are the circumstances in which it is in students' interests to work in a group in order to enhance their learning relative to working individually? It's important to ask that question because it cuts both ways:

- If group work can enhance the learning, then it is probably worth doing. Why wouldn't you?

- If the group work is unlikely to enhance the learning, then it's probably better not to do it. Why would you?

In working out the answer to the question, there are several variables to consider:

- The nature of the task and the extent to which the dynamics of working in a group could play a part in making the learning more effective, notwithstanding the practical constraints that may force group work on you due to the need for students to share resources and equipment.

- The make-up of the groups in terms of size, ability profile and attitudes to learning. It's important to be conscious of the Ringelmann effect[127] whereby individuals become less productive the larger their collaborative group becomes.

- The structure of the group in terms of the role of each person in it (defined roles or *de facto* roles): including, for example, the implementation of strategies to avoid Kagan's 'hogs and logs' syndrome[128] – where some people dominate while others are simply passengers.

- The extent to which prior knowledge is a prerequisite for the group task to enhance learning and the extent to which each student has the knowledge required.

- The time taken by the activity in relation to other types of activity and the extent to which this represents an effective use of that time compared to other possible activities.

So, let's not just assume that group work is inherently a 'good thing'. OR, that it's inherently a low-level activity that gives the illusion of students being busy and learning when actually they are not.

In my experience, when the basic requirements for excellent group work are in place, the learning is superb. In fact, over the years, I'd say that many of the best lessons I've seen have involved aspects of group work. The basic requirements as I see them are:

1. Each person in a group must be able to make a contribution: this requires thinking about group size and roles. In a Lesson Study process I took part

---

127. en.wikipedia.org/wiki/Ringelmann_effect
128. www.kaganonline.com/about_us.php

in we found that students in threes created a passenger and weaker students were more likely to be squeezed out. It also means making sure they have the knowledge and resources needed to add value to the group activity.

2. The learning outcomes need to dominate over the group dynamics. If students are unable to take turns, are excessively dominant or passive, then the content of the learning is going to be largely social, not intellectual. There is a case for teaching students how to function in groups – it's a learning goal in itself – but maybe not right now when you want to focus on some geographical analysis or the future tense in French.

3. The activity must deliver a learning experience that depends on interaction with others in order to achieve the learning aims; group work is not simply parallel individual work in a social huddle. Very often, effective group work is based around discussion to evaluate the relative strength of different ideas or where cooperation leads to stronger problem-solving power – or where it is an inherent element of the subject.

The implications are clear. Don't choose a group activity if students don't know enough in advance to make it meaningful and risk simply recycling their existing weak knowledge and misconceptions; if the group dynamics are such that the acquisition of knowledge you're after is unlikely to take place; or if they'd get more out of doing the same thing by themselves.

It's obvious enough that some subjects are more likely to lend themselves to meeting these requirements than others but, across the curriculum, I've seen countless examples where the requirements have been met.

Languages: Roleplay in German; Y8 students putting their books down, acting out discussions about a planned excursion, thinking on their feet in response to each other's questions and answers. This depended on each person having enough they could say to sustain the roleplay but it was an essential activity to give each student the opportunity to develop their capacity for recall, spontaneity and responsiveness.

English: Textual analysis through performance. Y12s working in groups to perform poems, using tone and gesture to communicate meaning. The group aspect was extended to assessing the quality of their own performances prior to re-running them with improved outcomes. Another example was a Y13 'text summary' activity with students working in groups to compare their interpretations of a play (Marlowe's *Doctor Faustus*) against a range of themes having read the play in advance at home, producing visual representations of the play highlighting the elements of structure, language, genre indicators and so on. Here the collective output was greater than any one student could have managed.

History: Y10 Students in groups of four studying the Russian Civil War between the Reds and the Whites *circa* 1920. Their task was to evaluate 20 stated features of the Red and White campaigns to arrive at an agreed view of the most significant factor. The group work was essential because different students expressed alternative positions that needed to be justified. It relied on good prior knowledge as ever; this was evident and was reinforced with good resources that captured the prior learning on one large A3 sheet.

Geography: Y12 tsunami warning activity using software that produces a tidal wave across a virtual coastal landscape after 15 or 30 minutes, requiring students working in groups to plan a strategy under time pressure to minimise loss of life. Whilst this could be done individually, the group element is a more accurate simulation whereby different people express alternatives and only one decision can be taken at numerous points.

Religious Education: Y9 students engaged in debates on various ethical issues. Here they needed to listen carefully to the views of others and construct their counter-arguments. The discussion was informed by good preparation and students were clearly refining their analysis in response to other people's views. You can't debate with yourself in a meaningful way; if debate matters then so does group work.

Maths: Group puzzles. Yes! I'd suggest that maths is an area where group work is less likely to be of inherent value compared to other subjects. However, I've seen tasks created that generated learning in an incredibly exciting manner, using group problem-solving as the driver. In one lesson students had ten problems to solve in pairs; they needed to select the order of the problems based on their difficulty with some solutions dependent on others. All the answers linked into an over-arching code-breaking puzzle. I've seen this done with Y12 on calculus and Y10 on quadratic equations. The main gain compared to just doing a set of questions from a book or doing the same task individually was in the need to agree an overall strategy; this involves high-level mathematical discussions. It creates great intrinsic motivation – a sense of purpose that yields significant gains in productivity. As one of many lines of attack in the teaching of maths, group work like this has its place.

Subjects like drama, PE and music are natural homes of group work for obvious reasons – collaboration is an inherent element of the subject. The question here is not whether to do group work, but how much freedom to give groups to organise themselves and make choices. A successful rehearsal of a four-piece band or a group performance or training session requires a certain degree of leadership and cooperation – skills that are certainly worth developing.

In science lessons, students work in groups a lot. I recognise that often this is simply because of the constraints on equipment. In class practicals, there isn't enough kit for them all to work individually so group work is a necessity. In that context it's not possible to say that the group work itself is adding value in terms of conceptual understanding and recall. It probably isn't. In fact it's worth asking whether they'd be better off working individually if they had the chance.

Social learning is an inevitable element of school life so students should learn to make the most of it. Any number of activities from simple think-pair-share questioning, to longer debates, discussions, presentations, practicals and data analysis tasks can be enriched by sharing and challenging the ideas and conclusions of others.

Overall, in a flow of lessons across a unit of work, an element of group work mixed in with other modes of learning is perfectly sensible and natural and can be highly effective. However, as far as possible, it should be a conscious decision to use group work because of the benefit to the learning derived from it rather than it being a default mode.

P6 Projects

One of the aspects of the curriculum that I love are the opportunities students have to pursue their own ideas in an extended project. The learning outcomes can often be extraordinary because students will invest significant time and energy into pursuing something that they're passionate about. To a large extent this is more of a curriculum planning issue than a pedagogical one. Often it depends on the subject choices that students make as to whether they'll have an opportunity to undertake a personal project.

Some examples include technology where a massive part of the course is to make something and to record the design process. Students are often hugely committed and invest heavily in the outcomes. The same is true in art. Art is the subject where I feel students have the greatest freedom to develop their own creative ideas – and, taught well, this is one of the most challenging intellectual experiences a student can have. If you talk to an art or technology student about their work, the level of personal investment is so evident. They gain so much from the freedom and challenge of making multiple creative decisions, of managing their time and materials so that they create something they're proud of – regardless of its status in the examination regime. My son had a similar experience with his GCSE media project, making a two-minute trailer for an imagined teenage drama. It was a genuine labour of love that stretched him in ways he had not foreseen: creative, technical, organisational, interpersonal.

Various other subjects offer this opportunity within the curriculum – or at least the option is there. In one physics course I have taught, the coursework element was excellent. Each student devised their own investigation and we give them ten hours of lab time to get stuck in. This was the closest they got to the art students' experience – taking ownership of their learning in a deep, hands-on manner.

Other examples include the Global Perspectives and Research Pre-U course (GPR)[129] and the Extended Project Qualification[130]. I have had the privilege of supervising a student's essay on Kuhn's paradigm shift, linked to 21st-century science and another on competing theories for dark matter in the universe. These research project programmes yield a range of fascinating 5000-word essays of the highest quality, reflecting each student's passion and personal interest.

In different schools, I've introduced a range of opportunities for students to embark on personal projects outside the curriculum. A particular favourite is the British Museum 'Family Learning' Project, run at both KEGS and Highbury Grove. At the most basic level, we simply asked students to go to the museum and 'do a project' with their family. We did also provide further guidance. This had some fabulous outcomes with students re-creating a range of artefacts, writing up superb accounts of one or more objects that took their interest – the Rosetta Stone was always popular.

Another example was an annual prize that we introduced at KEGS with various categories to encourage students to consider creative writing, producing significant pieces of art or to write extended essays. In our very first year the annual prize yielded some extraordinary work ranging from a full-blown original concerto, a 200-page novel, a truly remarkable poetry anthology, an extended piece of scientific research conducted in a professional lab over the summer holidays and an essay on global political ideologies. Unless we had put that structure in place, none of those things would have come to fruition. The prizes were quite significant but the main selling point was prestige: this motivated students to consider much more ambitious projects than regular school work would normally involve.

129. www.cie.org.uk/programmes-and-qualifications/cambridge-pre-u-global-perspectives-short-course-1340/

130. www.aqa.org.uk/subjects/projects/aqa-certificate/EPQ-7993

Several times I have also run a project scheme for younger students. These were called 'Gifted and Talented' projects at the time, but now I would think of a better title! This scheme led to a showcase of individual work at an annual exhibition which included compositions, videos, pieces of art, computer programs and much more besides.

In order to get this kind of work from students, first of all we need to provide students with these opportunities. That's the curriculum bit. In terms of pedagogy, what matters is to focus on the learning that the project generates. It's important to ask 'What has the student learned?' rather than 'What has the student made?'. The product is a vehicle for the learning – not the other way around. That helps to push students further, so that they don't look to make something polished and tidy as a priority over producing something challenging and deep.

With that focus, the next thing to consider is the balance between open-endedness, guidance, independence and quality. It's a balance because, without some guidance, some students will produce low-quality outcomes, below the standards they are capable of reaching. However, the major learning comes from having to solve problems and make choices using their own resources. In the Global Perspectives course and physics, this is built into the marking: you can tell a student, 'I could help you but it will cost you some marks...could you work that one out for yourself?'. Most often they can – but not always.

Finally, it can help to show students what others have done in the past. The focus there is to set standards, not to limit the outcomes. Once students can see what might be possible or draw inspiration from the level of ambition in previous projects, they are motivated to emulate them themselves.

P7 Keep it real: Authentic projects, products, experiences

In my view, where possible, the Rainforest canopy of learning possibilities should include authentic learning experiences. If an entire school curriculum was classroom- or even school-based it would be rather strange given that there is a world out there full of learning opportunities. There are plenty of students who don't get out into the real world enough, away from school, home, gaming consoles, social media. There are also some things you just can't simulate or recreate in a classroom; you need to do them for real.

Another avenue of authenticity is when the purpose or audience for a learning process is real. This changes the dynamics significantly; all of a sudden the outcomes become more meaningful and students raise their game to meet the challenge. Here are a few examples:

Local history walk

Every local community has a history and it is normally part of a good school curriculum to undertake a local history study. There is always a story to tell about how a town has changed and it's fascinating to see where the evidence for that can be found, alongside the key landmarks and places of historical significance. Getting out in amongst the living history of the places we live helps to convey the messages of continual change and the impact and characteristics of social and technological revolutions as they are happening. Most towns have war memorials which serve as an excellent way to connect to the stories you've been telling in the classroom. These were real people – just like us, living here.

Geography field trip; Outdoor education

At some point in every child's education I think they should get the opportunity to get out into the landscape to experience it and study it. Geography really comes alive once you are out in the field, knee-deep on a river walk or hiking past the rock formations you've studied in class. When you see an exposed rock face revealing the thousands of layers, discontinuities and puzzling upside-down curves, the ideas about rock formation of different kinds, patterns of erosion, the forces involved and a sense of geological timescales are immediately more vivid. Rocks become exciting. As mentioned in Chapter 3, the experience of walking through the forests and hills in your own country – ideally camping out or staying in a residential centre – make for good cultural capital, especially for urban children who rarely get out of the sprawl.

Writing a blog – real audience

When you publish something online, you have immediately opened up your work to a real audience – and anyone can do this. I have found the work of educators like Chris Waugh (@edutronic_net)[131] and David Mitchell, founder of @QuadBlogging[132], fascinating and inspiring. They use online blog platforms to post students' writing, inviting members of the public and parents to engage, support and comment. Chris created a sophisticated Wordpress blog site where each of his students had their own page where they would post a high proportion of their work. The comment feature allowed for dialogue with students during the writing process. The authenticity comes from the public scrutiny and engagement. QuadBlogging works by putting four classes of students together – often from different schools around the world – so they take turns in providing the audience for the others.

---

131. chris.edutronic.net
132. quadblogging.net

Feedback from Chris and David suggests that, because students know from the start that their writing will be read, they raise their aspirations and seek to deliver the best work they can. There's an inbuilt level of accountability that drives the process.

Project 9: Student-led IT Teaching Programme[133]

This was one of the best projects I have ever seen in a school. We started this at KEGS in 2010 and it is still going now. Project 9 involves students in the higher school years designing and delivering programmes in various aspects of IT or computing to students in Year 9. Students had about 10 hours of tuition during the project on a unit of their choice from a menu covering a wide range of topics: Raspberry Pi programming, Flash animation, stop-frame animation, Python, C++, Photoshop, PC building – to name a few. Most of these topics were ones that our teachers could not teach so we were capitalising on students' knowledge, gained from their private study and interests, to deliver an authentic part of the curriculum. The first year was so popular and successful that we committed to making this an inbuilt part of the curriculum year on year. It was wonderful when students would teach programmes on computing languages that they had started to learn on Project 9 themselves a few years before.

Student newspaper

In various settings, including schools I've run and some I have visited, I've seen an authentic student newspaper work brilliantly well. This is where a student group is given the responsibility, trust and resources to run their own newspaper, with support but without teacher control. This is very different from where a teacher or administrator runs a publication and students make contributions to it. If you set out the right parameters around editorial and production standards, students can be empowered to make all the decisions themselves and face the public accountability for what they publish. In some contexts you might need some pre-publication quality assurance – simply to avoid anything defamatory being published – but in others you really can build up enough trust to allow students to publish their own paper. This provides a support outlet for debate, humour, sharing student interests with major opportunities for developing a range of skills for those involved.

Similar opportunities can be created for organising drama productions, school concerts, charity events, sporting events, science exhibitions, poetry slams, equality group campaigns: these are real things with an authentic purpose and it always pays to give students maximum leeway for decision-making. The

---

133. teacherhead.com/2012/11/14/project-9-a-student-devised-student-led-it-programme/

tough part is to get as many students involved as possible, especially those who don't normally see this as something 'people like me' do.

P8 Get creative; learn to choose

A creative process involves exploring possibilities, making choices and then evaluating them to see if they work. Creative thinking can and should be built into the normal flow of lessons; it's an inherent feature of problem-solving, essay-planning, developing language skills and any one of the arts. However, sometimes, students can struggle to be creative. If students lack confidence in a particular subject or if they are excessively compliant in their thinking, students can worry a lot about being wrong and feel inhibited when given open-ended tasks that require their input and decision-making. I think students need to be given planned opportunities where they can learn to make low-stakes choices and develop creative confidence.

For me, a regular Mode B strategy is to give students some scope for making decisions about their learning using the open-format response strategy. If your students have done some research, explored some ideas or finished a topic, it can generate fantastic responses if you ask them to capture and consolidate their learning in any format they like: an essay, a PowerPoint presentation, a website, a video, a booklet, a 3D artefact – whatever they like. This leads to a lovely range of responses that can be shared in different ways. There's nothing worse than a class of PowerPoints to schlep through – but the open format method usually yields enough variety to make it possible to see everything.

This works because the knowledge content is secure so the creativity-inhibited students can focus on exploring a range of possible ideas to communicate their knowledge and understanding in the subject whilst learning some technical media skills in the process. Those that want to explore the subject in greater depth, in creative ways, are also free to do so.

Very often I find that students need reassurance – they are just so used to restricting their activities to what they have been told to do:

- Am I allowed to make a website? *Yes, of course!*

- Will it be OK if I film a discussion with my dad? *What a great idea!*

- Can I bring in a model that I made at home? *Oh yes, please do!*

You need to make sure the content is given due weight – it needs to be a rigorous piece of work that demonstrates their understanding. It helps to show them last year's stunning exemplars. The point to stress is that any format has equal value – it is just that they are different. With this process I have seen extraordinary work: models, graphic storyboards, extended essays, videos, websites and posters that defy the notion that a poster must necessarily be a bit lame: they can be graphic masterpieces. It was through this process that I learned that it is possible for a Year 7 student to create their own website without any help.

I will always remember a Year 8 girl at Highbury Grove who made a video – via her bedroom computer – where she gave a superb exposition of her ideas about animal adaptations – the topic in hand – with some graphic visual aids. The truth is that she was rather shy and I had never heard her speak for so long, with such gusto. Without this process, I would not have known that this was something she was capable of. It changed my view of her entirely.

Every so often, give your students permission to do whatever they like – but ask them to dazzle you. See the next idea, P9.

P9 'Dazzle Me' – Keeping it open

Building directly on **P8 Learn to choose**, open-ended tasks can play an important role in creating opportunities for students to explore their ideas; they can be a great source of top-end differentiation and lead to lovely, unexpected outcomes. But, they can also fall flat if the expectations aren't clear. It's no good just to hit and hope – because if one option is to produce something mediocre to complete a task, then that is what you'll get from some students: dross! At the same time, if you prescribe every detail, you may deter students from exploring things in ways you hadn't considered possible; you may actually limit them.

As ever, it's about getting the balance right. To illustrate this, here are a few of my son's pieces of work from his time in Year 6s and 7 (He gave me permission to include them).

RE Creation myth

In studying religions, creation stories emerge as a recurring feature. Asking students to devise their own creation story is a good way for them to explore the concept, using symbolism and narrative devices to communicate the story. My son was set this for homework and immediately saw it as an exciting project. The brief was simple – to write a creation story accounting for the formation of the Earth and to annotate it explaining each part. They were given a rough guide and were shown an exemplar from the previous year. He loved doing it, spending ages coming up with ideas, then writing it and organising the annotations on a big sheet to produce something he felt really pleased with. It's a lovely piece of work, full of imagination.

Here, a combination of factors made it work. There was enough structure and guidance given for him to know what to aim at; there had been an element of standard-setting with the exemplar but, beyond that, he had a high degree of freedom to make it his own and he got a great thrill from it. I quizzed him about what he learned from it and I was satisfied that it had also done the job of illustrating the value given to creation stories in religious teaching.

English dialogue

My son always enjoyed putting on voices when he told a story. He's got a whole range of characters he can adopt for comic effect when the opportunity arises. This English homework was a fabulous opportunity to put something he is quite good at to good use. They were asked to produce a play script that illustrated different modes of speech. This is packed with challenge in terms of writing. There were a few rules including the need for at least three characters. He loved it so much, he spent a whole evening writing it from planning it to typing out the dialogue. The final product was magnificent – and hilarious.

This task worked because it sparked his imagination. It's so open – he could write about any situation, with any characters, in any voice, for any length. It was set in a light-touch 'see what you can come up with' manner so he wasn't under any pressure to deliver. That gave him the confidence to be playful and experimental with his writing; he didn't have to be correct or overly formal. However, the teacher is one who is a natural standard-setter; he knew he couldn't turn in any old rubbish and expect her to be particularly impressed. That combination of freedom and high expectations delivered a great outcome.

Maths hat

This was an example of an open-ended task that didn't work out for my son. For World Maths Day during Year 6 they were asked to make a 'maths hat'. That was it. It was meant to be a fun activity to celebrate maths but my son didn't relate to that. He saw it as a task that was required but one that he didn't value. For him, maths could be fun anyway. He'd have happily done some actual maths of an interesting nature to celebrate Maths Day – but a maths hat? He found a woolly hat in his room with the number 67 sewn into it and saw his chance; three minutes later with some scissors and a stapler – job done! Maths hat finished. He had just added the multiply (X) and add (+) signs to the hat.

No doubt you could conjure up all kinds of creative ways to make a maths hat – and certainly his classmates went in with top hats of various shapes and sizes covered in geometry and algebra. But here, for my son, some ingredients were missing. There were no clear expectations or minimum standards; there was no link to the associated learning and no challenge. It might have worked at some level as an optional task explicitly for a bit of fun – but in this case the option to produce something rubbish was there and my son took it (To be clear, his teacher was fantastic and he got a top grade in maths – she knew her stuff. The maths hat was an aberration as far as my son was concerned, not a symptom of any deeper issue).

Here are some examples from my teaching experience:

Y10 Physics videos and other products

I normally use open-ended tasks when I feel that students can benefit from trying to synthesise information from research with the material covered in class into a format that they can share with each other. This could be a video, a publication of some kind or a presentation in some form. Where I am happy with the outcomes, it is normally because of a few factors:

- I have worked harder up-front to set out the parameters in terms of the standards expected. I've established the success criteria in advance with students and spelt out the things I don't want as much as the possible options I might want.

- I've encouraged them to use media devices and tools that they know, that they don't see as too much of a novelty and have the skill to use properly. There's nothing worse than sitting through a badly made video with dodgy sound quality that was meant to be saying something about science – if only they had kept the camera steady or the website links worked (If students can't do these things well, they need to be shown how before they use them in a new context).

- I've been very clear that the science content has to dominate over all else. The purpose of the activity is to give them the opportunity to use their knowledge and imagination to convey the scientific concepts in an interesting manner in order to develop their understanding – not to have a laugh making a hilarious video that will have their mates in stitches.

With those things in place I have had some real gems including a great set of 'Eco House' sales videos and websites that packed in tons of science about energy conservation and heat transfer with a fair degree of polish. Where I have been less happy, I've let some of the criteria slip and been subjected to bad PowerPoints, 'funny' (tedious) videos, lame leaflets, low-quality websites with lots of animation but no physics – and so on. It can feel like a horrible waste of everyone's time unless the set-up is done such that the outcomes are excellent.

Two final thoughts:

- If everyone in the class has slightly different subject matter, then there is a good reason for students to pay attention to each other's work. If they've all done the same thing, it's hard to get a class motivated to sit through presentations about things that they already know.

- Sometimes students respond to a challenge to go beyond your expectations. A former history teacher colleague asked her class to undertake a major piece of work researching aspects of the Renaissance and presenting their findings, within a week. She said 'I bet you can't do all of that in a week'. They said 'I bet we can'. She said 'Ok, then, get your ideas together and make something that will *dazzle me*'. And they did. Spectacular, breath-taking Year 8 work followed.

P10 Off-piste

I remember a visit to my school by students from a partner school. They spent a day with us and produced a report of their observations. Some of the things they liked about our lessons were:

- The lessons tend to start straightaway without lots of lining up and register-taking.

- Students do not have to copy objectives from the board every lesson.

- The teachers often deviate from the lesson plan to tell stories or share their personal interests. 'Our teachers never do this,' they said.

We hadn't anticipated the last point but, on reflection, it was certainly a feature of lessons. The students and teachers used to find great joy in the kind of spontaneity that allows anyone in the room to express their puzzlement, their curiosity or their sheer love of the subject. Diversions I've had in my own lessons have led us to consider the James May 'milk first' tea-making theory based on temperature gradient and specific heat capacity; how a bullet-proof vest works (following the input of a student materials enthusiast in my class) and what might happen in terms of g-force if we could fly through the sun. Is it on the syllabus? Not exactly ... but who cares?

Sometimes we just have to go off-piste; go with the flow – and do what we like, seizing an opportunity.

Lights out

When he was in Year 6, my son came home from school buzzing one day: 'We had the BEST lesson EVER'. They'd had a class discussion about ghosts, told some stories, explored the possibilities of UFOs and life on other planets ... lots of engaging deep thinking on big existential questions. Why was it so special? Because they were sitting in the dark for over an hour after a power cut! So, no writing or reading … just talking and listening. The teacher had capitalised brilliantly, letting their imaginations fire off in all directions. Of course, this agile teacher had made the most of a real situation … but why wait when these fabulous 'accidents' could easily be made to happen! If you have not yet read *Oops!: Helping Children Learn Accidentally*[134] by Hywel Roberts, then you should. He tackles this area superbly well.

Current affairs

Going off-piste can involve a teacher taking the opportunity to make connections to current developments, scrapping the planned lesson if necessary: there's an election, Venus is transiting the sun, Higgs' boson has been discovered, it is the anniversary of a publication by Darwin or Shakespeare, the biggest prime number ever has been identified, Richard III has been found and verified with carbon dating, there has been a tsunami, a new work by Van Gogh has been discovered…or vandalised…all these things are a reason to go right off at a tangent and bring learning into the real world. In fact, when these things happen, it is unforgivable not to.

Of course the very best reason to go off-piste is when a student blows your mind with their work. Sometimes you just have to down tools, get in a huddle and marvel at what someone has done.

Further possibilities

P11 Class forum

I am not a major advocate for education technology unless there is a very specific reason to use it. One of the best uses of technology that I have encountered and used extensively is an online class forum. I have used and seen a number of platforms for this: Moodle, Google Classroom, Edmodo, Tumblr, Wordpress – and I know there are many others.

I'm no expert on the merits of each of these platforms but I firmly believe that there is value to be gained from constructing an online forum that is dedicated to the work that you do in your lessons. To illustrate this, here are some of the ways that I used Edmodo with a Year 9 science class.

---

134. Roberts, H. (2012) *Oops! Helping Children Learn Accidentally.* Independent Thinking

Getting started: I spent an hour in a computer lab with three students to advise me as we tested out all the functions. We found that a combination of the website and the app on my iPad gave us the tools we needed. Here are some of the things we did with it:

Video/Image Capture: Using the iPad, my students or I could record a demonstration (a chemical reaction, for example) on video and upload it to Edmodo instantly; this was then a resource students could refer to again. This is useful and very easy to do. Students can re-watch a demonstration, including the audio commentary, to help them with homework and revision or simply (and most importantly) for interest. We made a video of the classic 'collapsing can' demo, undertaken by a student group; and another of the thermit reaction, a fabulous demo resulting in a big flash and some molten metal – one that is worth watching repeatedly.

Resource Sharing: At several points in the year, students posted resources that they have found and I did the same. This means that we did not have to be confined to the lesson slot to exchange ideas. If I saw something interesting that I wanted the class to see, I could upload it to Edmodo in a few seconds. The notification system means that they all received an alert to tell them there was something new to look at ahead of the next lesson or just for general interest. Students would share YouTube videos of interesting science experiments or news stories, for example.

Typically students would share any resources such as PowerPoint presentations they made for the lessons. The students know that the presentation will be put on Edmodo so they don't have to worry about copying everything down; they can listen and engage. Another example was after students had each researched some information about an interesting object in space, they shared their findings.

Homework Information: Edmodo cut out a lot of time spent setting and writing down homework in class. We normally got someone to post the information and subsequent clarifications and reminders could easily be issued. Here, two students gave instructions to their classmates as part of our co-construction process (see P15):

Easter Holiday HW: If you haven't done so already, you should finish your graphs measuring the resistance of the wire against the length. You should also write a short conclusion analysing your results. The test will be on Monday 28th. Could Asad and Reiss please share their revision guide for the Light topic. Thank you. Kieret and Alex.

General benefits: There are numerous other features of Edmodo that I've explored including using the markbook feature to log test scores. More generally, the online forum provided us with a means of communicating in-between lessons. That has a powerful effect on the way we talk about learning. We are not limited exclusively to the lesson-slot for exchanging ideas, resources or for doing the thinking. Simply by having a forum that can be accessed at any time, students start to talk about learning in their own time; that becomes normal. They also have access to their teacher out-of-hours if you allow it.

The effect of all of this, to my mind, is to strengthen some of the themes that I try to develop throughout my teaching:

- That learning is something you can and should do all the time and it's not confined to what the teacher tells you to do

- That you should take responsibility for your own learning but you also have a contribution to make to the group

- That it pays to emulate the most successful learners – to see what they are doing and try to match them

- That it's always rewarding to follow your interests and to share them with others

Another benefit is that you are able to model appropriate use of social media for learning purposes. In terms of pedagogy, it helps you to buy time. You don't have to cram everything in. Students can read things in advance or you can send the details later. You can give a demonstration knowing that they can watch it again on video; that affects the questions you can ask at the time. You can capture the work on your whiteboard in an image and send it on – that makes you invest in giving a good explanation that will be worth capturing.

All these little shifts in emphasis add up to being quite significant, especially when students learn to use the system and build it into their routines. In my experience, there are no net opportunity costs; only benefits. You can teach more freely and directly, knowing you've got a way to follow-through via the online forum whenever you get a chance.

Above all, I think the value from it comes from the sense of collective endeavour. We're a gang, working together to learn about this fabulous subject. This is our private space where we share stuff – and it's interesting, fun, challenging; and, for sure, we have to work really hard. But we're all in it together. I like that feeling and Edmodo helps to create and sustain it. All the other platforms would be the same once you get them up and running. In rainforest terms, this as much about 'establishing conditions' as 'exploring possibilities'.

P12 Reciprocal teaching

This is a tried and tested method that scores well in the Hattie effect-size rankings, for what they are worth. It's a process with a great deal of potential. From my experience, it works best when students are asked to go beyond explaining something they've understood themselves; they are actually asked to teach it so that other students also understand. As we all know, when preparing to teach a set of concepts, it requires deeper understanding than a straightforward explanation might; at the very least it demands a greater level of clarity in the way the explanation is communicated.

For example, my son's class in Year 4 had a lovely exercise to help them learn the language of giving instructions. They each had to teach their classmates a skill and write out a full script of everything they needed to say. My son taught them all how to play the 'Smoke on the Water' guitar riff during the class group-guitar lesson. In working out the sequence of notes and how to explain each chord, he reinforced his own knowledge. The class enjoyed several weeks where they were taught some interesting things by their peers each morning.

I've seen this method applied to lots of different subjects and in my own lessons, I find this very useful. If I am teaching something that requires a more extended exposition, to help ensure students have understood it, I then ask them to prepare to teach it back in the next week or so. It wouldn't work for them all to do it so I either select someone specific in advance or ask them all to prepare, knowing that I'll pick someone out to teach it back.

One favourite example in my subject is asking my Year 13s to teach one of my favourite derivations: the ideal gas equation from consideration of the motion of a particle in a box. It requires quite a lot of conceptual thought with lots of steps in the right order to lead to the final solution. By getting ready to explain this in depth to the whole class, the students will need to make sure they understand it in significant detail; it won't be enough just to learn it by heart without understanding it. This process also works as a form of formative assessment.

'Teaching it back' is a cornerstone of the co-construction process outlined in **P15: Sidekicks**. During that process I spent a bit of time with the leading team making sure they understood the concepts before they taught the class. Examples included students explaining how a lux meter works and how students can use it to explore the phenomena of absorption and transmission; explaining the ideas behind the pressure can demonstration; setting out questions relating to basic circuit theory leading to a practical where students tested their own circuits, measuring currents at various positions.

I have seen numerous other examples of reciprocal teaching across the curriculum:

- Y10s explaining the structural features of a poem, teaching the elements of sonnets

- Y8s explaining the grammatical structure of sentences in French

- Y13 music A level students explaining the use of harmonic elements in a set work

- A Y11 student showing their class the derivation of the rule for differentiation from first principles

- A Y9 student running through some gymnastic routines and warm-up drills in PE

- A Y10 student demonstrating a painting technique in art

One of the most important aspects of this process is to acknowledge and anticipate that students make mistakes; each mistake highlights an area where their conceptual understanding isn't as deep as you might like. Sometimes this is revealed from their teaching in a way that you might not have imagined was a problem from some more routine classwork. In giving their explanation in teacher-mode, they reveal more about what they do and do not understand. This is your cue to intervene to clarify or challenge as necessary. 'Teaching it back' is one of the best ways to flush out misconceptions, in my experience.

Occasionally, a student does the job so well, you feel you couldn't have done it better yourself.

P13 Flipped learning

Flipped learning is another of the 'exploring possibilities' ideas that sometimes gets bad press from more traditional teachers. It is often associated with new technology fads and is resisted on that basis. However, as Harvard Professor and flipped learning advocate Eric Mazur pointed out at an SSAT conference I attended[135], flipped learning has existed since we have had books: students are asked to read the material in advance of a lesson and then to bring their learning into the class as the basis for subsequent work. It's a timeless concept.

In my first ever job, teaching physics at Winstanley College in Wigan in the 1980s, the physics department had developed a fabulous method for teaching that was a form of flipped learning. It was a radical approach. Basically, the

---

135. Mazur, E. (2012) SSAT National Conference 2012 Keynote youtu.be/y5qRyf34v3Q

entire course was broken down into units (there were 42 exactly in 1987, which pleased *Hitchhiker's Guide* fans[136]). Each study guide directed students to read certain pages from certain books, to refer to specific diagrams, learn particular definitions and equations and then to practise some questions *before the lesson*. That was the key.

Students turned up to lessons with the notes already in their folders. Obviously it took time to perfect, building slowly over Y12, but by Y13, they were supremely good at it; it was automatic. Lessons were fantastic because all of our time was spent on questions, discussions, teasing out misconceptions, doing practical work and running demonstrations. We could zip through concepts where the pre-learning had been more straightforward and cut to the chase with more difficult issues. If I'd known how fabulous this system was at the time, I'd have kept a full set of all 42 guides … but I left empty handed!

This was 'flipping' in action; the students took responsibility for pre-learning the material prior to engaging with the teacher and each other. There are multiple applications for this including where online tutorials can play a part (see P14). Any subject where students need to engage in a lot of reading material or where they have the skills to embark on problem-solving unsupported can be enhanced by flipped learning. As a teacher it feels slightly risky to go into a lesson where you are relying on students having done the preliminary work in order for the lesson to work, but it's a risk that pays off handsomely most of the time.

Clearly, it only works if students can and will do the work that is required. In common with other Mode B strategies, there is a level of prerequisite knowledge that students need to have for it to be effective at any given level of learning. However, students can be trained to do this well; it should not be a case of sink or swim. Students can be trained to read for comprehension independently and they can be trained to make good notes. If you make the investment early on in a course, it pays dividends later. If you never train them, you will never feel confident that it is going to deliver the rigour you require.

P14 Online tutorials

One of the great features of the internet is that there are lots of superb online resources where people explain how to do things. These are incredibly useful if you want to build a shed or change a wheel or learn a magic trick. My kids used to like the piano exam models: videos of other kids (who did more practice!)

---

136. '42' is the answer to the Ultimate Question of Life, The Universe, and Everything in Douglas Adams's *The Hitchhiker's Guide to the Galaxy*

playing the same exam pieces so that they could hear what they are supposed to sound like! There are also lots of teacher videos and whole structures like the Khan Academy[137] where the core curriculum is broken down into small video segments with explanatory slides and questions.

I have found that, used selectively and precisely, it is possible to harness this wealth of material to support your teaching. These considerations are likely to lead to this process being more effective:

- Select specific videos in advance and direct your students to use them. This is important as a quality check – there is giant heap of junk out there – but it also ensures that the tutorial supports the learning in the way you want at the depth required. I would never ask students simply to 'find out about X on YouTube'. They will do enough browsing in their own time anyway. I want to be more precise. Over time I have found that there are specific video sources and individual clips that are especially good for my subjects. I used to love a particular video of a man explaining radioactive decay and the Khan Academy sequence on the properties of light was useful. In maths, video resources often have good pause cues for students to stop to think before answers were given; I've found these can be a good supplement to my own explanations of some quite basic operations.

- Make it a definite requirement to access the tutorials and monitor the students' engagement – through some form of formative assessment. Less motivated students, less confident students or, conversely, those who think they already know the material, will not necessarily go to an online resource simply because you suggest it is available. My experience is that you need to be quite precise about your expectations if you want students to watch a specific online tutorial in their own time. The drop-in resources that are there if you need them have very low hit rates.

- Use online tutorials for skills you don't have time to teach yourself. I discovered that students can often use online tutorials for using software packages such as spreadsheets. In one Year 10 class, I had a whole group making spreadsheets with a stopping distance calculator involving drop-down menus, formulas and vlookups. They used online tutorials to teach themselves how to use vlookups with great success. I got some superb results with minimal lesson time given to the spreadsheet business allowing us to focus on the science.

---

137. www.khanacademy.org

Again, had I not set the expectation, students would not have tried. You might find that only a few students can do this unsupported but, in the spirit of teaching to the top, don't allow that to hold you back from setting the challenge for those who can meet it.

I'm certain that online tutorials will never be a panacea or replace teacher-led instruction in a face-to-face environment but it is also certainly true that more and more material will become available and it pays to develop good strategies for harnessing this kind of learning experience to extend the possibilities.

P15 Co-construction: Sidekicks

It's an extraordinary human phenomenon that people will step up to the plate when circumstances dictate that they are needed by others to do so. As a school leader, I always found that, if I did things, other people would assume that they didn't need to; but if I created the conditions where they could take the lead, they did. The same goes with students. Very often I feel that people assume young people are not capable of doing things when they are all along; it's just that no-one ever thought to find out, to ask or to expect. So they don't. When it works, it's a question of giving students a clear role, trusting them and giving them enough space to feel that what they're doing is worthwhile and not tokenistic.

At KEGS, through my co-construction explorations and other observations, I came to believe that students are capable of making a significant contribution if the expectations are established. The focus of P15 is to celebrate the value of having a group of sidekicks to support the teaching process; it's great for them and it's great for you.

Before explaining how it works, let me give you a flavour for co-construction in action:

When working supported by my Year 9 Electricity Team, we had back-to-back lessons on a Monday and Tuesday. I'd taken the Monday lesson myself, delivering a teacher demo; I wanted to model some circuit-building processes and make sure that students were building good mental models for current, voltage and resistance. The next day, as I approached the lab, I remembered that I'd completely forgotten to organise the class practical or discuss it with my co-construction team. I started thinking of book-based alternatives; this was going to be an on-the-fly lesson. However, I needn't have worried. To my great joy, the Electricity Team, Kieret, Dominic and Alex, already had it covered. The previous week, without prompting from me, they had been to see the technicians and had organised the apparatus for this lesson – it was all ready to go. They'd taken their responsibility seriously and made sure the lesson they were due to lead was going to be a good one. It was. I'd just forgotten that it was their turn to lead. They also had a homework activity planned and took the books in to mark them.

On another occasion, with a Year 11 group, we were looking at how many lessons we had remaining to cover the syllabus. It was already October in the final year and it felt tight so we talked about the need for a detailed plan. Without actually asking for anyone to do this, the same evening I received an email from Taran. He had mapped out the whole course that remained against all the calendared lessons we had still to come. Taran's plan became our guide. He had built in time for revision, tests, holidays and contingencies. I couldn't have done a better job myself. He stepped up spontaneously and we all benefited. Taran was clever and conscientious but there will be Tarans in every school who could do this if the conditions are set up right.

I could list lots of other examples when these moments have happened. I'd suggest that whilst you may not wish to get involved in the whole co-construction process, there is great value in having a team of sidekicks working alongside you at any time. They can help to get things done; they give you a good indication of the students' perspective on how lessons are going and generally make life a lot easier and more interesting. Having a class communication tool like Edmodo, as described in P11, is a great help but it's not essential. Very often I'm in email contact with whoever is in my team at any time and that becomes part and parcel of how I teach.

In pedagogical terms, this starts to influence how you teach once it is an established, normal aspect of how the class functions. When running a sidekick process, in every practical lesson, I have a team helping me troubleshoot; I have people to log the homework; I have people who can capture the notes from a class discussion and bring them back the following day or post them online; I have students to tag with when it comes to explaining the key phenomena. At all times, we're in it together. I'm Batman. They are Robin.

Putting co-construction into action

In its most comprehensive form, co-construction involves students in planning and delivering an entire course, alongside you as the teacher. It becomes a joint enterprise where you harness their capabilities to maximum effect whilst remaining the central figure in driving and delivering the content. Students can plan, teach, mark, demonstrate, organise, model, explain, lead practice, ask questions. It's actually amazing what they can do in the right conditions.

However, you can always choose elements from the process to suit your context.

Introductory phase

I'll explain the process to the students and look at the scheme of work overview. I won't give them the details, just the topics. We will then discuss a sensible order of topics and the logistics of using each of our timetabled lessons. The order of topics is a great discussion; even if, as the teacher, you have a strong preference, you can steer them towards it or accept that some decisions are more arbitrary and let students decide. We will then seek out any 'wish list' items from the class. Are there any topics that they have a burning desire to study this year? The class can then decide whether to include them and where we'll place them on the timeline.

Next, we will establish a number of teams. In a typical class this might be eight teams of three or four students:

- I want one group to be the Core Planning Team. A group that monitors our overall progress, keeps us on track, administers the process of recording assessments and helps to liaise with the other teams from week to week. They will also plan cover lessons if I am ever absent.

- I want another group to be the IT Team. This group will set up and run a class blog, recording the content of the lessons we cover, posting resources and links and keeping a log of the homework that is set. They will need to decide an appropriate platform for doing this so I can communicate with them all in-between lessons.

- The other six groups will be Teaching Teams. We will allocate topics to each of them in advance and map out a rough timeline for the year so they know when they are taking charge.

The next step is to set out the parameters of the planning and delivery process

Roughly speaking, each team might have a flow of 8-10 lessons to plan across 5-6 weeks. They meet with me as we go along, to map out the details. Working with me, I will expect each team to do the following:

- Produce an overarching plan for their units, showing the lesson overview. This should indicate lessons where they will lead on giving teaching input; major front-bench demonstrations they will perform; lessons that I will lead as teacher; practical lessons for the class and any longer investigations that form part of the learning.

- Plan at least three of their key lessons in detail. This will include a fully structured lesson plan and should include the key learning objectives, the classwork and homework tasks and the key mode of assessment. It will also include a list of equipment that can serve as a requisition for the technicians and include a rough timeline for each lesson.

- Arrange a meeting with the science technicians to discuss their requirements. It is a solemn rule that students must do this themselves. When it is their lesson, I will not plan a back-up; they must take full responsibility.

The Core Planning Team and IT Team have a separate set of tasks and, in all probability, will need to devote more time to this than the others. They also chip in to some of the units so they get a taste for the teaching role. The remaining lessons will be planned more organically as we go along, taking account of student responses, giving time for feedback on homework and so on. It is hard to plan the exact sequence in advance so we need to be flexible.

We discuss various approaches to teaching and learning and establish firm expectations about the minimal use of PowerPoint presentations. They often need to be prompted to plan what the class will do and not just what they will do as the teachers of the lesson. They need to spend time learning about their topic areas and preparing good questions, with model answers. That is the key to this working. Once everything is up and running, I find that with a little bit of extra time commitment for me, with a few snatched planning meetings here and there, students are very capable of rising to this challenge. We evaluate each of their lessons so that they get better at doing them.

When you've invested in the process, the outcomes can be sensational: seeing students giving a demonstration, handing back the books they marked, supporting their peers with an experiment they have practised beforehand. The simple fact that they are trusted and expected to take a lead catapults them forward with the level of maturity they show and the extent to which they engage with the overall programme.

Does it work? In my experience, yes it does. I taught a unit of Year 7 RE on Islam and Christianity with this method and the creative ideas students had for their lessons were wonderful. Their ideas for the content were aligned closely to what was written on the official scheme: places of worship, life and death, the nature of God, rituals, attitudes to gender and sexuality – fabulous! I taught a full GCSE exam course with this method (the one with Taran's plan) that yielded amazing results – the best I've ever had for any class ever. Their grades would have most likely been exactly the same if I had taught them directly throughout but, with this process, I'm certain that they also gained a host of other skills and experiences on top. Co-construction is steeped in 'below the line' learning. Give it go!

P16 Independence: Tools and tricks

I think 'Independent learning' is one of the least well-handled terms in education. It is often cited as a desirable outcome for students; it is even claimed as the absolute priority for education in some schools. We want students to develop the capacity to pursue a learning process by themselves, using their own resources in a self-motivated manner so that they can continue to learn beyond school and into their adult lives: we want them to become life-long learners.

However, students do not simply become independent learners by osmosis. Independent learning isn't really a definable skill or mindset in itself; it is a collection of practical strategies that students can adopt alongside the disposition to use them voluntarily with certain learning goals in mind. In order to enable students to develop independence, we need to ensure that these practical strategies are available to them and that they know how to use them. As with many things, the more prior knowledge students have, the more independent of teacher instruction they can be – and that might be the key limiting factor in any given context.

There are specific strategies students might need to learn and rehearse if they are going to develop independent learning in practice. The Number 1 strategy is reading. Obviously. The more reading you do in class, the more you model the process of engaging with text – fiction and non-fiction; the better at reading your students become, the more likely they are to function as independent learners. Reading is the key; it's the lifeblood (or tree sap?).

However, there are other specific skills that can support reading in developing independent learning:

- Information Search skills: refining the search terms; applying a quality filter
- Self-assessment and self-quizzing routines; the FACE it approach (K18)
- Using dictionaries, encyclopedias and textbooks as resources
- Note-taking and organisation – *eg* Cornell notes, mind-mapping
- Reading for comprehension; skimming and scanning

- Task-planning – including essay planning; writing to time

- Proofreading for fluency, spelling, punctuation and grammar

- Technical troubleshooting and self-help; using online tutorials

- Project management and effective collaborative working: division of labour *etc*

- Understanding examination specifications and assessment criteria

Each of these skills can be taught in a standard instructional sequence: explaining; modelling, practising, assessing and giving feedback in the context of specific aspects of the content. It is worth investing in teaching these skills at a point when students need them and then reinforcing them thereafter.

Of course, the main stimulus for independent learning will be your mainstream instructional teaching. The more knowledge areas you explore, the more confidence your students develop with the subject material; the more inspired they are by the subject or rewarded by the sense of making progress, the more likely they are to develop their curiosity to know more and to generate the motivation needed to undertake independent learning beyond the classroom. In this sense, independent learning is an extension of firm teacher-led instruction, not a replacement for it.

P17 Structured speech events

Rhetoric is one of the three arts of the Trivium. As well as studying the grammar of multiple disciplines, we want to be able to express our ideas, share our thoughts and engage in debate. Communication is an embedded element of our social and political life, of academia and of any work place. Naturally enough we want students to be good at it – but developing excellent oracy skills doesn't necessarily just happen by chance; it needs a plan. Rhetoric needs to be taught.

Some people reject the idea that oracy skills as such exist. However, I find it a useful umbrella concept for a range of speech modes, whilst recognising that speaking well in different contexts will require different skills and background knowledge.

The term 'structured speech events' is the heading for a range of different activities that teachers can deploy where speech is being developed in a planned, structured manner. The structure in any activity is usually there to ensure that everyone participates, that the knowledge being explored remains at the core of the process and that the quality of speech is meeting the expected standards.

These are some of the activities that teachers might use:

- Individual or group presentations

- Speeches or recitations – deploying learning by heart strategies as in K19

- Pedagogical inputs – planned student-delivered instruction

- Structured discussions – such as the Harkness method[138]

- Role-plays or structured dialogues

- Debates – see strategy P18 for more specifics

Across the curriculum, it should be possible for students to engage with a range of these modes of speech at a frequency that is high enough for them to have regular opportunities to develop their confidence and skills. At Highbury Grove, led by our Head of English and oracy director, Andrew Fitch, we decided that instead of just hoping staff would pick up on this as an optional extra, we needed to map out a concrete plan to make sure that the coverage across the curriculum was planned and could be embedded. Here is an edited example to give you an idea of the process we embarked on.

Rhetoric Roadmap: Year 9

Autumn 1	Autumn 2	Spring 1	Spring 2	Summer 1	Summer 2
English: Role play – the trial of Macbeth and Recitation of a learned extract of Macbeth	English: Performance of Macbeth's 'Is this a dagger I see before me?' soliloquy	Science: Teach a lesson on an aspect of a chosen topic area	RE: Recitation – research, learn and deliver story in Hindu storytelling tradition	History: WWII Film making documentary	RE: Formal speech on treatment of ethical issues in *The Diving Bell and the Butterfly*
Maths: Formal presentation: Angles and Polygons (proof /problem- solving (notes)	Geography: Presentation on glacier (from memory)	Geography: Structured discussion on 'food security'	French: Formal presentation: *'Ma vie Sociale, la Sante, Les Ambitions'*	RE: Formal presentation Select two different cultures and provide a comparison of their moral norms	English: Role play S&L assessment based on *Kindertransport*

---

138. See Carl Hendrick's article: learning.wellingtoncollege.org.uk/harkness-teaching-and-uk-education/

Media Studies: Pedagogic session on the deconstruction of a TV advert	RE: Formal debate on topic of either Preventing Extremism or Contemporary Sunni/Shia Conflict	English: Formal debate on whether dystopia is too depressing	English: Performance of their original dystopian story	Maths: Formal presentation: Probability problem-solving (notes)	Music: Formal presentation on their favourite song

The table shows that in any given half-term, students had several planned structured speech events lined up but only a few for any one subject. This was coordinated to balance out the type of events across the year. It was rather ambitious as a starting point but it meant that most staff were engaged in the programme at some level. I hope the elements are largely self-explanatory – a mixture of recitations, presentations, speeches and roleplays. The pedagogical inputs varied from subject to subject. In maths the most common format was for students to be given specific questions to explain to the class. They would prepare them in advance and then explain model answers in detail during a lesson, taking turns across the term.

This classroom-based programme was reinforced by some wider initiatives such our 'Project Soapbox' led by English teachers where students in Year 8 were asked to give a speech to an audience of 40-50 other students on a topic of their choice. Some did it from memory; others used prompt cards. Over 95% of students took part with some very special results. It was wonderful to see this coming to fruition. Philosopher kids, out in the agora? Not quite yet, but this is a good way to start.

P18 Debate

First, a cautionary tale.

I remember teaching a Year 7 unit in geography at Alexandra Park where students were studying human impact on the environment. There was a case study about a new ski resort in the Italian Alps and the impact of tourism. Part of the unit was to conduct a debate. Students were placed in groups representing different stakeholders: the local people, farmers, the developers, environmentalists, the local politicians. The aim was to explore all the issues through the debate format. I tried to put this in place but it was a disaster. Rather predictably, even though we had studied the unit and undertaken some preparatory work, the students simply did not have enough knowledge about the context, the issues or the significance of the different roles for the debate to be meaningful. They resorted to repeating lines from their worksheets but, beyond the direct prompts, they could only guess what to say and it fell apart. It was play-acting, not debating.

This is not what debating is for. If we want students to acquire new knowledge, Mode A teaching is far more likely to be successful. Debating comes into play when students have the knowledge required and where the question in hand is genuinely worthy of debate, with legitimate opposing views that students can engage with from a position of some authority. As we explored in **P2 Ambiguity and uncertainty**, there is plenty of scope for legitimate debate and it certainly pays to build selected opportunities into the curriculum.

Preparation for a debate is a superb vehicle for deepening learning around a certain topic. Students have to prepare an argument that they can support with some facts; they then need to consider how to construct a persuasive argument using appropriate oracy tools. They also need to anticipate what the opposition will say and prepare rebuttals. All of this can form a very rigorous piece of research work, group work and writing if pitched with the right level of rigour.

The performance of the elements of the debate are great vehicles for developing voice projection, to read notes fluently, to listen and respond spontaneously to other arguments in a formal setting. If you get the right balance of formality and rigour with competitive, challenging arguments, debates can be great fun as well as feeling that they are extending the learning.

The English Speaking Union Schools' Mace[139] provides a good model: they use a two-person debate team format; one team proposing a motion; the other opposing the motion. After the initial proposition, each successive speaker will rebut the arguments of the opposing team as well as delivering their own arguments and summarising their case. The World Schools Debating Championships[140] use two teams of three and there are other models to explore. With twos and threes, you can run practice sessions with multiple debates happening around the class so everyone is involved – as well as creating a class audience as pairs of teams go head-to-head. With two or three per team you are also reducing the risk of students being a passenger.

Once debating becomes a regular feature of the school curriculum, students can develop a real love of it. This is one of my absolute favourite memories from KEGS.

---

139. www.esu.org/our-work/schools-mace
140. www.esu.org/our-work/world-schools-debating Note that HGS's Andrew Fitch coached England to be World Champions in 2016! Kudos.

One lunchtime I found a group of about 12 lower-school students in a classroom (11 to 14-year-olds). Everyone else was outside playing football. They were sitting in a rather formal seating arrangement. I asked what they were doing and was delighted to be told that this was the new Lower-School Debating Club; the students had just set it up on their own initiative. The motion was: This House Would Invade North Korea. I stayed a while to listen in – and it was massively impressive. This is the ultimate goal: to create a culture where debating is actively sought out by students in their own time. It's not necessarily likely in some settings, but having seen it, I know this is possible.

P19 Third time for excellence

This is a simple idea derived from Ron Berger's *An Ethic of Excellence* and Austin's Butterfly as discussed in Chapter 5. Although redrafting can become a routine element of a student's curriculum experience, it can still be the case that some students never experience what it is like to produce work that is truly excellent. Students can muddle through producing one mediocre piece of work after another, albeit with slight improvements.

My suggestion is that students should have the opportunity, at least at one point in the year for every subject, where they are given the time to continue to work on something until it really is excellent. In practice, this often means giving students three attempts. The first gets them started, exploring the challenge in the task; the second is to engage with the first round of feedback to push themselves further. However, it is the third draft when students really start to deliver work of the highest quality they can. We trialled this approach at Highbury Grove through some pioneer 'excellence units' with some fabulous results.

In art, students had produced paintings that were abstractions from a still life. When laid side by side – versions one, two and three – the transformation from first to third was fabulous. Students made so much progress because they were given the time and structure to continue working on the same thing. In English, history and French, we saw pieces of writing develop significantly from draft one to draft three. The final pieces were exciting to read.

Third Time for Excellence is a strategy that certainly takes up time – which is why you might not be able to use it in every case. However, if you build these opportunities into the overall scheme so that students do manage to experience excellence in your subject, it can be enormously motivating as well as providing them with a stronger sense of what excellence actually looks like.

P20 Excellence exhibition

My final suggestion for 'Exploring the possibilities', the culmination of our exploration of the Learning Rainforest, is to celebrate the fabulous work that students produce. Some of the highlights of the school calendar are events like the annual art exhibition, concerts and drama productions. They are great because you get the chance to see students' talents come through, to see the progress they make and the results of the effort you see them putting in. I've always felt that other subjects rather miss out from having this kind of exposure so, at various schools, I've worked with staff to create exhibitions of student work from across the curriculum.

It is possible to create accessible displays of student work – in their books, on computers, on display-boards, on the walls and tables – that allow visitors to engage with learning products of all kinds. If books are laid out, people will sit down to read them; it doesn't have to be 'display work' – the original work is what people want to see. If students are present to talk about their achievements and their thought processes, so much the better. Listening to students talking about work that they take pride in is always enormously inspiring.

Events of this kind are always hugely celebratory and can provide another form of authentic experience for students: they know that people will see the work they produce. I strongly recommend making an Excellence Exhibition a routine feature of school life, one that every student can contribute to.

CONCLUSION: A FINAL WALK THROUGH THE LEARNING RAINFOREST

'In a forest of a hundred thousand trees, no two leaves are alike. And no two journeys along the same path are alike.'
Paulo Coelho, Aleph[141]

'Il faut cultiver notre jardin.'
Voltaire, Candide[142]

Across the world, every teacher will be working in a unique context with their own collection of unique individuals to teach; each child a complex character with their unique background, motivations, ambitions and interests. Each child's path through the curriculum they experience will be different – however standardised it may appear on the surface. However regimented, turbulent or demanding any education system is, teachers will need to 'cultivate their gardens', doing the best they can to succeed in their immediate environment, with the students in front of them.

For all the complexity and contextual diversity, teachers everywhere will face the same basic challenges:

- Establishing conditions: how to design a rich, broad, inspiring curriculum and create conditions in which learning can take place effectively.

- Building knowledge: how to contribute to the process of building a knowledge structure that supports each child's understanding of the world they live in.

- Exploring possibilities: how to ensure that each child flourishes, finds fulfilment and develops a love of learning – *as philosopher kids* – by exploring the learning possibilities in their context.

---

141. Coelho, P. (2011) *Aleph*. Harper Collins
142. "*We must cultivate our garden*" Voltaire, and Constantine, P. (2005) Candide, or, Optimism. New York: Modern Library.

The three elements of the Learning Rainforest tree metaphor, supported by the debates and research outlined in Part 1, and all the strategies included in Part 2 to bring them to life, are merely a rough guide. Every teacher and reader of this book will find that the ideas resonate in different ways depending on their values, their experience, their school context and the needs of the individuals they teach. For sure, I would expect vigorous debate about the 80:20 split I suggest for Mode A: Mode B teaching as different values and contexts come into play.

The fusion of art and science in teaching is at the core of what makes it so fascinating and rewarding. On one hand there is a great deal in the year-on-year experience of teaching in real classrooms that is predictable and straightforward; learning is not a complete mystery. Great teachers accumulate wisdom that allows them to be highly effective in securing superb outcomes for their students. At the same time, there is no end to the ways in which students can and will continue to surprise and delight or confuse and confound us in the way their learning and our teaching interact.

I hope that I have managed to signpost a path through all the complexities, contradictions and uncertainties. The three-part tree model provides a way to deliver a Trivium-style curriculum in practice; managing the tension between the progressive and traditional ideas about education examined in Chapter 2, replacing absolute choices with a more subtle balancing of principles and practice over time, depending on the stage students have reached in their learning journey.

The philosophical debate is linked directly to the details of the enacted curriculum that students actually experience. In the Learning Rainforest, we are ambitious for what students will learn: a broad and deep body of knowledge and skills across multiple domains; a range of personal dispositions and as much cultural capital as we can expose them to. If we are serious about educational equity, this all needs to be mapped out deliberately not merely left to the chance allocations of teachers with particular interests.

As we explored in Chapter 5, the assessment paradigm that has dominated our schools for so long, is ripe for change and I'm optimistic that the shift we need is going to happen. Increasingly we will see that assessment thinking focuses on the purpose of improving student learning, on the detail of what needs to be learned, as close to the action as possible. I am also extremely optimistic that, increasingly, teachers will ensure that their ideas, practice and deliberations are informed by evidence from research as our knowledge and understanding of the learning process deepens. Research within the three category areas of climate, instruction and memory will continue to yield findings that we will all have to take note of. This will often be as much a case of debunking myths and protecting ourselves against fads as suggesting definite strategies that might be said to work.

Looking back on my personal experience as a teacher – which is where I began the rainforest journey in Chapter 1 – I am certain that my successes have come from situations where the three elements of the Learning Rainforest came together; my failures have been where one or more of the elements was too weak to support the others.

Some of the teaching episodes I remember most vividly are from my earliest teaching days. When studying for my PGCE[143] in 1987, during a placement at a low achieving South Manchester comprehensive, I took on a feisty Year 10 Physics class from a man who was so disillusioned, he literally told me to '*get out while you can*'. He meant I should leave the profession I had only just joined! Ignoring his pessimism, one day I took the class outside onto the playing fields. Our goal was to measure the speed of sound using an echo method. This involved standing 50 metres from the gym wall, measured with trundle wheels, and timing a 'bang-echo-bang-echo-bang' sequence created by banging some heavy wooden blocks together in a rhythm with the echoes. Once we had performed the calculations whilst still out in the field, we shared the results. They were truly magnificent. My students – who were never allowed outside and had spent most lessons copying words they did not understand from the board – were ecstatic. My PGCE tutor happened to be there to see it. He'd hovered in the background with his clipboard. I'll never forget what he said: '*Well, that was risky ... But it was totally brilliant.*'

The students had risen to the occasion. The conditions were good: my expectations were high; the curriculum content was challenging; I had already established a positive rapport with the class. We were building knowledge: the method and calculation process has been well rehearsed in advance; the experiment was supported by a good understanding of the key ideas – waves, reflection, the speed-distance-time equation. And here we were exploring the possibilities – getting our hands (and shoes) dirty, exploring the dialectic of real science out in the field. This was a microcosm of the Learning Rainforest.

I'd like to say something romantic like '*I never looked back*' – but that wouldn't quite be true.

I could run through multiple success stories but, actually, it is your struggles

---

143. Post Graduate Certificate of Education

and failures that often teach you the most. With all of my years of experience to draw on, I still found the very last Year 10 GCSE class I took one of the most challenging.

Teaching maths, I found the process of designing the most appropriate learning sequence a continual challenge. I had to work on establishing the basic conditions for learning continually: behaviour routines, work habits, mindsets, relationships. I had to work hard to build a solid knowledge structure, to identify and breakdown numerous mathematical misconceptions in order to rebuild better schema to cement deeper understanding and long term recall. How often did a student who could deliver $6^2=36$ in any lesson or drill, revert to $6^2=12$ in a test or forget the basic methods for column addition or long division?! Students' models for these operations were massively insecure and needed very careful nurturing.

Here, I was very much micro-managing my section of the Rainforest. The class consisted of outwardly robust individuals who were actually very fragile specimens in learning terms, years spent developing their convincing bravado to mask low self-esteem as learners. Exploring possibilities felt like a distant hope at the point I took them on given that, without doubt, many of them had missed out on some important formative mental model-making experiences with numbers and shapes earlier in their education.

This scenario is one where, as a teacher, you are forced to question all your basic assumptions, to examine the research, seek out ideas and draw on your experience to design an effective curriculum and assessment plan. This is where you are truly tested. Of course it is at precisely these moments that you need to keep your eye on the big picture and the wider goals; to remain motivated by a vision for 'educating the whole child', never to let the challenges diminish your expectations but to persist. It's through persistence that the breakthroughs come; those moments when, finally, things start to fall into place and that intangible, ephemeral idea – 'learning' – takes form and we feel like we're winning again.

Fortunately, over the years I have enjoyed lots of successes including plenty of those air-punch triumphs that bring a tear to your eye as students either succeed against the odds or simply blow you away with the scale of their wonderful achievements. I've had wonderful classes in every school where the relationships and the learning were fabulous as we set out on our rainforest journey together. I've witnessed the tears of joy as students have reached high, gaining a university place they had never dared dream could actually happen for them – a reward for their years of persistent hard work; I've wept tears of pride as a student has given an impassioned assembly speech about overcoming their once-debilitating stammer or their journey as a member of the LGBT community, finally finding the confidence to express their identity, to finally be themselves amongst their peers. I've sat in awe as various students have demonstrated their learning: a breath-taking robotic bomb disposal system, a student's astonishing poetry anthology, an exhibition of extraordinary art work or the award of national accolades for academic excellence.

One of my favourite success stories was from Alexandra Park School. In 2004, when we analysed the results of our first ever cohort to pass through the school from Year 7 to Year 11, we found that one student had made bigger gains than anyone else by some distance. This was a Turkish boy who I'll call Sercan. He had arrived with a low level of English but through hard work and dedication had progressed to gain excellent GCSE grades. Sercan was never in amongst the highest attainers and, when I taught him science, he often seemed to struggle in comparison to his first language English-speaking peers; he needed a mix of firm pushing and positive encouragement to get the best from him.

Eventually it all began to click and he achieved better results than he or anyone else had hoped for. On results day I told Sercan privately that he had been the student to make the most progress in terms of exam grades. You could not wish to see a happier soul. He asked me to put this in a letter for his parents and when he translated the news for his mother who only spoke Turkish, her pride in her son was overwhelming. He later took A Levels and progressed to university to study engineering. He wrote to tell us how grateful he was for what the school had given him which was, above all, self-belief. That is the power of a great education.

A career in teaching is always going to be a journey. Perhaps the three-part model works for teachers too. We need to invest in creating conditions in which we all thrive as professionals; we need to continually build our professional knowledge structure, deepening our understanding of our subjects, of assessment methods and of the learning process; and, finally, we need to continually explore the possibilities for what teaching in real classrooms can be and what constitutes success in delivering a rounded, broad, inspiring curriculum.

The detailed ideas and overarching philosophy of the Learning Rainforest have developed alongside my career that began over 30 years ago. And I'm still going. From the beginning I have been keen not to present this book as anything other than a kind of status report: this is just how I see things right now. There is still so much more to learn and explore from educational research, from the debates that are ongoing, from my own teaching and from other teachers; I am certain that my ideas will continue to evolve for as long as I am still involved.

I say this because it is my great hope for the teaching profession as a whole that successive generations of teachers pick up the baton and continue the search for deeper insights and greater clarity in our collective understanding of the important work that we do. Of course there will always be competing values systems at play: there will always be tensions around the purposes of education and the content of the curriculum; most teachers will experience a degree of cognitive dissonance as they seek to align the theories and principles about teaching methods with the lived realities of the classroom. But this is the essence of our dynamic profession: reflection, debate, research, experimentation, innovation, collaboration – opening our ideas to challenge, sharing everything we find and learning from each other and from every source of expertise in the wider global education community.

Despite the many challenges teachers and schools face, I remain fiercely optimistic for the future of education because I meet so many talented, energetic and committed teachers and school leaders who are so dedicated to the professional learning process. I hope that *The Learning Rainforest* provides a structure and a set of ideas that can help you in what you do, ultimately leading to enhancing the educational experience of your students.

This book is my contribution to the process of passing the baton to the next generation. If that includes you – it's over to you to continue the exploration. I hope that you enjoy the journey and find your rainforest experience as rewarding as mine has been.

BIBLIOGRAPHY AND REFERENCES

This includes the books and other key sources cited. Websites, online sources and other texts are referenced in the footnotes. It also includes other books that have helped to shape my thinking though not directly referenced.

Allison, S. and Tharby, A. (2015) *Making Every Lesson Count*, Crown House.

Berger, R. (2003) *An Ethic of Excellence*, Heinemann, Portsmouth NH, USA.

Birbalsingh, K. (ed.) (2016) *Battle Hymn of the Tiger Teachers*. The Michaela Way. John Catt. Woodbridge.

Black, P. and Wiliam, D. (1998) *Inside The Black Box: Raising Standards Through Classroom Assessment* GL Assessment Ltd.

Christodoulou, D. (2013) *Seven Myths About Education eBook*. The Curriculum Centre.

Christodoulou, D. (2016) *Making Good Progress? The future of Assessment for Learning* Oxford University Press, Oxford.

Claxton, G. (2002) *Building Learning Power: Helping young people become better learners*. TLO Limited, Bristol.

Claxton, G. *et al* (2011) *The Learning Powered School. Pioneering 21st Century Education*. TLO Limited, Bristol.

Coe, R., Aloisi, C., Higgins, S. and Major, L. E. (2014) *What makes great teaching? Review of the underpinning research*. Sutton Trust.

Didau, D. and Rose, N. (2016) *What every teacher needs to know about psychology*. John Catt. Woodbridge.

Dunlosky, J. (2013) *Strengthening the Student Toolbox, Study Strategies to Boost Learning*. American Educator Fall 2013.

Dweck, C. (2008) *Mindset. How you can fulfil your potential*. Ballatine Books.

Hattie, J. (2009) *Visible Learning: A synthesis of over 800 meta-analyses relating to achievement*. Routledge.

Hirsch, E. D. (2016) *Why Knowledge Matters: Rescuing Our Children from Failed Educational Theories* Harvard Education Press.

James, D. and Warwick, I. (eds) (2017) *World Class: Tackling the Ten Biggest Challenges Facing Schools Today.* Routledge.

Ko, J., Sammons, P. and Bakkum, L. (2014) *Effective Teaching.* Education Development Trust.

Lemov, D (2015) *Teach Like A Champion 2.0.* Jossey-Bass.

Nuthall, G. (2007) *The Hidden Lives of Learners.* NZCER Press, Wellington, NZ.

Robinson, M. (2013) *Trivium 21c: Preparing young people for the future with lessons from the past.* Independent Thinking Press.

Robinson, M. (2016) *Trivium in Practice.* Independent Thinking Press.

Rosenshine, B (2012) '*Principles of Instruction: Research-Based Strategies That All Teachers Should Know', American Educator* Spring 2012.

Rovelli, C (2017) *Reality is not what it seems. The journey to quantum gravity.* (English Translation) Penguin.

Sherrington, T. (2014) *Teach Now! Science. The Joy of Teaching Science.* Routledge.

Wiliam, D. (2011) *Embedded Formative Assessment.* Solution Tree Press.

Wiliam, D. (2016) *9 Things Every Teacher Should Know* – TES article (2/9/2016)

Willingham, D. (2010) *Why Don't Students Like School? A Cognitive Scientist Answers Questions About How the Mind Works and What It Means for the Classroom.* Jossey-Bass.

Yeager, D. *et al* (2013) '*Addressing achievement gaps with psychological interventions', Kappan* February 2013.

ACKNOWLEDGEMENTS

This book is dedicated to all the teachers I have worked with and learned from over the last 30 years. Teaching is a wonderful profession and I'm grateful for all the opportunities I have had to work with so many talented, committed people, giving their all to provide their students with a fabulous education. I'm also grateful to all the students I have met and taught over the years. Without knowing it, they have helped to shape the ideas in this book, providing inspiration and challenge in equal measure.

Writing *The Learning Rainforest* would not have been possible without the support of lots of different people. My family have been incredible. Not only have they encouraged and supported me during the heavy writing days when I have been locked away in my study typing away for hours, they have made a contribution to the content. My wife, Deb, who has shared my rainforest journey with me, is a constant source of inspiration. Our daily conversations about education have provided the raw material for so much of the book. She also provided the FACE It strategy alongside numerous other ideas. Our lovely children, Daisy and Sam, have allowed me to feature snippets of their school experiences. My mum, Karin, proofread the entire book and helped me with my French; my stepdad, Larry, provided material for learning by heart and the awe of medieval poetry. It's been a family endeavour.

I am grateful to Alex Sharratt at John Catt for giving me the opportunity to publish the book and for his effusive encouragement throughout the process. Our serendipitous email exchange in February 2017 kicked the whole thing off. I wrote to Alex asking if he would publish my book literally simultaneously as he wrote to me asking if I would write it. Destiny! Thanks also to Jonathan Woolgar and Jonathan Barnes for the thorough proof-reading and editorial tweaking in the final stages.

Working with Oliver Caviglioli on the graphics and design has been a real joy. I have loved our email exchanges and meetings, talking about the ideas and the different ways to present information. I could not be happier with the visuals in the book – the wonderful rainforest cover and all the chapter summaries. It's a real honour to have a book branded with the Caviglioli style.

My long-standing friend and colleague Tom Andrew-Power provided much-needed support and guidance on the detail as the book was written. Reading every chapter as I finished it, Tom was a constant virtual presence in my margin, nudging, questioning and encouraging with the occasional euphoric reaction that lifted my spirits no end.

Various other people have also helped to shape the ideas in the book at different points: Peter Hyman, Leila Mactavish, Carl Hendrick, Sam Gorse and Martin Robinson all provided helpful suggestions and encouragement at just the right moment. I am especially grateful and honoured that Martin agreed to write the foreword. His *Trivium 21c* has been a major influence on me and I'm thrilled that, having championed his book for years, he now features in mine.

Finally, I would like to acknowledge the support I have received from the readers of teacherhead.com and my @teacherhead followers on Twitter, particularly in the last year. *The Learning Rainforest* is the product of the blogging that has provided me with such an amazing testing ground and platform for sharing ideas. I'm continually bowled over by the level of support and engagement from readers around the world and by the kindness and camaraderie that emanates from our online community. I hope that the book will now help to extend the dialogue into the real world that teachers inhabit every day.

STRATEGIES INDEX

Establishing the conditions

Building the knowledge structure

Exploring the possibilities

INDEX

A

Arnold, M. 54, 62, 68, 78
assessment
– *authentic* 10, 127, 131-132
– *formative* 127-138, 196, 210-215
– *summative* 126-128
Austin's Butterfly 133, 148, 265

B

behaviour 52-53, 161-170
bell curve 117-126
Berger, R. 29, 133-134, 265, 273
Bjork, R. 103, 109-110, 117

C

Christodoulou, D. 10, 30, 54, 57, 127-128, 131, 273
Claxton, G. 54- 56, 61, 104, 273
co-construction 49, 88, 101, 250, 252, 256, 257
Coe, R. 59, 102, 104, 106, 107, 110, 273
Cognitive Load Theory 103, 108
cognitive science 3, 84, 92, 112, 117, 127, 171, 193
cultural capital 29, 30, 53, 65, 78, 80, 86-88, 227, 242, 268

D

differentiation 106, 147-148, 154, 178, 245, 253

E

EAL 146-147, 184
explaining 190-195